Monsoon Postcards

Monsoon Postcards

Indian Ocean Journeys

David H. Mould

Ohio University Press   Athens

Ohio University Press, Athens, Ohio 45701
ohioswallow.com
© 2019 by Ohio University Press
All rights reserved

Printed in the United States of America
Ohio University Press books are printed on acid-free paper ⊗ ™

29 28 27 26 25 24 23 22 21 20 19   5 4 3 2 1

Cover photo: Flooding in Dhaka, Bangladesh, July 2017. Courtesy *Daily Star*
(photographer Amran Hossain)

Unless otherwise noted, photographs are by the author.

Library of Congress Cataloging-in-Publication Data
Names: Mould, David H., author.
Title: Monsoon postcards : Indian Ocean journeys / David H. Mould.
Description: Athens : Ohio University Press, [2019] | Includes
  bibliographical references and index.
Identifiers: LCCN 2019012001 | ISBN 9780821423714 (hc : alk. paper) | ISBN
  9780821446775 (pdf)
Subjects: LCSH: Mould, David H.--Travel--Indian Ocean Region. | Indian Ocean
  Region--Description and travel.
Classification: LCC DS337 .M68 2019 | DDC 910.9182/4--dc23
LC record available at https://lccn.loc.gov/2019012001

Contents

Illustrations

Figures

Maps

one

Traveling with a Purpose

"How do you like Madagascar?" The waiter at Ku-de-ta—the name is a tongue-in-cheek tribute to the country's history of illegal power grabs—asked me the question he probably asked all foreigners at the restaurant.

His timing was bad. I was exhausted and dispirited. I wanted to say, "Not as much as I did yesterday," but my French wasn't up to the linguistic nuance and I didn't want to make a well-meaning waiter feel uncomfortable. Instead I smiled, mumbled something affirmative, and reached for my beer.

We all face setbacks in our lives and are supposed to grow stronger because of them, but my colleague Andrew Carlson and I were feeling unusually fragile and insecure as we tried to process what had happened earlier that day in March 2016. We had made our first visit to Antananarivo, Madagascar's capital, eighteen months earlier to launch a large-scale research project for UNICEF, the United Nations Children's Fund. It was a wide-ranging study of knowledge, beliefs, and practices in health, nutrition, hygiene, water, sanitation, education, and child protection, key issues for the agency. Our six-person international team had worked with colleagues from the University of Antananarivo and the national statistics agency to design the study, conducted in three coastal regions. Earlier that day, we were informed by e-mail that, after more than a year of work and almost $500,000 spent, UNICEF had decided to reject the research report and shut down the project. We had been given no advance warning. The only reason given was a vague reference to "inadequate data analysis." We were upset and confused.

When you're feeling down, it's easy to vent your frustration at your environment—the place, the people, the waiter at Ku-de-ta. But as Andrew and I enjoyed an exceptional lunch and rounded it off with a *rhum arrangé* (the flavored rum that is customarily offered as an after-dinner digestive), our mood mellowed. We were at one of Antananarivo's best restaurants, savoring French haute cuisine at incredibly reasonable prices. Outside lay a picturesque, historic city built on sacred hills where every walk or taxi trip yielded new sights and sounds. I was looking forward to a weekend trip to the countryside with my Malagasy university colleague, Richard Samuel, to visit his hometown and family tomb.

This was my fifth visit to Madagascar, and I had become enthralled with the country, its people, and its culture. My bad mood, I decided, had everything to do with our shabby treatment by the UNICEF office and nothing to do with Madagascar.

The waiter brought the bill. "You know," I said, "I like Madagascar very, very much." He smiled, and I did too.

Itinerant Academic Worker

I've been fortunate enough to have visited more than forty countries on five continents. Born and brought up in Britain, I'm grateful to my parents for introducing me to travel on family camping vacations in France and Spain. In the 1970s, when I worked as a journalist, my first wife Claire and I took budget trips to Mediterranean countries—Portugal, Spain, Italy, Morocco, Greece, and Turkey—traveling by bus or hitchhiking, camping or staying in youth hostels or fleabag hotels that didn't rate a single tourist star.

I moved to the United States for postgraduate study in 1978, began university teaching two years later, and didn't travel much for the next fifteen years. Since the mid-1990s, most of my travel has technically been for work, not pleasure. I say "technically" because I enjoy most trips, even though I work long days in sometimes difficult conditions. That's because I am traveling with a purpose. By contrast, I've had vacations that didn't give me much pleasure. I find beaches boring, resorts unappealing. I'm not a gambler or souvenir shopper, don't play shuffleboard or mini-golf, and don't like Las Vegas shows; I don't think I'd enjoy a cruise.

My trips have been as a teacher, trainer, researcher, project director, and some other titles I've forgotten. Unlike the typical business traveler, I can get away with dressing academic casual—a shirt and khakis. There are ties (mostly gifts) in my closet. On average, I wear a tie once a year. Not every year. Fortunately, the organizations that hire me are looking at my proposal, résumé, and experience, not my wardrobe.

In June 2010, I officially retired from Ohio University after a thirty-year academic career. There was no way I was going to take up golf, bridge, or bingo, enroll in classes in pottery or furniture making, let alone sit on the front porch drinking iced tea and comparing Medicare supplement plans. For me, to retire was to move on—to have the time and freedom to work in interesting places.

It's often difficult to describe to strangers what I do. Sometimes, I dodge the question and tell them I'm a consultant. That's a convenient but unhelpful response, because no one (not even those who use the word on their business cards) can easily describe what it means to be a consultant. It's a catchall that covers a range of services—from training mercenary armies to appraising antiques. "Oh, a consultant, that must be interesting," is the usual reaction. "Sometimes," I reply. That's when the conversation usually ends.

Recently, I've taken to describing myself, somewhat mischievously, as an "itinerant academic worker." I can go wherever my academic and professional credentials take me. No regular classes to teach. No students to advise. No faculty meetings. No research expectations. It's the academic open road.

The real bonus and joy of travel has been to write about the places I've seen, the people I've met, the experiences I've had. Since cameras went digital, many travelers record their memories visually, posting images on websites, social media, and sharing sites. I shoot some pictures, but mostly I take notes and ask questions. What are they harvesting in that field? Are those houses made of bamboo? What does that road sign mean? What's the name of this village? What are we eating? Is that a wedding celebration? Did you see that elephant we just passed on the road?

I don't want to suggest that all travel is interesting. Travel writer Thomas Swick put it well: "Readers sometimes say to me, 'You always meet the most interesting people when you travel.' I tell them, 'Not really, I just write about them when I do.' Most of the time I'm wandering around lonely and aimless. In my own way, I am as guilty as the cliché mongers of perpetuating the idea of travel as a continuously fascinating activity—though all writers shape their experiences into an unrepresentative series of highlights; otherwise our stories would be too boring to read."[1]

Traveling with me can be tiring, especially for those who want to sleep. I rarely do. In a bus or car, on a train, or on foot, I am constantly scribbling in my notebook or on whatever piece of paper I have handy— an airline boarding card, a restaurant menu, or even the background briefing paper I promised to read on the way from the hotel to the office. I write down what I see and learn because that's the only way I can connect the dots later. Even in a place filled with new sights, sounds, and smells, what is interesting and unexpected on first encounter is more familiar the next time around, and less worthy of recording. The Antananarivo I first visited in September 2014 was a fascinating new place, unlike any other city I had ever seen. I described it as "Paris with rice paddies." On my second visit three months later, it was interesting but less surprising; by the time of my fifth visit in March 2016, the city seemed less noteworthy. I made many notes on my first and second trips, but fewer on the later ones. However, even in places I've visited before, I always learn something new. Often, it comes in chance conversations—in buses, trains, taxis, and shops, at roadside cafes and markets. Indeed, the best insights are often gained by just hanging out with people. You strike up a conversation with the desk clerk or the passenger sitting next to you. You never know where it will lead.

Much of the time, I rely on colleagues to translate. I mean this in the broadest sense—not only the literal translation of words and phrases from another language but interpretations of history, society, and culture. I have also learned not to take what I am told at face value. In any country, there is no single, accepted history or vision for the future; instead, there are many perspectives, and they are constantly in motion, fanned by the winds of politics, nationalism, and identity.

I've been weaving my notes into narratives, trying to put places and people in historical and cultural context, since my travels to the former Soviet republics of Central Asia in the mid-1990s. I have also written articles for newspapers, magazines, and online outlets. The Central Asia stories, originally sent as e-mail letters to family and friends, formed the basis for my first offbeat memoir, *Postcards from Stanland: Journeys in Central Asia,* published in 2016. It recounted my travels and work in Kyrgyzstan, Kazakhstan, Tajikistan, and Uzbekistan.

This book has a broader geographical sweep, describing a broad and circuitous arc around the Indian Ocean with insights into the history, geography, politics, economy, climate, and belief systems of four countries where I've traveled over the last decade. My journey begins in Madagascar's chaotic capital, Antananarivo, then wanders through the Central Highlands, the eastern rain forest, and the savannah and desert of the southwest, offering glimpses of the history, culture, and politics of a beguiling but desperately poor country. From Madagascar, I make the long leap northeast across the Arabian Sea to the Indian subcontinent. India defies all generalizations because of its social, ethnic, and religious diversity. My narrative begins in the capital Delhi, then broadens out in space and time, exploring the colonial legacy, the partition of British India, and the country's demographic, economic, and environmental challenges. From the north, I move to the ancient kingdom of Hyderabad, and finally to the underdeveloped "chicken-neck," the northeastern states of Assam and Meghalaya. Then I follow the Brahmaputra River south to Bangladesh, a country defined by its rivers and struggle for independence. From the traffic jams and garment factories of Dhaka, I travel to the rice bowl and commercial centers of western Bangladesh, to the tea gardens of the northeast, and to the delta region—the front line for climate change. My journey ends in Indonesia—at Banda Aceh, ground zero for the 2004 tsunami, the noise and traffic of the capital, Jakarta, ancient Yogyakarta, and the beaches and backcountry of Bali.

Ambivalent about Development

My first experience in international development work came in December 1995 when, at short notice, I took an assignment to set up a journalists' training center in southern Kyrgyzstan, a region that had experienced ethnic conflict over land, resources, and political power. My US embassy liaison flew with me to the city of Osh, stayed a couple of days, and then left, wishing me good luck. I spoke only a few words of Russian and had few contacts. I hired a student as interpreter, found an apartment, visited local media, launched a search for a center manager, and enlisted Peace Corps volunteers to teach English classes in exchange for Internet access.

Four years after the fall of the Soviet Union, Kyrgyzstan's economy was still in freefall: factories and collective farms had closed, the currency devalued, pensions almost worthless, and power cuts frequent. Often I was the only diner in a restaurant where a sad-faced waiter apologized that most items on the menu were not available. In subzero temperatures, families squatted on the broken concrete sidewalks, their possessions—kitchen utensils, auto parts, school textbooks, old clothes, Soviet memorabilia—spread out on blankets. I don't know who was buying because most passersby were just as poor as the sellers.

Before my work in Kyrgyzstan, the problems of the developing world had seemed remote and abstract to me—a wire service report on the latest famine or civil war somewhere in Africa, a TV charity appeal with images of suffering women and children. Now I was seeing them for myself. My experience convinced me that I had the skills and temperament to work effectively in an unfamiliar and challenging situation. A quarter of a century and two revolutions later, the Osh Media Center is still going strong, despite political and financial pressures.

Over the next twenty years, I returned frequently to Central Asia—to Kyrgyzstan, Kazakhstan, Tajikistan, and Uzbekistan. For my university, I took student groups to Hungary, the Czech Republic, Ecuador, and Thailand and managed an exchange program between Indonesian and US television journalists. I had two Fulbright Teaching Fellowships—in Kyrgyzstan (1996–97) and in Kazakhstan (2011). In Asia and southern Africa, I have worked for a veritable alphabet soup of international and government organizations. I have conducted workshops on training techniques for broadcast managers and worked with journalists to improve their reporting on social, economic, and environmental issues. For six years, I led a team that offered a global training course on communication for development (C4D) for UNICEF staff, with workshops held in Ohio, Johannesburg, and Hyderabad. The Madagascar research fiasco was followed by a successful two-year project to introduce C4D curricula at universities in Bangladesh and improve the research skills of faculty.

To work in development, you have to believe you can make a difference, however small, in people's lives. It's all too easy to become frustrated—by bureaucracy, ill-conceived project goals, and especially unrealistic timelines. Social and cultural change occurs slowly; no mass media campaign, however creative or far-reaching, will suddenly transform people's attitudes and behaviors. It may take a generation for people to change the way they think about issues such as child marriage or girls' education, and another generation to do something about them. Yet donors demand fast, measurable results that will show up as a good return on investment in annual reports and press releases. They account for the funds they receive on a yearly basis and have to report results. The "annual report syndrome," as an eloquent critic of top-down approaches to development, Alfonso Gumucio Dagron, calls it, "is one of the worst enemies of development" because it "forces a chain of lies and exaggerations from the grassroots level up to the implementers and funding institutions."[2]

The "lies and exaggerations" often begin earlier in the cycle, when government and international development agencies invite bids for contracts. In the United States, a relatively small number of not-for-profit and private-sector organizations, most of them in the Washington, DC area (earning them the sobriquet of "Beltway Bandits"), compete for lucrative contracts—not only from the US Agency for International Development (USAID) but from the Departments of Treasury, Commerce, and Agriculture, as well as from other agencies. Because all the bidders are staffed by seasoned professionals and have a host of consultants on their rosters, it's difficult to pick a winner based on expertise. More often than not, the agency awards the contract to the bidder who promises the most for the least money and has lined up an impressive list of partners and collaborators. After winning the contract, the organization spends months negotiating a work plan; inevitably, goals and activities are scaled back, and partners dropped, because there isn't enough money to do what was originally promised.

Although development agencies pay lip service to the idea of community participation, most projects are designed and implemented by professionals to meet donor priorities. In many sub-Saharan African countries, more people die each year from malaria or diarrhea than from AIDS and sexually transmitted diseases, yet more money is earmarked for reproductive health than for mosquito nets and oral rehydration kits. Even when reproductive health is a priority, aid comes with conditions; USAID contractors are shackled by Congressional guidelines that specify the percentage of funds to be spent on abstinence programs, even if condom distribution has more impact.

"The more we invest in development, the more we contribute to the growing of the cemetery of development." That's Gumucio Dagron's gloomy assessment. Newly built schools are closed because no money was allocated to pay teachers or buy desks and books. Water and sanitation systems are abandoned because no one knows how to maintain them. Gumucio Dagron offers a catalog of failed projects—abandoned hospitals, broken-down vehicles, and "two thousand post office mail boxes rusting under the rain in a village of five hundred illiterate families who neither received nor wrote letters."[3]

I cannot be as pessimistic as Gumucio Dagron, but I have my own catalog of ill-conceived and botched development projects that have failed to make a difference in people's lives. I've also seen well-planned projects that have helped lift people out of poverty, improved their health, and provided their children with education. In my experience, the best investments are in human resources, in helping people gain the knowledge and skills they need to make a difference in their own countries. That's why I've gained the most satisfaction from education and training programs. Of course, not all my workshop participants apply what they have learned to become better managers, journalists, or C4D professionals, but some (maybe more than I realize) do so. And when they are passing on what they have learned to others, I know I have achieved something.

I continue to worry about the unintended consequences of development aid. We need to feed the hungry, but will massive food shipments depress prices on the market and drive local farmers off the land? International charities urge individuals to buy desks for schoolchildren so they do not have to sit on the dirt classroom floor. Would the money be better spent on population control, reducing average family size (and the number of schoolchildren)? In some countries, foreign aid accounts for almost half of the government's annual budget and a significant percentage of Gross Domestic Product (GDP). Are we creating a culture of dependency, a neocolonial relationship between the donor and receiver countries, by making them continue to rely on foreign aid?

Put me down as ambivalent about development.

Postcards

I am from a generation that enjoyed sending and receiving postcards. I haven't received many recently. It's easier to post a selfie to Facebook from under a beach umbrella than to get out of your chair, find a shop, buy a postcard, write it, buy a stamp, and mail it. But I miss sending and receiving them. For me, the pro-forma "Weather lovely, wine cheap, *pâté de foie gras* gave me indigestion, wish you were here" greeting was never enough. I bought cards with the largest possible writing space and usually managed to cram more than one hundred words about my travels into the left-hand side.

This book, like *Postcards from Stanland,* combines personal experience, interviews, and research. It is not intended as a travel guide. It's not an academic study or the kind of analysis produced by policy wonks, although it offers background and insights. Think of it as a series of scenes or maybe oversized postcards (with space for a few thousand rather than one hundred words) that I would have sent if you were on my friends and family list. Which you can be, if you send me your e-mail address.

two

Indian Ocean World

"Historians visualizing the Indian Ocean," wrote the Sri Lankan academic Sinnappah Arasaratnam, "have been like the five blind men in the old Indian fable conceiving of an elephant by feeling different parts of its anatomy. They have come up with partial views of sections of the Ocean, or of the Ocean viewed from sections of bordering land or from the perceptions of different people who traversed the Ocean."[1] But not the ocean as a whole. The Indian Ocean world stretches far beyond coastal areas—in other words, it is a region linked to, but not limited by, a body of water.

The ocean-as-world perspective is generally attributed to the French historian Fernand Braudel of the *Annales* school who used the Mediterranean Sea, not territorially bounded units such as kingdoms or principalities, as the framework for study. Similarly, the Indian Ocean world is a vast interconnected region, from interior Africa to the Middle East to China, whose boundaries have shifted in time and space as military, economic, and cultural empires have risen and fallen. It was built on commercial networks, including the slave trade, the movement of peoples and their cultural assimilation, and the spread of religions, particularly Hinduism and Islam. In his introduction to the essay collection *Trade, Circulation, and Flow in the Indian Ocean World*, Michael Pearson concludes that "ties and connections, elements of commonality, stretching all over the Indian Ocean" mean that "we can indeed write of an Indian

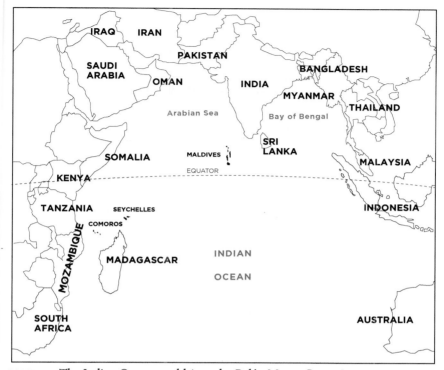

MAP 2.1 The Indian Ocean world (map by Belén Marco Crespo)

Ocean World." With the rise of India and China and competition for sea lanes, oil, and African minerals and markets, "the Indian Ocean world represents a strategic arena where the forces shaping a post-American world intersect most visibly."[2] Foreign policy analyst Robert Kaplan describes the Indian Ocean as "the coming strategic arena of the twenty-first century."[3] The concept of an Indian Ocean world allows me to venture beyond coastlines and port cities to interior regions, linked to the ocean by rivers, colonial conquest, trade, migration, and culture.

What ties together four seemingly diverse countries—Madagascar, India, Bangladesh, and Indonesia—besides their proximity to the Indian Ocean and its historic trade and settlement routes?

First, there is the monsoon. It has different names and comes at different times, but it always comes. The monsoon determines when you plant and harvest, when and where you travel, even when you get married, have children, or bury your dead. It is both a curse and a blessing. It brings death and destruction yet provides the water vital to survival. In northeastern Madagascar, the cyclones of January and February sweep away bridges and roads and leave communities stranded; six months later, farmers harvest cash crops of cloves, lychees, and vanilla. In Bangladesh in 2017, the first rains came early (in April), ruining the first rice crop in several regions. When I returned in August, the waters of the Padma (Ganges), Jamuna (Brahmaputra), Meghna, and their tributaries had left northern regions under water, washed away roads, bridges, and railroads, and forced as many as eight million people to abandon their homes. Yet when the waters recede, they deposit the alluvial soil that makes Bangladesh one of the most agriculturally fertile countries in the world.

Second, each country is the creation of a colonial power—the British, French, or Dutch. Even Madagascar, which makes the most geographic sense because it's an island, was formed only when one ethnic group subjugated others, a conquest that was administratively consolidated by the French. In the others, European powers cobbled together tribes, ethnic groups, and independent kingdoms (maharajahs, sultans, and emirs) into colonies where unity remained fragile. At independence, British India and the Dutch East Indies were sliced and diced, creating new fissures. Despite half a century of nation building, the boundaries drawn in the colonial era remain a challenge to unity and identity.

There are common threads to the national narratives of colonialism, and to a historical schizophrenia in which the colonizer is both resented as the agent of oppression and exploitation, and admired for transforming the economy, building infrastructure, expanding education, and establishing political institutions. As Shashi Tharoor, a former UN diplomat and Indian cabinet minister, notes: "Whether through national strength or civilizational weakness, India has long refused to hold any grudge against Britain for 200 years of imperial enslavement, plunder and exploitation."[4] This ambiguous relationship to the colonial past has shaped national development and public discourse. As my Malagasy colleague Richard Samuel puts it: "All actions by our government are taken in support of France. It's neo-colonialism. More than half a century after we declared independence, we have still not achieved it."

Third, all four countries face daunting environmental and climatic challenges—devastating floods, droughts, earthquakes, tsunamis, urban pollution, saline intrusion, deforestation, and desertification. The benefits of economic development—from mining to cash crops, from logging to tourism—come with social costs. Governments, foreign and domestic business interests, international agencies, environmental groups, and local communities are engaged in high-stakes conflicts over land, natural resources, and water. The technocrats who decided to address the Madagascar government's budget deficit by leasing more than half the country's agricultural land to a South Korean conglomerate did not consult with the people farming the land, let alone offer them any compensation. In the furor that followed, the government was overthrown in a coup.

Fourth is the movement of people. Internal and external migration are most often driven by economic factors: historically by the global and national slave trades and the transportation of indentured laborers to rubber and sugar cane plantations; today by economic opportunities, particularly in the Persian Gulf, where remittances from migrant workers support families and boost domestic GDP. Some migrations are caused by natural disasters or climatic shocks. Yet the most disruptive population movements are occasioned by war, civil conflict, or political change—interethnic conflict in Madagascar, the 1947 partition of British India, Bangladesh's 1971 Liberation War, separatist movements and conflicts in regions of Indonesia.

Fifth is political change. Since achieving independence, and throughout the Cold War era, these countries have vacillated between autocracy and multiparty democracy, between state control of the economy and media and open markets and press freedom. Even in India, where political institutions are well established, strong leaders have emerged—Nehru and the Gandhi dynasty, and today, Narendra Modi. In other countries, where institutions are more fragile, the leaders of anticolonial resistance movements all too often became homegrown despots, amassing power and wealth for their families and associates and ruthlessly suppressing opposition, often with support from the West or the Soviet bloc.

Are We in Africa—or Asia?

It had been a long lunch at Ku-de-ta. Andrew and I decided to walk for an hour or so before returning to the hotel to try to figure out if we could rescue the UNICEF research project. We strolled to the ridge of the *haute ville* where a great stone staircase descends to the market area and looked west toward the hills and the rice paddies. Most of the people on the streets, with their dark brown skin color and straight black hair, were Asian in appearance. If it weren't for the French-language signs, cobbled streets, and colonial-era architecture, we could have been in a hill town in Indonesia.

It was more than a millennium ago—somewhere in the Malay Archipelago, near where my journey ends—that a small group of people set sail in their outrigger canoes, heading west with the trade winds across the Indian Ocean and avoiding the monsoon. They stopped for water and supplies at harbors in the Bay of Bengal and Arabian Sea before sailing south and landing on a large island, previously uninhabited by humans. It's a journey that took years, maybe even generations, with trade and intermarriage along the way. They were Madagascar's first settlers.

three

Land of the Merina

Of Kings and Drunken Soldiers

"We're on our way to Arivonimamo—the town of a thousand drunken soldiers."

Richard Samuel laughed at his own joke as he edged his dented Nissan pickup through the chaotic traffic of Madagascar's capital Antananarivo, weaving around aging Citroën and Renault taxis, potholes, and hand carts hauling furniture, metal fencing, and sacks of charcoal.

The name of Richard's hometown evokes the heyday of the Merina, the highland ethnic group that ruled Madagascar during the nineteenth century and is still prominent in politics and business. In an early campaign, the Merina king Andrianampoinimerina dispatched a thousand soldiers to capture a market town in the rice-growing region about thirty miles west of Antananarivo. Facing little resistance, the soldiers didn't have much to do except get drunk on home-brewed, sugarcane rum and give the new garrison town its name. In Malagasy, "Arivo" means thousand and "nimamo" drunks.

Richard is proud of his Merina heritage and claims descent from "a former king (*roi*)." In Madagascar, the word "king" needs to be treated with caution. Until the French colonized the island at the end of the nineteenth century, the central highlands were a bit like medieval Europe, albeit with nicer weather. Local lords, supported by armed retainers, ruled the villages and their rice fields from fortified hilltop positions. To call them kings is a stretch; my colleague Luke Freeman, an anthropologist who has worked in Madagascar for more than twenty-five years, more aptly describes them as kinglets (in French, *roitelets* or petty kings).

Whether *roi* or *roitelet*, Richard's ancestors were local nobility, their power measured by the size of their domain and the number of zebu—the humped oxen that are the mark of wealth in rural Madagascar—in their herd. Today, descendants of noble families still claim moral authority because of their lineage and, in some cases, their healing powers.

"I have inherited, along with all the members of my extended family, the power to cure burns," Richard told me. "It's not a skill, it's a gift. All the members of my family have it. My son, my daughter, my sisters, my brothers—all can cure." It was, he said, a matter of noblesse oblige. No traditional healer in a community hangs out a shingle like a doctor or dentist. People simply know which family has the power to cure this or that ailment. Richard says he does not expect payment; his power is a gift from the ancestors, and he must use it to benefit others. Some traditional healers take cash payments, but Richard says it's more common to receive a gift—a bag of rice or cooking oil.

I met Richard at the University of Antananarivo (UA) in September 2014, on my first trip to Madagascar for the UNICEF research study. He was soft-spoken, modest about his own experience, and respectful of others' opinions. We bonded quickly, and on my visit in March 2016 he invited me to travel to Arivonimamo.

Richard lives in two worlds. He has advanced degrees in economics and development studies, has worked in senior positions for government ministries, and is on the sociology faculty at the country's leading teaching and research institution. As the descendant of nobility and a traditional healer, he inhabits another world, far from the pressures of life and work in the city. As often as he can, he returns to Arivonimamo—to the modest home of his parents, to the Catholic high school where he was educated by Canadian friars, to the church where he was baptized and had his first communion. On the main street and market, people stop to ask for his advice on all sorts of matters. Most of his family members still live in the area. A few miles west of the town is the new house Richard and his wife Tina have built for weekend getaways and their retirement. It's next door to the family cemetery.

FIGURE 3.1 Richard Samuel, academic, political activist, minor nobility, traditional healer

Island or Continent?

If people have an image of Madagascar, it's usually of a beach, a baobab tree, or a cartoon lemur. The island's name recognition was boosted immensely by the 2005 computer-animated comedy hit from DreamWorks about four animals from New York's Central Park Zoo who, after spending their lives in happy captivity, are suddenly repatriated to Africa and shipwrecked off the coast of Madagascar. Two sequels and a spin-off, the implausibly titled *Penguins of Madagascar,* put the "big red island"—so named because of the red, claylike soil of the central highlands—on the movie map and may have given a minor boost to tourism.

It wasn't always an island. It was once part of the supercontinent of Gondwana, sandwiched between Africa and India. Gondwana started breaking apart about 180 million years ago, but it was another 100 million years before Madagascar detached itself from Africa and floated off into its present position in the Indian Ocean. Stretching almost 1,000 miles north to south and almost 375 miles across at its widest point, it's almost the size of Ukraine and a little larger than Texas; it's in the top fifty countries in the world for land area, larger than Kenya, Thailand, or Spain. It's often ranked as the world's fourth-largest island, after Greenland, New Guinea, and Borneo. But is it an island? Its long geologic history, wide range of vegetation and climatic zones—from semidesert to tropical rainforest—and biodiversity arguably place it in the "continent" category; indeed, some (including, of course, the tourist companies) call it the "eighth continent." Neither geologists nor biologists, writes geologist Maarten de Wit, "have a definition that is capable of classifying Madagascar unambiguously as an island or continent." Which gives de Wit a catchy subtitle for his scientific journal article: "Heads It's a Continent, Tails It's an Island."[1]

Because it was separated from other landmasses for eighty million years, Madagascar developed a unique ecosystem, with plants and animals found nowhere else in the world. It has more than twelve thousand plant species, almost ten thousand of them found nowhere else, almost 350 reptile species, and forty-three primates, including the signature cuddly ring-tailed lemur. The biodiversity makes Madagascar what de Wit calls "the world's hottest biodiversity hot spot," attracting thousands of well-heeled tourists, mostly from North America and western Europe, who take guided tours through the jungles, cactus forests, and deserts. It's also a favorite, safely exotic destination for French vacationers, who come mostly for the beaches, nightlife, and excellent haute cuisine. In the French tourist brochures, it sits alphabetically between its two main tropical rivals—the French-speaking Caribbean islands of Guadeloupe and Martinique.

There are no cave paintings, parchment scrolls, or even oral traditions to tell us when Madagascar was first settled by humans—a lack of evidence that has led to a long and vigorous debate over origins. However, most scholars agree that in the scheme of human history, settlement came late, probably not before the fifth century. By that time, trade routes had been established across the Indian Ocean, linking Southeast Asia, India, the Arabian Peninsula, and east Africa.

Geographically, one might expect the first settlers to have come from Africa, making the relatively short (250–400-mile) journey across the Mozambique Channel. Astonishingly, they came from the other side of the Indian Ocean—from the Malay Archipelago, or what today is Indonesia. Although it is not known who they were or when they arrived, the historical evidence is persuasive. The Malagasy language borrows words from Javanese, Malay, and the languages of Borneo and Sulawesi; its nearest linguistic relative is a language spoken in southern Borneo. Some crops— rice in particular—are found throughout southeast Asia. On the coast and rivers, Malagasy travel in outrigger canoes like those used in Indonesia. Ethnomusicologists compare the simple Malagasy xylophone to one used by tribes in Borneo. Conclusive scientific evidence came in a 2012 study of matrilineal lineage that made a statistical comparison of the mitochondrial DNA of people from Madagascar and Indonesia. The team, led by Murray Cox of New Zealand's Massey University, concluded that Malagasy and Indonesian DNA separated about twelve hundred years ago, close to the date when historians believe the island was first settled.

What were the reasons for settlement? At the time, much of the Malay Archipelago was part of the Srivijayan Empire, a major trading power that had the ships and men to mount an expedition; however, there is no historical evidence that it did. "Most likely, then," notes the *Economist* in an analysis of the settlement evidence, "the first Malagasy were accidental castaways, news of whose adventure never made it back home. But there is still a puzzle." Because people inherit mitochondria only from their mothers, the study tracked only the female line of descent. That means that the first party of settlers must have included some women—perhaps as few as thirty, according to Cox. Most ships' crews were male, so why were women on board? One explanation is that the women were the cargo, and that Madagascar's original inhabitants ended up on the island by chance after a slave ship wandered off course or was wrecked on the reefs.[2]

Whichever historical narrative is applied—that the first Malagasy were traders or shipwrecked slaves—it is unlikely that they were heading for Madagascar, or that they even knew where they would end up after they left the Malay Archipelago. Even with favorable winds, trading ships could not have made a direct crossing of the Indian Ocean. It is almost four thousand miles from the west coast of Sumatra to Madagascar, and the ships would have run out of fresh water and food after a few weeks. Instead, they took the long way around, stopping at ports in the Bay of Bengal and the Arabian Sea before heading south along the east coast of Africa, a journey that may have taken years. Although most trading ships returned home with cargoes, some did not, their crews deciding to settle and seek their fortunes in ports around the Indian Ocean. They intermarried with the indigenous people, creating the racially mixed population that is typical of many coastal communities.

Archaeological evidence shows that Bantu peoples from East Africa may have begun migrating to the island as early as the sixth and seventh centuries. Some were herders from the Great Lakes region, and they brought their animals with them. Linguists have noted that most Malagasy words for domestic animals have Bantu-language roots; for example, the word for the humped cattle zebu is *hen'omby*, from the Swahili word for beef, *omby* or *aombe*. Other historical records suggest some Bantus were descendants of sailors and merchants from the east coast—from modern-day northern Mozambique north to Somalia—who crossed to western Madagascar in their dhows to trade. Finally, some may have been transported to the island as slaves. Migrants cultivated crops found throughout the African continent, such as manioc and sweet potatoes.

The early settlers from the Malay Archipelago are referred to in some sources as the *Vazimba*, as if they were a distinct ethnic group that occupied a specific region during a certain period. It's a convenient way for historians to box them into a timeline to fit a narrative of conflicts, cattle raids, and slavery. From a Malagasy perspective, history is more complicated. As Luke notes, the Malagasy use *vazimba* as a word for any unknown population that was in a place before they were and "left enigmatic traces of themselves such as abandoned tombs or a standing stone." Throughout the island, "there are traces of lost people who settled and moved on and whose history and passing are lost in time. So *vazimba* are not really the 'original' or even 'early' people of Madagascar, just vanished predecessors, just people doing what all Malagasy people do: settling, moving on, fading away." The problem, as Luke points out, is the use of the definite article; once you talk about "the Vazimba" rather than "vazimba," you elevate their status from "just people" to that of an ethnic group.

A second wave of settlers from the Malay Archipelago arrived between the eighth and twelfth centuries. They were the Merina, Richard's ancestors. They brought with them their traditional clan organization and agricultural practices, particularly rice cultivation. They settled mostly in the highland regions where the landscape of rice paddies today looks as if it could be anywhere in Thailand or Indonesia. Their skin color and straight dark hair make them Asian in appearance. However, many communities, especially in the coastal regions, are racially mixed, with generations of intermarriage between people of Asian and African descent, Arab seafarers, and later Chinese and Indian traders and European settlers.

From the seventeenth century, Madagascar became important in the Indian Ocean trade in silks, spices, and slaves, and a haven for pirates who preyed on merchant ships. Although successive European powers— the Portuguese in the sixteenth century, followed by the Dutch from the Cape Colony, then the French and the British—tried to establish trading and military posts, most settlements were short-lived. Other Europeans ended up on the island by accident, shipwrecked on its notorious reefs. The tribes, especially in the south, were often hostile, and disease and climate took their toll. The only group that adapted relatively successfully were the pirates who used the harbors of the east coast as bases to prey on merchant ships sailing to India; they had goods to trade for food, and some took Malagasy wives. By the mid-eighteenth century the British navy had sent most of the pirates scuttling back to the Caribbean. While other areas of Africa fell under European rule, Madagascar, relatively isolated and lacking exploitable agricultural or mineral resources, remained off the colonial radar. The island was divided between three large kingdoms and small feudal domains headed by warrior chieftains. They were almost always fighting each other, stealing zebu and taking captives to use as slave labor.

By the end of the eighteenth century, the Merina chieftain Andrianampoinimerina had subdued his rival kinglets and created a unified kingdom in the central highlands. He vowed that the Merina kingdom would have "no frontier but the sea." In their imperial ambitions, the Merina kings had a willing ally in the British, who were competing with the French for military and commercial dominance in the Indian Ocean. The British struck a deal with the Merina kings—guns for slaves. In return for stopping the export of slaves to the French colonies of Réunion and Mauritius, Britain recognized Merina sovereignty over the island and provided economic and military aid, including firearms, enabling the kings to extend their domain outside the central highlands. The Merina replaced local chiefs with civil servants who collected taxes and imposed labor quotas. The irony is that while restricting the export of slaves—and so dealing a severe blow to the French plantation economy on Réunion and Mauritius—British support for the Merina boosted the internal slave trade. By the mid-1820s, the British-trained, musket-toting armies of Andrianampoinimerina's son, Radama I, had conquered or subdued most of the island, capturing or taking as tribute thousands of Malagasy. A century after Britain abolished slavery in its empire, Madagascar's slave markets were booming. Britain's emissaries diplomatically ignored the Merina use of slave labor—either imported slaves or those from coastal areas—in plantations and factories. Although slavery was officially abolished in 1877, the institution remained until the end of the monarchy.

As the European colonial carve-up of southern Africa continued apace, British interest in Madagascar and support for the Merina monarchy waned. In January 1895, the French landed fifteen thousand troops on the northwest coast. Although half the force died or had to be evacuated because of disease, the Merina army proved no match. After a one-day artillery bombardment of Antananarivo, the Merina surrendered. The monarchy was abolished, slavery banned, and taxes imposed; French settlers arrived, coming to dominate agriculture, commerce, and industry. The great Merina landholdings were broken up, and local leaders replaced Merina in administrative positions. The Merina kings had allowed Protestant missionaries to establish churches and schools, and many had followed the lead of the royal family, which converted in 1869. With French colonization, pragmatic Malagasy Christians sensed the way the winds were blowing and found the Catholic mass more politically and socially agreeable than the Methodist or Lutheran service. Madagascar remained a French colony until independence in 1960.

Although maps and guidebooks show the island neatly divided into eighteen ethnic groups, each supposedly protecting its own cultural terrain, ethnicity in Madagascar is muddled. There's no single criterion for defining an ethnic group; some are based on racial origins, some are alliances of clans that resisted Merina conquest, some are classified by economic activity, such as fishing or zebu herding. Throughout its history, Madagascar has experienced almost constant migration, both from other regions of the Indian Ocean and internally, as people moved to flee conflict, find better farmland, or work in mines. Except in isolated rural areas, most communities have an ethnic mix.

The historical divisions between the highland peoples of Asian descent, including the Merina, and coastal peoples (*côtiers*), primarily of African descent, are key to understanding Malagasy society. The highland peoples have a complex social structure; at the top of the hierarchy are the noble clans (the *andriana*) that ruled the island until the French arrived; further down are the *hova* (commoners) and clans with less land, zebu, and political clout; at the bottom of the social strata are marginalized clans of migrant workers and the descendants of former slaves. Depending on whom you talk to, intermarriage between the highland peoples and *côtiers* is either taboo, extremely rare, or, in urban areas, a lot more common than it used to be. The ethnic mix has not yet melted.

Ethnicity is a complex and sensitive issue. I respect the views of Richard and others who believe that colonization by the French destroyed the national unity the Merina kings had built. At the same time, other ethnic groups, especially in the south, have long regarded the highland Merina as oppressors. In the nineteenth century, the Merina conquered their lands, stole their zebu, and sold them into slavery; today, the central government, dominated by the Merina political elite, taxes them without providing schools or social or medical services. Although the monarchy collapsed in 1897 when France took control, the Merina have remained the most politically and economically powerful ethnic group in the country. In the nineteenth century, the *andriana* ruled from their palaces and traveled in sedan chairs; today, the Merina elite rule from ministries and corporate headquarters and travel in SUVs.

The research study focused on five areas—health, nutrition, water and sanitation, education, and child protection. UNICEF wanted to know whether certain ethnic groups had specific attitudes and practices. Did one group fear needles and refuse to have their children vaccinated? Did another have food taboos? Did another believe that water from the river was cleaner than treated water from a well? The first time we asked our mostly Merina colleagues at UA about ethnicity, we faced a stone wall. "There are no ethnic groups in Madagascar, we are all Malagasy," was the collective response. Knowing that most Malagasy identify by village or community and hold ceremonies to honor their ancestors, we came up with a roundabout way of asking about ethnicity in our questionnaire: Where are the tombs of your ancestors? If we had that information, we could be reasonably confident about ethnic origin because the boundaries of tribal regions roughly correspond to those of old kingdoms. Again, we were stymied. When the final versions of the questionnaires were translated from French to Malagasy, the question was cut.

When You Die, You Live Together in the Same Tomb (Malagasy Proverb)

You'd expect a road called Route Nationale (RN) 1 to be a major highway. Typically, the number one national route in any country is a major artery, connecting the capital with important regional centers, helping to drive the national economy. On that measure, Madagascar's RN1 is a disappointment. It starts in the right place—the capital Antananarivo, familiarly known as Tana—as a divided highway heading confidently westward toward the coast. Outside the city, it reverts to a two-lane that winds lazily through the highlands. Seventy-five miles west of Tana, RN1 seems to hesitate and divides into two branches. They are reunited 60 miles further west at Tsiroanomandidy on the edge of the highland plateau. That's where RN1 and the blacktop end, still more than 125 miles short of the coast and what should be its terminus, the fishing port of Manitrano. The fizzling out of RN1 is symptomatic of Madagascar's infrastructure problems; without better road or rail connections, or electricity-generating capacity, economic development will always be hampered. For those traveling on from Tsiroanomandidy to the coast, the dirt road descends from the highlands to the savannah grassland, and then to the coastal plain. It's a bone-rattling fifteen-hour trip by 4x4 or high-riding vehicle. In the dry season, the trip by *taxi-brousse* (bush taxi) costs 70,000 *ariary* ($23); in the monsoon season, it's 100,000 ($32). The people of Manitrano call it "the devil's route."

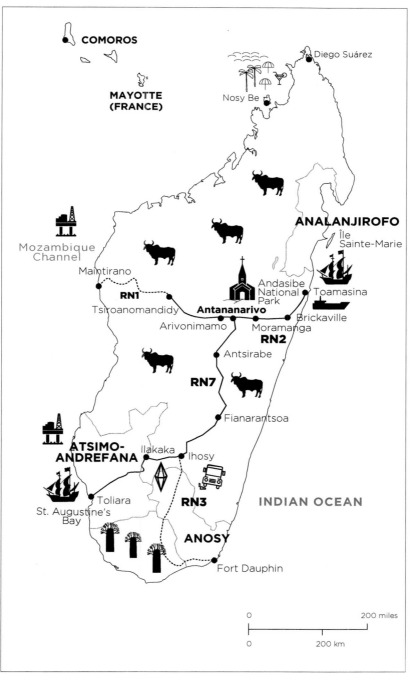

MAP 3.1 Madagascar (map by Belén Marco Crespo)

The highland region west of Tana is called Imerina, literally the homeland of the Merina. RN1 winds gently up and down the low hills, skirting fields of corn, rice paddies, and secondary-growth stands of pine and eucalyptus; along the roadside, billboards feature images of politicians planting trees and declaring their commitment to environmental conservation. Brick kilns dot the fields; with most wood used for charcoal, homes are built from rough mud bricks fired from the red-clay soil of the region. The towns are agricultural and commercial centers, selling farm implements, seeds, and supplies and shipping produce to the capital.

Richard, Tina, and I stopped at the roadside to eat fresh corn, grilled in cocottes over charcoal fires. "This is an agricultural region, but the farmers are not self-sufficient," said Richard. By tradition, land is divided among sons, so over generations farm plots have become smaller. The national average for a family farm, Richard said, is half a hectare—about half the size of a football or rugby field. "You can't survive on that, and the population continues to grow. That's why the people go to Tana every day to do *petit commerce,* selling farm produce, secondhand clothes or cheap consumer items."

We stopped for lunch in Arivonimamo, the town of a thousand drunken soldiers, and visited Richard's family home and the Catholic

FIGURE 3.2   Cooking corn in cocottes on charcoal grills at roadside on RN 1, west of Antananarivo

FIGURE 3.3 On the market at Arivonimamo—manioc, a staple in the Malagasy diet

lycée where he studied. The first armed rebellion against the French occurred here in late 1895, soon after Tana surrendered, and the queen
signed a treaty establishing a French protectorate. Some regarded the
Merina monarch and political leaders as traitors for abandoning the religion and traditions of the ancestors, converting to Christianity, adopting Western ways, and accepting defeat and occupation. A force of two
thousand men seized Arivonimamo and murdered the Merina governor,
two Quaker missionaries, and their child. The force planned to regroup
in Tana on market day, with arms concealed in their clothes, to attack
the royal palace, the French residency, and the European quarter, but
the plot misfired, and French troops were sent to Arivonimamo to quell
the uprising. Insurrections broke out in other parts of the island in 1896
before the French were able to assert control.

A few miles beyond Arivonimamo, we pulled off into the red dirt
driveway of the new family home. Like all residential construction
projects, this one had been going on longer than Richard and Tina expected, but they seemed stoic about the delays. Richard's brother, wearing a yellow-and-green Brazil football T-shirt, was sitting on a stone wall
waiting to greet us.

FIGURE 3.4 Lala and Richard Samuel at new family home near Arivonimamo. Go Brazil!

Richard introduced us. "His name is Relax," he joked, then corrected himself. "Lala."

I wondered for a moment if the Richard of the city and university was envious of his brother's simple, unhurried lifestyle as a subsistence farmer. Their parents had seven children. Three brothers had died, leaving Richard, Lala, and two sisters. Richard was the only child to go to high school and university. The others remained in the Arivonimamo area.

Richard, Lala, and I walked outside to the terraced garden with sweeping views from the ridge to the south. Tina had planted manioc, coffee, and lychees, as well as herbs; a patch of ground had been excavated for a fish pond. From the garden, it was just a few steps to the family cemetery—half a dozen above-ground stone and concrete tombs. Two zebu wandered among the tombs, grazing on the long grass. I thought to myself that when Richard and Tina die, they won't have too far to go.

I pointed to one grave dug in the earth and decorated with flowers. "In 2014, we lost an elder brother," said Richard. "And soon after we buried him, a cousin died. We will move them into the tomb at the proper time. You can't just open up a tomb when someone dies."

For the Merina, the proper time is the *famadihana*, literally the "turning of the bones," a three-day celebration when extended families gather to open the tombs, exhume the corpses, and rewrap them in silk shrouds (*lamba*). For many Malagasy, death is the passage between life on earth, which is ephemeral, and life beyond, which is eternal. The ancestors' spirits, writes Madagascar historian Sir Mervyn Brown, "watch over every aspect of daily life. . . . The concept of the ancestors as a collective entity embodying traditional wisdom reinforces the unity and continuity of the family."[3] In life and death, family ties are unbroken. Richard quoted a Malagasy proverb: "When you are alive, you live together under the same roof. When you die, you live together in the same tomb."

The *famadihana* is the opportunity to communicate with the ancestors, to seek their blessing for health and wealth. "You pray to be successful in business and to have many zebu," said Richard. The standard ethnographic view of the ceremony, writes anthropologist David Graeber, is "that the living wish to give honor to the dead, and that by doing so they receive their *tsodrano* or blessing—a blessing that will ensure their continued health, prosperity and fertility." However, in attending

FIGURE 3.5   Richard Samuel and brother Lala at family tombs

seven *famadihana* in the Arivonimamo district, Graeber found a darker side to the practice—a fear of ancestral violence. This is linked to what the Malagasy call *fady* (taboos). There are *fady* on plants that should not be grown or eaten, on stealing from members of one's clan, on selling ancestral land to outsiders, on intermarrying with lower castes, particularly the descendants of slaves. When Graeber asked people what would happen if *famadihana* was not performed, the answers were unequivocal: their children would die, their health would fail, or the family would fall deeper into poverty. When asked about "the origins of the dark, murderous specters that disturbed children's sleep or otherwise plagued the living, most people immediately suggested they were ancestors whose descendants 'no longer took care of them.'" Memory of the ancestors, writes Graeber, is double-edged—they are both celebrated and feared.

The *famadihana* has a set ritual and sequence of events. It begins with a procession to the tomb led by an astrologer, usually accompanied by men carrying photographs of the most important ancestors and followed by neighbors, guests, and women carrying straw mats. After uncovering the stone door to the tomb, the men descend the steps with candles or lamps and carry out the bodies, rolled in the mats, in order of seniority, calling their names as they emerge. The crowd shouts for joy, and the band cranks up the beat as the men dance the corpses around the tomb. Placed on the laps of the women, the corpses are sprinkled with rum and honey, then rewrapped in new white silk *lamba*, and held by family members who pray silently. The music picks up again and mixed groups of men and women dance the corpses around the tomb one more time. The mood, writes Graeber, is one of "delirious abandon," with the corpses "twisted and crunched about a great deal before finally being returned to their places inside." As the crowd begins to drift away, the tomb is sealed with earth. Later, the astrologer and a few assistants return to perform a *fanidy*, symbolically locking the tomb by burying magical objects around the doorway. If done correctly, writes Graeber, a *fanidy* should ensure that "the ghosts of those within would remain there, unable to emerge again and trouble the living."[4]

The *famidhana* is a joyous occasion, but an expensive one. A huge feast is prepared, one of the few occasions when a zebu is killed for meat. There are the costs of the silk *lambas*, the band, the bottles of homemade rum. Family members are expected to contribute what they can, handing over an envelope of cash to the host. The event can cost from $1,500 to $2,000, more than many families earn in a year. "It is usually held in winter after the harvest when families have the means," said Richard. Winter is also the dry season; for public health reasons, the government has banned the exhumation of bodies during the monsoon months.

There is no set interval between the *famadihana,* although some say that once in seven years is common. "It depends on a family decision, and financial means," said Richard. Lala was suggesting it was time, and maybe they could do it in September. "We need to consult everyone in the family," Richard replied. By then, he hoped, the house would be finished so everyone could stay overnight.

The practice of *famadihana* has been criticized. A *Washington Post* article attempted to link it to the spread of bubonic plague in Madagascar, although the connection seemed weak;[5] in a country where over 75 percent of the population live on less than $2 a day, many people live in unsanitary conditions that provide fertile breeding grounds for rats and fleas. Attempting to ban a strongly established cultural practice because it may result in a few cases of plague diverts attention from the structural problems of poverty, sanitation, and lack of infrastructure. The government could achieve more by picking up the trash and enforcing sanitary regulations than by banning *famadihana.*

Richard did not forget Lala's request. The family agreed to hold the two-day *famadihana* in mid-September. I was sorry I could not attend, but Richard posted photos to my Facebook page.

Paris with Rice Paddies

Most travelers arrive in Madagascar at Tana's Ivato international airport, about eight miles from the city center. There are daily flights from Paris, Johannesburg, Nairobi, and Maputo (Mozambique); connections to Indian Ocean destinations—Mauritius, Réunion, the Comoros, and Seychelles; and weekly flights to more offbeat destinations such as Bangkok and Istanbul. The Bangkok passengers include gem dealers with illegal shipments of rough sapphires sewn into their underwear or in bottles labeled as vitamin tablets. Others travel to buy electronics and upscale consumer goods for resale to middle-class customers. Until the domestic market grows enough to make it viable to use air freight, business owners will continue to make shopping trips, stuffing cheap luggage with designer-label clothes, iPhones, and cosmetics.

Domestic flights are on Air Madagascar. Or "Air Maybe," as one passenger described it. "Sometimes they fly, sometimes they don't," she said. "You can never be sure." The airline seems to suffer from the same disease as the government that owns it, staggering from one financial or management crisis to the next. Sometimes it's bankrupt. Sometimes the pilots are on strike. Sometimes there is no fuel. You should never book too far ahead on Air Maybe.

The road to the city from the airport passes through a densely populated area. After a few hotels and the Chinese casino, it's the typical African or Asian street scene—honking cars, slow-moving trucks, hole-in-the-wall shops, children playing on the narrow sidewalk, porters lounging on hand carts. Change the language on the signs and it could be almost any city in India, Bangladesh, or Indonesia. A mesmerizing array of small retail establishments are crammed into narrow storefronts—a tire repair shop next to a beauty salon, then a halal butcher, a one-room health clinic, a furniture workshop, a SIM card recharge outlet, a shop selling *friperie* (secondhand clothes), a small hotel, a lumberyard, a used car parts store, another beauty salon. Then a wall plastered with posters for music concerts and religious revivals, almost obscuring the *Défense d'Afficher* (forbidden to post) sign. A jumble of colorful hand-painted signs, mostly in French or Malagasy with a sprinkling of English—Good Auto, Rehoboth Shack, Smile Pizza, Quick Fix Oil Change, Flash Video. For the last four miles, the road runs along the levee of the River Ikopa. The low-lying areas around the city are crisscrossed by canals supplying water to the rice paddies. Among the paddies are islands of shacks, with chickens, geese, and ducks (some destined to be pâté) running free, and zebu grazing on patches of grassland. Then past the fifteen-thousand-seat national rugby stadium—home of the Makis (the lemurs)—to a retail district centered, without any sense of ideological irony, on a square dedicated to a communist hero, the Place de Ho Chi Minh.

Situated just over four thousand feet above sea level, Tana, with its hills and narrow, winding streets, feels like a tropical, slightly rundown version of Paris with rice paddies. From the original *rova* (fortress) built by the Merina king Andrianjaka in the early seventeenth century, the royal real estate expanded, with new palaces and royal tombs built on the highest points of the ridge. The residential topography of Tana (as in other Merina towns and villages) reflected class distinctions. Down the hill from the palaces were the houses of the *andriana,* the noble class; the commoners, the *hova,* lived further down the slope, and the slave caste (*andevo*) and rural migrants on the plains to the west. Members of castes were required to live in designated districts and return to them after working in other places. Nonnobles were not allowed to build wooden houses or keep pigs within the city limits. As the population grew, the Merina kings used forced labor to construct a massive system of dikes and paddy fields around the city to provide an adequate supply of rice.

Tana temporarily lost its status as the Merina capital in the early eighteenth century with the death of the king Andriamasinavalona. The kingdom split into four territories and for the next seventy-odd years, Merina kinglets fought, intrigued, allied, married, and died as they competed for supremacy. The eventual winner was Andrianampoinimerina from the eastern district, who conquered Antananarivo in 1794, ending the civil war. His former capital, Ambohimanga, was designated the spiritual capital of the Merina, and Antananarivo the political and commercial capital. Andrianampoinimerina created a large marketplace at Analakely, the lowland area between the two ridges, and it remains the city's economic center.

By 1810, when Andrianampoinimerina's son Radama I ascended the throne and began expanding the Merina empire, Antananarivo, with a population of more than eighty thousand, was the largest and most important commercial city on the island. Radama's successor, Ranavalona I, helped launch Madagascar's modest industrial revolution. British missionaries introduced brickmaking, and a shipwrecked French craftsman, Jean Laborde, established factories to produce construction materials, agricultural tools, and weapons for the army; in Antananarivo, two massive staircases were built to connect the market at Analakely to the growing residential areas on the two ridges.

Until the mid-nineteenth century, all houses in Madagascar were built from wood, grasses, reeds, and other plant-based materials deemed appropriate for structures used by the living; stone, as an inert material, was reserved for the dead and used only for family tombs. In 1867, after a series of fires destroyed wooden homes in Antananarivo, Queen Ranavalona II lifted the royal edict on the use of stone and brick for construction. The royal palace was encased in stone. The first brick house built by the London Missionary Society in 1869 blended English, Creole, and Malagasy designs and served as a model for a new style built in the capital and across the highlands. Termed the *trano gasy* (Malagasy house), it is a two-story, brick building with four columns at the front that support a wooden verandah. In the late nineteenth century, these houses quickly replaced most of the traditional wooden houses of the *andriana*. As Protestant denominations and the Roman Catholic Church gained adherents, stone and brick churches were constructed.

In the early twentieth century, under French administration, the city spread out along the lower hilltops and slopes in *la ville moyenne* (the middle town). In the *basse ville* (lower town), northwest of the Analakely market area, French urban planners laid out the streets on a grid pattern aligned with a broad boulevard, now called the Avenue de l'Indépendance, with the city's Soarano railroad station at its northwest end. Engineers drilled tunnels through two large hills, connecting isolated districts; streets were paved with cobblestones, and some later with blacktop; water, previously drawn from springs at the foot of the hills, was piped in from the Ikopa River. Since independence in 1960, the city has spread out across the plains in every direction, and urban growth has been largely uncontrolled. In the sprawling districts of the *basse ville*, where roughly built houses are vulnerable to fire and flooding, many

FIGURE 3.6 Madagascar's capital, Antananarivo, "Paris with rice paddies"

residents splice into city power lines to steal electricity. Informal settlements, without adequate water supply and sanitation facilities, have grown up on agricultural land on the outskirts.

Today, the historic *haute ville* retains its late nineteenth-century charm. *Trano gasy* houses with steeply pitched tiled roofs, verandas, and flowering cactus line the cobbled streets snaking up the hillsides; alleyways with stone steps descend to the Analakely market and shopping streets branching off from the Avenue de l'Indépendance. Among the most impressive buildings are the stone-built churches on the summits. Below the Malagasy Montmartres, people cook over open charcoal fires, draw water from hand pumps, and sleep in doorways. The official population of the Tana metropolitan area is more than two million—about one-tenth of the total population of Madagascar—but that does not count unregistered migrants from rural areas who arrive every day to work or engage in *petit commerce.*

The French influence is still apparent—in language, the architecture of public buildings, the bakers selling baguettes and croissants, the escargots and pâté de foie gras on the restaurant menus. At the Soarano railway station, the Café de la Gare resembles a brasserie in a French provincial town, with its dark wood paneling, chandeliers, candlelit tables and white-shirted waiters. The best hotel in the city, the Colbert in the *haute ville,* founded as a handful of rooms above a café in 1928, reeks of colonial extravagance with its marble-clad lobby, patisserie, hair salon, perfume shop, spa, and casino. At the nearby Café du Jardin, overlooking the Analakely market, the large-screen TVs rebroadcast French provincial rugby matches.

My guide to the city was Luke, who had worked in Madagascar on and off for more than twenty-five years. He arrived in Tana in 1989 as the country was emerging from more than a decade of what some termed "Christian Marxism" (Marx would have turned in his grave). He was supposed to be fulfilling his university foreign-language requirement by spending a year studying French. He had another motive. "Saying you're going to Madagascar to study French is rather like saying you're going to Nigeria to study English," he said. He improved his French but concentrated on learning the Malagasy language and studying the culture. Since 1989, he has returned to Madagascar almost every year. As an anthropologist, cultural study meant more than wading through dissertations, books, and articles on kinship, tradition, and religion. Luke worked as a rice farmer and herded zebu across the southern deserts.

It was in 2004, while Luke was on a zebu drive, that he was summoned to the capital by the so-called yogurt king Marc Ravalomanana, winner of the December 2001 presidential election. The president wanted to reduce Madagascar's dependence on France and open trade links with English-speaking countries, particularly the United States and South Africa. Luke was appointed the president's English speechwriter and communication adviser. "One day, I was sleeping under a tarpaulin," Luke recalls. "Three days later, I was in a luxury hotel in Addis Ababa, writing a speech for Ravalomanana to deliver to the African Union." He moved to Tana and worked for Ravalomanana before returning to the UK to take a university position.

Luke had been a late addition to our research team, stepping in when another member withdrew for medical reasons. His knowledge of the history, geography, economy, and culture of Madagascar proved indispensable; he was the first to make us aware of the divisions between the Merina and the *côtiers* and their implications for the research study. He helped us understand how our UA colleagues viewed the project, and what they hoped to gain from it. In Tana, he knew where to shop and where to eat (he introduced us to Ku-de-ta). Like anyone who has lived long enough in another country, Luke knew how to get things done. A case in point: most bureaucratic transactions require an official stamp. When Luke applied for an extended visa, the immigration authorities demanded a stamp from his institution, at that time the London School of Economics (LSE). LSE does not have a stamp, but Luke had to come up with one. He went to the bazaar where a skilled artist created a mirror imprint of the LSE logo and made a stamp. It was good enough for the immigration authorities.

Luke helped us understand Madagascar's complex, love-hate relationship with its former colonial master. French rule brought law and order, roads and railways, schools, a health system, nice restaurants, and good pastries, but it also forced people to leave their homes to work on plantations. France is still the leading foreign investor (although China is catching up), and French tourists bring in much-needed foreign exchange. France is still seen as the place to receive higher education, and maybe to migrate for work. At various times since independence, nationalists have discouraged the use of the French language, yet it is still taught in schools and widely spoken, especially in urban areas. Madagascar-historian Sir Mervyn Brown, who served as UK ambassador in the late 1960s, recalled that French nationals still occupied senior positions:

> It is normal when a country becomes newly independent that colonial officials should remain in important positions for a short time. . . . But in Madagascar, even ten years after independence, the French were still there in force. In the President's office his secretary general was French, and the head of security was French, the head of his personal staff was French, a gendarmerie colonel; and they weren't very discreet about it. Neocolonialism was very evident.[6]

I wondered what people would think of my rusty French. I need not have worried. As I emerged from a mobile phone store after buying a SIM card, I told Luke that the staff must have been snickering over my mangled syntax. "They don't care," he said, "It's not *their* language."

Vive le Renault 4L et le 2CV!

"Do you have a lot of 4Ls in the United States?"

Richard asked the question as our Renault 4L taxi hurtled down a cobblestone hill in Tana. It was a jarring, noisy ride. I gripped the door handle, which appeared to have been re-riveted to the frame more than once. At the bottom of the hill, the driver crunched into low gear and began a slow climb.

I told Richard I had never seen a 4L in the United States. His question puzzled me but, as I looked out at the chaotic traffic, I realized why he had asked. In his urban landscape, the 4L was a dominant species.

When I traveled in France in the 1970s, the Renault 4L was a common sight. With its functional, box-like design, it sat high (for its size) on its chassis, its front end leaning slightly down as if it was getting ready to dive into the potholes and muddy farm fields. It was introduced in 1961, aimed at the lower end of a market dominated by the two-cylinder Citroën 2CV, the celebrated *deux chevaux* (two horses), a small front-wheel-drive sedan marketed as a people's car in the same class as Germany's Volkswagen Beetle. The 4L, like the 2CV, was seriously underpowered, taking several minutes to reach its preferred cruising speed of about 80 kilometers (50 miles) per hour. Once it made it, it chugged along happily, using much less petrol than anything else on the road. For the new driver, the gear shift on the 4L and 2CV was a challenge—you pulled it out directly from the dashboard, then twisted it left and right, forward and backward, in a complex series of motions. In my twenties, living in Britain, I owned first a 2CV and then the slightly upmarket (but no more powerful) Citroën Diane. I soon became expert at the contortions required to shift gears.

I visit my sister and her husband in southwestern France every couple of years. There, it's unusual to see a 4L or 2CV on the road, although I've spotted a few rusting in barns. But they are still the most common taxis on the roads of Tana. Many are survivors of the city's traffic wars, with battered panels and out-of-whack alignment. On some, the ignition no longer works, so the driver hot-wires the engine. As you rattle up the cobbled streets you try to forget that there's almost no suspension and just marvel that the car is still running.

The history of the French automobile industry lives and breathes— or rather wheezes—in Tana and other Madagascar towns. I've seen other Renault and Citroën models, the Peugeot 204, 304, and 404, and even the occasional Citroën DS (Goddess), the sleek, streamlined car with a hydraulic system that looked years ahead of its time when it was

FIGURE 3.7 His pride and joy, a Renault 4L taxi

introduced in the mid-1950s. There are gas-guzzling SUVs on the roads of Tana, but in a country where all indicators—unemployment, poverty, health, literacy—put it in the "least developed" category on global indexes, you're fortunate if you own a 4L or a 2CV. The last ones came off the production line in the early 1990s, but they still command high prices on the used-car market, more than $2,000 for a model with a few dents, a cracked windshield, and worn seats.

With spare parts no longer available, except from specialty dealers at high prices, how do drivers keep their cars running? The answer is "bricolage" (from the French verb *bricoler*, to tinker), loosely translated as "do-it-yourself." "We Malagasy always manage to find a bricolage solution," Richard told me. The auto parts trade, he said, is controlled by Indian and Pakistani shopkeepers who import parts from factories in Mumbai and Karachi. Many either fit the old cars or can be made to fit with a little bricolage. For that service, you go to one of the many metal fabrication shops that cut and weld made-to-order fencing, pipes, market stall frames, and agricultural implements. They can take a Tata or Mahindra part and make it work for your 4L; if not, they'll just make you a new part. When cars eventually break down and cannot be repaired, the parts are salvaged and resold. "In this economy, there's almost always a new use for something," said Richard.

Madagascar Recycles

You'll find the most ingenious examples of recycling and bricolage on Tana's markets. Not the upscale markets where middle-class Malagasy, expatriates, and tourists shop, but the regular markets that serve most residents. Luke took me to the Isotry quartier, one of the poorer districts of central Tana, south of the Soarano railroad station. The Isotry bazaar is off the tourist route, and the more interesting for it. Live geese, ducks, chickens, and turkeys are crammed into straw baskets. Scrawny cats, tethered by string to the baskets, are also on sale; the point-of-purchase message is that if you buy a cat to keep down the vermin, it will not attack your poultry. There are live crabs in buckets, and stacks of *friperie* (secondhand clothes) and shoes. There's new stuff, of course, including the bizarrely branded Chinese T-shirts and underwear—Tokyo Super Dry, Cool My To Rock, Hugo Premium Fashion Boss. Because it was early December, vendors were hawking artificial Christmas trees and decorations. In the consumer electronics section, it took me a few minutes to figure out why stalls displayed guitars, amplifiers, car batteries, and solar panels together. It's because electricity is still not available in some communities around Tana, and city districts experience power cuts. The band must play on, so musicians travel with their own power supply.

At one stall, we found a selection of farming hand tools, with blades of different lengths, widths, and angles designed for every task, all forged from scrap metal. Richard had told me that the scrap metal trade is controlled by ex-zebu herders from the south, a tough bunch who drive hard bargains. Next door, the vendor was selling hand weights fashioned from car gears. Bottles and jars are washed and reused. I bought jars of homemade *lasary* mango hot sauce, a specialty of northwest Madagascar, and *sakay,* made from red chili peppers with ginger and lemon juice. To carry the jars, I used a shopping bag made from polyester straps used to secure boxes for shipping. The Malagasy have long learned to recycle and reuse—not through any sense of environmental consciousness but because in a poor country there's no alternative.

One section of the market is devoted to traditional medicine. The stalls are piled high with wood sticks, bark, shells, bottles, and packets of remedies. One promised to cure almost anything—diseases of the heart, liver, lung, and stomach. Others claimed to improve fertility or build muscles. To ward off evil spirits, there are amulets to wear and incense to burn. It occurred to us that perhaps UNICEF should commission research on the market. The use of traditional medicine is not confined to remote rural regions and ethnic groups; here in the capital city there were dozens of stalls, most offering the same range of merchandise, and people were buying.

An Ample Supply of Vowels

In April 1996, at the height of the Balkan crisis, the satirical newspaper the *Onion* reported the latest US initiative to bring peace to the region:

> Before an emergency joint session of Congress yesterday, President Clinton announced US plans to deploy over 75,000 vowels to the war-torn region of Bosnia. The deployment, the largest of its kind in American history, will provide the region with the

critically needed letters A, E, I, O and U, and is hoped to render countless Bosnian names more pronounceable.

The deployment, dubbed Operation Vowel Storm by the State Department, is set for early next week, with the Adriatic port cities of Sjlbvdnzv and Grzny slated to be the first recipients. Said Sjlbvdnzv resident Grg Hmphrs, 67: "With just a few key letters, I could be George Humphries. This is my dream."[7]

Far be it from me to criticize US foreign aid policy—even a satirical version of it—but I feel obliged to point out that large stocks of vowels are lying idle and unpronounced in other countries. If the State Department had done its research more thoroughly, it could have purchased an ample supply from Madagascar, giving a much-needed boost to the country's foreign exchange earnings. Americans should be asking why their government is sending its hard-earned vowels overseas when some American schoolchildren are struggling to form syllables. We need to keep our vowels at home to help make America great again.

Unlike some African countries that have many languages and even more dialects, Madagascar has a single, vowel-rich national language—Malagasy—with French as the second language for most educated people. There are regional differences, of course. Standard or official Malagasy is the dialect of the highland Merina, the government, and national media. Outside the highlands, especially in racially mixed coastal areas, dialects are spoken; people understand official Malagasy but do not use it in everyday life.

Malagasy is not related to other African languages, although it imported words from Bantu and Arabic, and later from English and French. It belongs to the Malayo-Polynesian branch of the Austronesian language family; its nearest linguistic relative is a language spoken in southern Borneo. Madagascar has a long and rich oral literary tradition, expressed in *hainteny* (poetry), *kabary* (public discourse), and *ohabolana* (proverbs); the *Ibonia* epic poem, about a folk hero of the same name, has been handed down in different forms across the island, and many stories, poems, and histories are retold in musical form. From the seventh century, *ombiasy* (wise men) transcribed Malagasy using an Arabic script called *sorabe* to record sacred knowledge. Written, Western-inspired literature developed shortly after colonization by France at the end of the nineteenth century, and it flourishes today.

Malagasy positively brims with vowels. Of course, some unstressed syllables are dropped, and diphthongs compress vowels, but that's cold comfort for the tongue given the abundance of *a*, *e*, *i*, and *o* in many words. A simple greeting, "Hello" (two vowels in English), has seven in Malagasy—*Manao ahoana*. That's manageable, but the names of some people and places seem bewilderingly long to the non-Malagasy speaker. The chieftain who unified the Merina clans in the late eighteenth century to form a powerful kingdom in the highlands went by the polysyllabic name of Andrianampoinimerinandriantsimitoviaminandriampanjaka. Presumably, some rival Merina chiefs surrendered after failing to successfully pronounce his name, a small triumph for syllables over armed conflict. Later, he adopted the shorter, easier-to-recall name, Andrianampoinimerina (the lord at the heart of Imerina). His son, who expanded the Merina empire, made it easier for his foes to negotiate terms. He was called simply Radama I.

As in other languages, the name tells a story about the position or lineage of its owner. The name of some kings begins with "Andriana," a term that denoted the noble caste of Merina society. In the extended form of Andrianampoinimerina, "Andria" appears three times, indicating that the king ruled over three regions. It's a well-worn monarchical marketing strategy to project power by accumulating titles, so the Merina king was doing no more than European rulers had been doing for centuries. Andrianampoinimerina's British contemporary, the unfortunate George III, was officially King of the United Kingdom of Great Britain and Ireland, Defender of the Faith, King of Hanover, and Duke of Brunswick-Luneburg. Napoleon I made himself Emperor of the French, King of Italy, Protector of the Confederation of the Rhine, and Mediator of the Helvetic Confederation. All of which makes the Merina king's name look rather modest. The difference, of course, is that in Malagasy, the titles run together in a compound word.

The Merina kings followed the playbook of all conquerors, renaming places to imprint their own version of history. "The imperial tactic," according to Luke, "was to inscribe the Merina presence in the mythology and identity of local places." In many cultures, the clearest markers of settlement and land ownership are ancestral tombs; when these are removed by a conquering army, the original inhabitants' historical claims to the land are erased. In the early seventeenth century, the chieftain Andrianjaka expelled the inhabitants of Analamanga, a village at the highest meeting point of two forested ridges, and built a *rova*. According to oral tradition, he deployed a garrison of one thousand soldiers to guard the *rova*. A later king, Andriamasinavalona, renamed the settlement Antananarivo, the "city of the thousand," in honor of Andrianjaka's soldiers, and it became the capital of the Merina kingdom. A hundred miles west of Richard's home town of Arivonimamo (the "town of a thousand drunken soldiers"), on the edge of the highland escarpment at the terminus of RN1, is the town of Tsiroanomandidy where "two shall not rule," which is reportedly what the Merina king told the local ruler when he conquered the place. East of Tana on RN2, place names commemorate the passage of the Merina kings and queens and their retainers. There's Manjakandriana, which literally means "where the king passed through." Nandihizana is "the place where there was dancing," marking the arrival of the Merina queen and the cue for the local population to turn out and boogie.

Madagascar has had eight presidents since independence in 1960; the names of six begin with "Ra"—Ramanantsoa, Ratsimandrava, Ratsiraka, Ravalomanana, Rajoelina, and Rajaonarimampianina. When I first reviewed the list of our UA colleagues, I was similarly dismayed: they included Rabaovololona, Ralalaoherivony, Randriamasitiana, Ravelonjatovo, Rakotonirina, Rasolofoniaina, and Ramamonjy. The lineage of most highland Malagasy is represented through their names, which position them in relation to their clan, region, or village. Remembering them is easier when you mentally lop off the honorary "Ra" prefix, which means "Mr." or "Ms." But there are still a lot of vowels and syllables. Even for the Malagasy. Antananarivo is usually abbreviated as Tana, except on the iconic French red and white kilometer road markers, where it is uncomfortably squeezed into an ugly "Ant/rivo."

Divide and Rule

For even the experienced analyst, Madagascar's politics are infuriatingly complex. Since independence in 1960, the country has vacillated between dictatorship and freewheeling democracy, between socialism and unbridled capitalism, while maintaining a close but uneasy relationship with its former colonial master. Five successive presidents were forcibly ousted from office. In a continent that has seen more than its fair share of coups, Madagascar is near the top of the league table; in the first decade of the twenty-first century, it had at least four actual or at-tempted coups. The name of that Tana restaurant, Ku-de-ta, is no joke.

"Parties keep changing their colors," said Richard. "Today, a party is in opposition, but tomorrow it will rejoin the alliance of the party in power and in return has to be given a ministry." Richard served in government positions under three presidents and criticizes a system that is "100 percent influenced" by politics. Ministers are, of course, political appointees, but party membership is also required for department heads who, in another country, would be career civil servants. Ministers and their staffs are constantly changing. Richard recalls a test question on the entrance examination for first-year sociology students: Who is the minister of public services? "No one knew. It changes so often."

Richard credits his political activism to his father, Rasamoelina, who worked as a barber in Arivonimamo. Rasamoelina was a member of the Democratic Movement for Malagasy Renovation (MDRM), formed by French-educated nationalists after World War II to push for independence. The MDRM hoped for a peaceful transition, but the French government refused to consider any degree of political autonomy. The French colonial minister, Marius Moutet, cabled the high commission in Tana to "fight the MDRM by any means." As tensions rose, Rasamoelina's smoke-filled barber's shop became a hotbed of political discussion. In 1947, a revolt broke out in eastern Madagascar, with rebels attacking French commercial interests, including plantations and mines. The revolt spread to other regions. In Arivonimamo, Rasamoelina, aged thirty-two, left his family and shop to join a rebel unit. He was lucky to survive.

The suppression of the 1947 rebellion is regarded by historians as one of the most brutal of the colonial period. There were few French casualties because most fighting was done by Senegalese—an example of one colonial people being used to suppress another. Psychological tactics were employed—rape, torture, and the burning or razing of villages. In one town in the southeast, prisoners were thrown from an aircraft on a so-called death flight. In Tana, prisoners were herded into railroad cars; at Moramanga, on the line to the east coast port of Tamatave (now Toamasina), the doors were opened, and the prisoners machine-gunned. French colonial reports put the death toll at eighty to ninety thousand, although later figures lowered it to eleven thousand. The discrepancy has never been satisfactorily explained. Perhaps no one will ever know how many died from hunger or disease after fleeing from their villages into the forest.

In Arivonimamo, Rasamoelina's rebel unit was forced to flee to the hills ahead of advancing Senegalese troops. The group was captured, but Rasamoelina and a few others escaped from trucks while being transported back to Arivonimamo. A few months later, after the fighting was over, he returned to the town. Family connections enabled him to stay out of prison.

Richard was born seven years later, but the struggle against the French shaped his politics and passions. "My father always talked about how hard it was to achieve independence. We paid with many deaths, with torture, with forced labor." Men were sent to build roads, and women and children conscripted into the civilian labor corps.

Richard criticizes the French for fomenting ethnic divisions in Madagascar. "My father talked about how the colonizers lit the fire between the coastal peoples [the *côtiers*] and those of the high plateau. It was the kings of the high plateau [the Merina] who united the island, after conquering the small coastal kingdoms. But when the French came to colonize, they told the coastal peoples, 'We're liberating you from subjugation.' It was a policy of divide and rule."

Too Many Coups

The nationalist leader Philibert Tsiranana, a *côtier*, became the country's first president in 1960, but postindependence euphoria soon evaporated as the country struggled with debt and a poor economy. In 1972, popular protests forced Tsiranana to hand over power to the army commander, General Gabriel Ramanantsoa. Political turmoil continued, and in 1975, after surviving several coup attempts, Ramanantsoa stepped down. His successor was assassinated within a week of taking office, and another coup brought Admiral Didier Ratsiraka to power. He weakened relations with France and aligned Madagascar with the Soviet Union.

Although paying lip service to socialist principles, Ratsiraka sought to impose revolution from above. Madagascar even had its own "Red Book" (*Boky Mena*) to guide the actions of the five pillars of the revolution: the Supreme Revolutionary Council, peasants and workers, young intellectuals, women, and the Popular Armed Forces. The Red Book advocated a foreign policy of nonalignment, with domestic policies focused on economic development through rigorous planning. Political parties were suppressed, and strict censorship enforced. Because of its situation on the Mozambique Channel—a major shipping route for oil and other commodities—Madagascar became a key proxy in Cold War geopolitics. Although the government had nationalized some French companies, France maintained a large embassy and a major aid program. When Malcolm McBain arrived as UK ambassador in 1984, he found a "considerable diplomatic presence."

> It was also important to the Russians. [They] had a large embassy. There were about forty diplomatic missions, resident missions in Madagascar, plus numerous non-resident missions and a large European delegation. . . . The Communist Chinese were running an aid programme, and rebuilt the key road linking the capital with the main port. The Japanese were there, with some valuable aid. Also represented by embassies were the North Koreans, the Libyans, the Indians, the Indonesians, the Cubans and the Vietnamese. The African National Congress had a representative there, the Egyptians, the Yugoslavs, the East Germans, of course.[8]

The Soviet Union deployed thousands of technical staff and advisers— on everything from aviation and the military to sports. Russian was introduced to the secondary school curriculum; the best students went on to study in Moscow and Leningrad. North Korea built Ratsiraka a new concrete presidential palace, modeled on the *rova,* outside the city. However, life for most Malagasy did not improve.

"The state controlled everything, all the wealth," said Richard. "The only jobs were with the government, and you needed connections." The French colonists had been replaced by a new group of homegrown oppressors. When Ratsiraka came to power, Richard was studying at UA, working at night in a *gargotte* (a roadside restaurant) to support himself. He joined the Proletarian Party and took part in student antigovernment protests. "We were reading Che Guevara, and running around at night, plastering posters on walls," he recalled. "We were always running away, and in danger of being shot by the security forces. It was a great adventure."

With Ratsiraka in power, most French faculty left the university, to be replaced by Soviet professors. "They brought with them lots of books on scientific communism," said Richard. "They were serious about their mission and taught all subjects using Marxist-Leninist principles, but the students didn't read most of the books. Fortunately, the students were exposed to two perspectives because the Malagasy professors stayed."

Strikes and student protests continued as economic conditions worsened. In 1979, when Richard's first child was born, almost everything—food, milk, medicines, soap—was in short supply. "You needed to belong to the cooperative of the revolutionary party to have coupons for supplies," he said. "There were always shortages, but we were told we needed to make sacrifices to reach the socialist paradise."

In 1989, Ratsiraka was returned for a third seven-year term in what many regarded as a rigged election. For the next four years, the country was paralyzed by general strikes and riots. In 1993, opposition candidate Albert Zafy defeated Ratsiraka, ending his seventeen years in power and sending him into exile in France. Three years later, Zafy was impeached by the parliament. To the surprise of the international community, and many Malagasy, Ratsiraka returned to win the 1996 election.

With the end of the Cold War and the collapse of the Soviet Union, Ratsiraka abandoned the socialist experiment, imposed neoliberal reforms, and restored diplomatic and economic ties with France. The economy improved, with a boom in tourism and textile exports to the United States; from 1997 to 2001, foreign direct investment grew tenfold, and in 2001, the economy grew by 6.7 percent, one of the best performers in Africa.

Two Presidents, Two Capitals

Ratsiraka's opponent in the December 2001 election represented a radically new direction. Marc Ravalomanana, the so-called yogurt king, had built his dairy products company Tiko into a business empire before being elected mayor of Tana in 1999. He was credited with cleaning up the capital, repairing roads, installing street lights, and putting more police on the streets. The city experienced a building boom, with new offices and supermarkets opening. The youthful Ravalomanana made much of his devout Protestant faith, and his TIM (I Love Madagascar) party ran a slick, media-savvy campaign. His TV and radio stations bolstered his candidacy, and his face was everywhere—on T-shirts, bags, and baseball caps. He favored economic links with the United States and South Africa, rather than France, and printed English-language slogans on Tiko's bottles of milk and mineral water. He was a Merina, popular in Tana and the central highlands. Ratsiraka was a métis (mixed race) with Merina and Betsimisaraka lineage, so he had support across ethnic lines; however, his power base was in the port of Toamasina on the east coast, and much of his support came from the *côtiers* of African or mixed descent.

Officially, neither candidate gained an absolute majority in the election. Ravalomanana claimed the count was rigged and crowds in Tana turned out to proclaim him president. Ratsiraka denied election shenanigans and called for a constitutionally mandated runoff. For the next six months, Madagascar had two presidents, two prime ministers, two parliaments, and even two central banks. The economy went into freefall. The banks could not extend credit, and businesses could not repay debts; textile factories closed, tourists canceled vacations, and investors fled. Donors could not dispense aid because they did not know which government was in charge.

Ravalomanana's government controlled Tana and the central highlands; Ratsiraka, backed by five of the six provincial governors and military top brass, set up a rival capital in Toamasina and controlled most coastal regions. His supporters built barricades and blew up bridges along RN2, the main road from the coast to the capital, halting supplies of food, fuel, and other goods. The *Economist* reported in May 2002 that at Brickaville, where RN2 turns west toward the highlands, "the country's main commercial route is reduced to a narrow concrete path. . . . Men totter over it in single file under sacks of cement, crates of tinned food and baskets of chickens. Others wade across the river, pushing barrels of smuggled petrol. . . . Brickaville is becoming a border town, and a rough one at that."[9]

The military eventually threw its support behind Ravalomanana, and in April 2002 the High Constitutional Court declared him the outright winner. TIM won a convincing victory in elections for the National Assembly. Ratsiraka was forced to admit defeat and return to exile in France. Ravalomanana embarked on a business-friendly reform agenda, providing tax breaks for foreign investors. The government improved roads, schools, and hospitals and fought corruption. Textile factories opened in tax-exempt free zones, and multinational companies started exploiting mineral resources. And the president hired Luke as his speechwriter and communication adviser.

Ravalomanana easily won a second term in 2006 but faced opposition when he proposed constitutional amendments that increased the power of the presidency and allowed him to stand for two more terms. The changes were narrowly approved in a referendum. Although the economy continued to grow, food prices rose, and opposition mounted to the free rein given to foreign investors. In July 2008, Ravalomanana signed an agreement with the South Korean conglomerate Daewoo for a ninety-nine-year lease of half of the island's arable land to grow grain. South Korea, with a growing population and limited land and water resources, certainly needed the grain, but the decision was both legally and morally dodgy. The prospect of selling off ancestral land to foreigners horrified many people. What was to happen to the subsistence farmers who had used the land for centuries to grow rice and herd zebu? Would villages be moved from ancestral lands? Would Daewoo bulldoze family tombs to clear land for planting? This time, Ravalomanana had gone too far.

Richard, who had taken part in the popular uprisings against Ratsiraka in 1991 and 2001, was back on the streets in January 2009 to call for the resignation of Ravalomanana, the leader he had previously supported. For months, the president was locked in a power struggle with the young mayor of Tana, Andry Rajoelina, a former disc jockey, whose party had swept local elections. A week of rioting, looting, and burning in the capital left up to one hundred dead.

Ravalomanana's ascent to the presidency had reduced French influence. The Anglo-leaning president actively sought commercial and political ties with the United States and promoted the English language as a way for Madagascar to compete in the global economy. With the discovery of offshore oil deposits in the Mozambique Channel, France claimed drilling rights around two of the Îles Éparses (Scattered Islands), small coral islands that were French territories and had no permanent population. Ravalomanana claimed the islands for Madagascar. His diplomatic saber rattling worried the French, who decided to support his rival and provided Rajoelina with refuge in their embassy. The public mood changed when the presidential guard opened fire outside the palace, killing twenty-eight protesters and injuring more than two hundred. The government lost control of the army and police force, and tanks moved into the capital. On March 17, a few hours after declaring he would fight to the death rather than resign, Ravalomanana stepped down, transferring power to a trio of loyal military leaders. A few hours later, the trio were arrested and handed over power to Rajoelina. Ravalomanana fled to Swaziland, then South Africa. He was sentenced in absentia to life imprisonment on charges relating to the shooting of protestors outside the palace. The coup was roundly condemned by the international community, including the African Union (AU), but the AU was not ready to take on Madagascar's large and well-trained army. Rajoelina was effectively left in power, with international bodies accepting his promise to call early elections.

Promises, promises. From March 2009 Rajoelina promised—and then postponed—elections every year until 2013. Meanwhile, the economy tanked; most foreign aid, which had accounted for 40 percent of the budget, was suspended; licenses for mining projects were revoked, and foreign investors were scared away. In polls, two-thirds of Malagasy described their financial situation as bad or very bad, compared with one-third before the coup. The main stumbling block to an election was the conflict over who could run. Eventually, a deal was brokered that barred both Rajoelina and Ravalomanana, but each endorsed a proxy candidate. In October, the proxies—former finance minister Hery Rajaonarimampianina for Rajoelina and former health minister Jean Louis Robinson for Ravalomanana—fended off thirty-one other candidates to go into a December runoff. Rajaonarimampianina was the eventual winner. The donors returned, followed, somewhat nervously, by the mining companies and other foreign investors.

Richard holds France partly responsible for Madagascar's political instability and lack of economic progress. "When British colonies became independent, Britain did not meddle in their affairs and they were left free to develop," he said. By contrast, through a policy sometimes dubbed *Françafrique*, France continues to intervene, militarily, politically, and economically, in its former colonies. "France wants our president to be on its side for political and economic reasons—for the oil of the Mozambique Channel, for mineral resources. French financial interests are still strong. All actions by our government are taken in support of France. It's neocolonialism."

Over his career, Richard has served in government for more than a decade, under three presidents—Zafy, Ratsiraka, and Rajoelina. Yet he also joined the street protests that led to the overthrow of three presidents— in 1991, 2001, and 2009. Like his dual roles as college professor and traditional healer, he sees no contradiction between his political positions. Yet he despairs of lasting change. "Since independence, Madagascar has had four republics. Each time we change the republic, we change the constitution. Each party, each faction rewrites the constitution to meet its needs." He shrugged. "We're always having referendums. It's very tiring."

four

On and Off the Road in Madagascar

Not-So-Wild Madagascar

UNICEF had booked a resort hotel in a national park east of Tana for a weeklong workshop to launch the research project. Away from the noise and bustle of the capital, free from classes and meetings, our five-person team and our colleagues from UA could huddle in break-out sessions, share meals, and build personal relationships. In the jungle, mobile phone coverage was patchy and the Internet slow. There wasn't much to do when the sun went down except sit on the veranda, enjoy a *rhum arrangé,* and listen to the lemur lullabies.

It's just over ninety miles from Tana to Andasibe National Park on RN2, the highway to Toamasina, the main port on the east coast. If the weather is clear and the traffic light, you can reach Andasibe in two hours; our outbound and return trips both took three hours, an average of thirty miles per hour. Trucks hauling fuel and containers wheezed up the hills; every few miles, we came across one stranded by the roadside, its driver sprawled across the open engine, or the trailer precariously jacked up, teetering on the edge of a cliff. Almost all freight to the capital and highlands is transported on this road. The single-line railroad the French built along the route could carry heavy freight, but the truck owners' cartel has put pressure on the politicians to withhold funding for maintenance, and the track has fallen into disrepair. We saw only one train.

From Tana's so-called ring road, the surreally named Boulevard de Tokyo (built with Japanese aid), RN2 rises through the hills. It's a similar landscape to the Imerina region west of the city, with most land devoted to rice cultivation. The paddies stretch out over the bottom lands and the lower slopes of hills where farmers build terraces; water flows from springs into the terraces and then to the lower paddies through channels or pipes, where flow is controlled by sluice gates. In the fields, wood-fired brick kilns stand like sentries, and large stacks of rough red-mud bricks line the roadside; in several places, the granite outcrops have been gouged to quarry stone for road and home construction.

In 1817, the Merina king Radama I led an army of twenty-five thousand along this route to subdue the Betsimasraka and capture Toamasina. The Betsimasraka (the "many inseparables") was a loose confederation of clans that ruled a large stretch of the eastern seaboard and had long-established trading relations with Europeans. The kings periodically processed through their domains to remind the kinglets of who lived in the largest *rova,* who had the troops and cannon, and who had the support of the British Empire. The royals and other *andriana* were carried up and down the hills on sedan chairs by teams of bearers. Depending on the royal weight, there were two or four bearers up front and at the back. It was an exhausting but prestigious job carting around the royals and, later, French colonial officials and missionaries. According to Luke, those at the front of the sedan needed different strengths from those at the back, so they developed muscular specialties. You can almost hear the negotiation. "OK, I'll go back right on *Monsieur, le colonel.* My rate is ten francs a kilometer on flat stretches, fifteen up hills, and three meals a day. An extra charge if he's more than eighty kilograms."

As RN2 descends from the highland escarpment, the hills on either side are clear cut or covered with second-growth eucalyptus forest. A hundred years ago, old-growth forest extended over much of the highlands and northeast, but most has been destroyed by slash-and-burn agriculture and the cutting of timber for charcoal, firewood, and home construction; perhaps as much as 90 percent of the island's original forest has been lost. The French planted the fast-growing eucalyptus to provide fuel for the railroad and steam engines used on plantations, and today these trees are the main source of charcoal. It is estimated that 95 percent of Malagasy households, including those in urban areas, use firewood or charcoal for cooking and heating. Along RN2, the trees are cut down to their stumps, and the wood is slowly burned in earth ovens to produce charcoal. Sacks are piled by the roadside; the local price is about $2, making it worth the trip to transport charcoal to Tana, where it fetches $6 a sack. The eucalyptus stumps soon sprout again, but it is a stubby new growth. Any wildlife that once lived in these forests has fled or been hunted. Only in the protected areas of the national parks do the eucalyptus trees and native varieties grow high, providing shelter and food for wildlife.

Today, mining poses a deeper threat to the environment. For many years, foreign investors shied away from Madagascar, deterred by political instability, corruption, and poor infrastructure. What was the point in building a mine or factory if the politicians were going to nationalize it or grab the profits? Or if there were no roads, reliable power supply, and skilled workforce? Recently, multinational mining companies have started to exploit the vast and largely untapped resources.

Since 2005, the British-Australian company Rio Tinto has invested almost $1 billion in an operation near Fort Dauphin (Taolagnaro) on the south coast to mine ilmenite, which is used to make titanium dioxide, the white pigment commonly found in paint, toothpaste, and cosmetics. Global demand has been growing, especially in China and India, and the Rio Tinto mine—20 percent owned by the government—was expected to give a major boost to the economy and provide jobs in one of the poorest regions of the country. From the start, the project was mired in controversy. No agricultural land was available to compensate those who gave up land for the mine, so the company paid them in cash. Construction created a temporary employment boom, but when production began in 2009, few jobs were available. Critics claim only 10 percent of employees are locals; Rio Tinto says it's 70 percent. Whatever the real number is, mining transformed the local economy. Hotels sold out for two years, ruining the local tourist business. Sex workers spread STDs. And people who had been living on less than $1 a day suddenly had more money than they would previously have seen in a year. Some used it to set up small businesses, but most failed. "People were buying cars, TVs, generators, drinking," one construction worker recalled. "It was like a party every day."

The party ended violently in January 2013 when several hundred protesters armed with spears and slingshots blocked the mine access road, complaining about high unemployment, corruption, and inadequate compensation for landowners. For a time, the company's chief executive and 178 staff were trapped inside the compound. Eventually, troops using tear gas dispersed the crowd. The protests made Rio Tinto wary of future investment; it shelved plans for a second, and larger, mine in nearby St. Luce.[1]

Madagascar's other major mining operation is off RN2 near Moramanga, the site of the massacre of prisoners during the 1947 rebellion. The Ambatovy nickel and cobalt mine, built by a Canadian-Japanese-Korean consortium at a cost of $8 billion, claims to be the largest-ever foreign investment in the country and one of the largest lateritic nickel mines in the world. The ore is strip-mined and sent to a preparation plant; the nickel and cobalt ore slurry is then piped underground for 136 miles to a processing plant and refinery south of Toamasina, where it is separated and loaded onto ships.

Critics say the government granted the mining license with minimal study of its potential impact. Rather than employing and training local people, the company brought in a foreign workforce (mostly South Asian and Filipino) to build the mine and pipeline. The influx of foreign workers and money transformed Moramanga, a regional market center, into a boomtown, its streets lined with import shops, hotels, restaurants, and karaoke bars. Rents soared, forcing local people to move out of town. Crime and prostitution levels increased, with teachers reporting that most teenage girls had dropped out of school. There was more money to be made working the streets than working the rice paddies. That went for the men as well as the women. The streets of Moramanga are crowded with brightly painted *pousse-pousse* bicycle rickshaws. The drivers, who rent their machines by the day, must hustle hard to make money.

The tourism industry, while less destructive than mining, is changing the country in other ways. There are two types of tourists. One heads for the beaches and tropical islands; there are direct flights from Paris to Nosy Be (Big Island), the largest and most developed resort area off the northwest coast. The tourists never see the urban sprawl and poverty of Tana, or the rural central highlands. The second type comes to see the lemurs and other wildlife in the national parks. They stay at tastefully designed lodges with manicured gardens where diesel generators provide backup power, the showers always have hot water, the juice is freshly squeezed, and the buffet offers a mix of European and

Malagasy dishes. Andasibe National Park has half a dozen lodges catering to foreign tourists who come in small parties (no large buses) and sit at dinner tables reserved for "Wild Madagascar" or "Jungle Adventure." Then they go off to see the lemurs.

We did too, on an afternoon break from the workshop. You don't have to venture too far into the jungle to find your photographic prey. At the Wakona Lodge, most lemurs live on a small island in a river (a thirty-second canoe paddle from the parking lot). They do not hide in trees but bound out of the undergrowth to greet you, climbing on your head or shoulders in the hopes you brought bananas. This is wildlife at its most accessible. Most of these lemurs were donated by people in Toamasina who had kept them as pets. I'm sure they're happier living on the island than in cages, but calling this "Wild Madagascar" seems a stretch. However, it's enough for many tourists who don't want to walk too far to get their photographs. They can go home with stories of the jungle and make donations to wildlife charities to protect Madagascar's biodiversity. They may not think much about the people of Madagascar or economic or social conditions. The national statistics for poverty, health, education, safe water, and other indicators are woeful, but also tedious and easy to ignore, especially for tourists on jungle tours. Poor people are not nearly as cuddly as lemurs.

Jungle Prisoner of Sociological Theory

The UA sociology professor leaned across the table. "I'd really like to talk about Max Weber," he whispered. As session chair, I weighed my options. I could say no and risk a minor academic diplomatic incident. I could feign an apology, claim it was time for the coffee break and hope he would not remind me later. Instead I did the diplomatic and, in hindsight, the right thing. I surrendered to sociological theory. *"Mais bien sûr* [but of course]," I said.

I wondered how he was going to connect Weber's antipositivism to childhood vaccination rates, school enrollments, the building of latrines, or any of the topics UNICEF had selected for the session. I need not have worried. In his ten-minute monologue he made no reference to the practical research issues on the agenda.

My colleagues and I knew that working with the UA faculty would require patience and tact. Looking back, I'm sure the UA faculty felt the same about us. It was not only the language barrier. The main challenge was that most of the UA faculty had a traditional French academic background that emphasizes theory and language over practice. They had little experience in the applied research that can help a development agency such as UNICEF improve health or education. Weber does not offer guidance on how to persuade people to use latrines or wash their hands before eating.

We felt frustrated. Our colleagues seemed more interested in discussing theoretical issues than in hashing out topics and questions for the study. It was tough for the interpreters, grappling with three-way simultaneous translation—Malagasy to English, French to English, and English to French. The day reached a low point when I heard this through my headphones: "The real problem is situated somewhere between the problematic and the problematization."

We felt like prisoners in a jungle of theory. I thought briefly about running off into the real jungle to hang out with the lemurs. Yet over the next few months, we came to realize that the lecture on Weber and other apparent diversions into Marxist, literary, or linguistic theory were not academic posturing. They were, to use development jargon, capacity building. UNICEF had asked our team to build the capacity of UA faculty and postgraduate students to conduct social research. We knew how to design a study, do the data analysis, and write the report, but we knew little about Madagascar, its culture and turbulent history, or how our Malagasy colleagues regarded research. Rather than writing us off as the latest group of foreign academics to show up, run around the country, and leave without learning anything, they couched their critique in the shared language of theory. Their priority for the workshop was not to draft questionnaires but to build an equal, trusting research partnership. Capacity building goes both ways.

A Marriage of Convenience

It had been an arranged match with UA, without even a blind date. In the bidding process, we worried that our proposal would not make the cut because of our modest French-language skills. My recent experiences were at holiday parties at my sister's home in the Dordogne region of France, where the conversation usually focused on wine, food, plumbing, and knee replacements, not sampling, focus groups, or multivariate analysis. A few months later, we learned we had been awarded the contract. It was time to pull out the maps, bone up on French research phrases, and get to know our academic partner in what UNICEF was grandly calling the "international research consortium."

Madagascar's development challenges are daunting. The country has long languished in the "low" category on the UN Human Development Index for health, education, and income levels. Coups and political instability have scared away donors and foreign investors. Three-quarters of households live on less than $2 per day and over one-third are classified as food insecure. The maternal mortality rate has been rising and child vaccination rates declining. Many households lack access to safe water, and open defecation is common. Only three out of ten children who begin primary school complete the cycle. Child marriage is prevalent, with close to half the female population aged fifteen to forty-nine married before eighteen years of age. Sexual exploitation and violence against children are major concerns. Almost every year, the country experiences cyclones and floods on the east coast, and sometimes drought in the south.

UNICEF had stacks of demographic data—tables, line graphs, bar graphs, and pie charts presented in glossy reports and PowerPoints complete with stock images of happy children in classrooms, women engaged in ecofriendly, income-generating craft cooperatives, and villagers sitting under trees earnestly debating local issues. The data were descriptive and demographic—how many (or what percentage) of urban or rural children in which family income bracket had (or had not) had all their shots, completed the primary school cycle, or met a global nutrition standard. The statistics were listed by year to indicate possible trends, and by region for comparison. What they did not tell us was the why— the reasons people believed and did (or did not) do something. Or, if they believed in something, such as keeping children in school, why they did not do it in practice. Why did women give birth at home? Why were girls married off in their teens? Why did people think water from a river was purer than water from a tap? Were the barriers to better health, nutrition, sanitation, and education the result of culture or other factors? Who influences attitudes and behaviors—clan leaders, traditional healers, midwives, mothers-in-law, or radio broadcasts? Working with UA, our task was to design and undertake research on knowledge, attitudes, and practices, or, in bureaucratic shorthand, a KAP study.

The UA campus sits on a ridge in Tana, with commanding views across the highlands. Founded in 1955, it's the country's leading institution, with master's and PhD programs and links with French and Western universities. It is also, like the education system in general, woefully underfunded. Faculty pay is low and working conditions are difficult. The red-brick and concrete buildings, most dating from the 1960s and 1970s, have cracks in the walls; inside, paint peels from the plaster and classrooms with wooden desks and chalkboards line dimly lit corridors. Power cuts are frequent, and the water supply unreliable; on a day when we discussed how to phrase questions about hand washing, we could not wash our hands because there was no water in the building. UA reminded me of the not-so-genteel decay of universities in Central Asia that I wrote about in *Postcards from Stanland*. The only saving grace is that it never gets too cold in Madagascar, so you don't have to wear an overcoat, hat, and gloves to teach.

Although UA was paid for the research, and although being part of an international research consortium may have a certain cachet, the strongest motivation for the faculty and postgraduate students was the research experience they would gain. Under our contract, we were supposed to build capacity at the same time as we conducted the study. Balancing the two tasks and staying on schedule and on budget proved challenging.

Who Are the *Vazaha?*

The first Malagasy word I learned was *vazaha*. Translated literally, it means "foreigner," and it aptly described the members of our multinational team—from the United States, the UK, South Africa, France, and Nepal. At the lodge in Andasibe National Park, there were good-natured jests about throwing the *vazaha* into the river to feed the crocodiles. But the banter suggested deeper social rifts. The word *vazaha* is also a disparaging term for a person of higher economic, social, or political status—an outsider, a government official, or an aid worker in a SUV.

Most faculty and postgraduate students at UA are Merina. If the research study had been conducted in the central highlands, where Merina form the largest percentage of the population, there would have been few barriers to data collection. However, the three regions selected by UNICEF were all coastal—two (Anosy and Atsimo Andrefana) in the south, and one (Analanjirofo) in the northeast. The researchers would be working in areas where people were mostly of African descent, where the cultural terrain, including the dialect, was unfamiliar.

The major barrier to development in Madagascar is poor infrastructure. On the maps, the Routes Nationales (RNs) are confidently marked in solid red, suggesting adequate connections between population centers. But just a few miles outside Tana, vehicles slow down to dodge the potholes or mudslides. In the south, some RNs are little more than dirt roads. During the cyclone season in Analanjirofo, which is crisscrossed by several rivers, travel is difficult as floods sweep away roads and bridges. We had used geographic and economic criteria to classify communities into four types: interior, subcoastal, coastal, and urban. Some interior communities were two days by zebu cart from the main dirt road; to include them would have lengthened the project and strained the budget, so we had to compromise.

Most people in southern Madagascar depend on subsistence agriculture or fishing. Access to health services and schools is poor. The government is resented for taxing and exploiting natural resources without giving back. The view from the capital is that "parts of the south are ungoverned, and parts may be ungovernable," said Luke. The army, police, and even health workers venture into the so-called *zones rouges* (red zones) at their peril. Local people, according to Luke, see it differently, maintaining that their own social systems and norms preserve order. They are naturally suspicious of outsiders who ask about living conditions and household income (even if they also ask about vaccinations). Are they really university researchers, or are they gathering data for the tax agency?

To their credit, the UA researchers worked hard to build trust in the communities where they did interviews, focus group discussions, and observations. But they faced research fatigue. People have seen data collectors come and go and have not seen any benefits. Why should the latest group of researchers with their notebooks and audio recorders be any different? Community members will not turn away researchers, but their answers, according to Luke, may be "terse, evasive . . . politely subversive." During a later workshop, one team reported that people in Mahavatse, a low-income community of fishermen, small traders, and rickshaw drivers in the south, were reluctant to talk to them. One reason was that as Merina "we looked different—some people said we were *vazaha.*"

Because of its relative isolation and ethnic diversity, Madagascar has been a happy hunting ground for anthropologists. In a study commissioned by UNICEF, the depressingly titled "The South: Cemetery of Projects?" the authors compiled sixteen single-spaced pages of books, articles, and dissertations with titles such as "Funeral Rites of Betsileo Princes," "Identity and Descent among the Vezo" and "The Sakalava Poiesis of History." The sheer volume of studies makes it tempting to think that traditional beliefs and practices dominate every sphere of life.

Our study indicated that traditional practices persist. Many pregnant women still drink a noxious potion called *tambavy*. After birth, the umbilical cord is buried near the ancestral tomb or cast into the river at a sacred site. Food taboos (*fady*) remain. Traditional forms of marriage are still practiced. However, many barriers to improving health, sanitation, nutrition, and education are practical—distant health facilities, bad schools and untrained teachers, poor infrastructure. Changing people's beliefs was not the issue. It was about providing better services.

Our UA colleagues did not deny the role of tradition. They simply said that it was not the only or even the most important factor. They reminded us that for many people in Madagascar, survival remains a daily challenge. In May 2015, with the project already months behind schedule, we politely asked when data collection could begin. The chair of the communication department, Lucie Rabaovololona, reported that in Analanjirofo roads were still closed by floods and mudslides. Meanwhile, the two southern regions were experiencing drought and food shortages. The project timeline had to be amended, she said. Her rationale was simple yet evocative: "We should not be asking people questions about nutrition when all they have to eat is cactus."

Abide with Me

The sound of the group singing drifted in from the courtyard of the Norwegian mission on a sunny December morning in Tana. The tune was familiar, but in my early-morning stupor after a long flight I couldn't place it. Then it came to me. It was my father's favorite hymn, "Abide with Me," a Church of England standard. I had sung it during my childhood, usually at school assemblies or compulsory Sunday church attendance; it closed the funeral service for my father in 1985. I recalled the opening line, "Abide with me, fast falls the eventide," although it seemed surreal on a warm morning in the middle of Madagascar's capital city. I wondered how this hymn had traveled across two continents and been translated into Malagasy.

For that cultural exchange, we can credit the Norwegian Lutherans and other Protestant missionaries who have worked in Madagascar for two centuries. The London Missionary Society (LMS), a product of the evangelical revival of the late eighteenth century and composed mostly of Congregationalists and other nonconformists, was the first to plan a mission to Madagascar. The British seizure of the Indian Ocean island of Mauritius from the French in 1810 provided a base for operations. In August 1818, two twenty-two-year-old Welshmen, David Jones and Thomas Bevan, arrived in Toamasina from Mauritius and opened a small school. Their wives and young children followed, but by the following January Jones was the only survivor, the others having died from the fever. Jones persevered and in 1820 was welcomed to the court of Radama I. Other LMS missionaries followed and within a decade had established schools and gained converts in the highlands.

Radama was personally indifferent to religion but wanted to improve the economy by adopting Western technologies. He welcomed the LMS because the missionaries included artisans—a tanner, a carpenter, a blacksmith, a cotton spinner, and a printer—who taught new skills; one, the Scot James Cameron, introduced brick making. By the time of Radama's death in 1828, the LMS missionaries had established twenty-three schools with twenty-three hundred students, one-third of them girls. The missionaries began transliterating Malagasy into a written script, using the Latin alphabet. The LMS shipped a printing press, and by 1828 the missionaries were printing spelling books and readers, as well as gospel tracts. By 1830, three thousand copies of the New Testament in Malagasy had been printed.

After almost two decades of openness to trade, religion, and other European contacts under Radama I, the Merina kingdom turned inward and xenophobic under his successor, the capricious and bloodthirsty Queen Ranavalona I. Her reign began with the ritual murder of all potential rival claimants to the throne, including Radama's mother and brother-in-law. The traditionalist party gained dominance at court and lobbied for cutting trading and diplomatic ties with the French and British. For a few years, the missionaries were allowed to continue teaching, preaching, and distributing religious texts, but from 1831 the government started clamping down on their activities. The queen's hostility was fed by reports that Christian converts were contemptuous of ancient customs and regarded the royal talismans—sacred wooden objects carried on military campaigns and state processions to protect the kingdom—as idols. In 1835, she banned Christianity and ordered all who had been baptized to confess and recant. Most did, but those who refused, or continued to practice religion in private, were vigorously persecuted.

The lucky ones—mostly members of the noble *andriana* caste—lost their property or official position. Some were sold into slavery or exiled to unhealthy regions of the island, where they succumbed to disease within a few months. Other converts were executed in public, with cruelty designed to strike fear into the population. They were speared to death, burned at the stake, or hurled off a cliff below the queen's palace. Some were placed head-down in a rice pit; boiling water was poured on them, and the pit was filled with earth. A few survived the notorious *tangena* ordeal by poison. The accused was made to swallow three pieces of chicken skin and some rice, with scrapings from the poisonous *tangena* nut, then drink a large quantity of rice water to induce vomiting. If all three pieces of skin were vomited up whole, the accused was considered innocent but then often died anyway from the effects of the poison.

In 1835, all missionaries left Madagascar, but many converts held to their faith, worshipping in private homes or in the countryside, hiding their Bibles in caves and holes in the ground. The martyrdom suffered by Malagasy Christians served only to strengthen their resolve. When, in 1861, the new king Radama II restored freedom of religion and declared an amnesty for all condemned for their beliefs, thousands flocked to newly opened places of worship. Christianity was no longer a foreign import because the Malagasy Christians had their own martyrs, preachers, and ordained pastors. Protestantism became established, even socially fashionable, among the ruling classes, when the new queen, Ranavalona II, and her prime minister, Rainilaiarivony (who married her, in accordance with political custom), converted in 1869. Soon after the marriage, the queen ordered the burning of the royal idols, completing a symbolic break with ancestral beliefs.[2]

With the field opened again for missionary activity, the LMS faced competition from other Protestant denominations, including the Anglicans. The Jesuits, based on the French island of Réunion, established small missions on the west coast and by the 1860s were competing for souls in the central highlands and on the east coast. Like the Protestants, the Catholic missionaries contributed to education, establishing primary and secondary schools, but the two groups were always in competition.

The LMS, Anglicans, and Catholics were followed by Norwegian Lutheran missionaries. They were young men from the farms and fjords, who set off for a long sea trip to an unknown island in the southern Indian Ocean. Some left young wives behind, promising to return when God's work was done. Most never did, entering into accepted, but unsanctified, unions with Malagasy women. The first two missionaries arrived in 1866, establishing a church south of Tana. This precipitated a turf war with the LMS, but eventually both sides agreed to reserve the region of Betsileo in the southern highlands for the Lutherans. The Norwegians were followed by American Lutheran missionaries from Minnesota; they founded a small mission in Fort Dauphin in the south where they were never in competition with other Protestant missions.

After Madagascar became a French colony in 1896, the Catholic Church gained strength. Today, about one-fifth of the population (four million) is Catholic; the Church of Jesus Christ in Madagascar (FJKM), which united the LMS with the Quakers and other evangelicals, is the largest Protestant group, with about 3.5 million adherents. The Malagasy Lutheran Church (FLM), with 3 million, comes in a strong third; the Fifohazana, an indigenous revival movement, has made the Malagasy church one of the fastest-growing Lutheran churches in the world. The alliance of these three with the Anglicans in the Malagasy Council of Churches (FFKM) has been an influential force in Malagasy politics; in the disputed 2001 presidential elections, the FFKM rallied behind the Protestant candidate Marc Ravalomanana, whose electoral slogan was "Don't be afraid, only believe." Evangelical churches with charismatic preachers, meeting in sports stadiums and other large venues, have gained followers; Tana now boasts at least one "megachurch." Muslims constitute about 7 percent of the population. Many Malagasy comfortably combine their religion with traditional beliefs, observing *fady* and consulting with astrologers on the most auspicious days to build a house, plant a crop, or hold a wedding or funeral.

The Norwegian mission is in the Isoraka district, high on one of the city's hills near the Embassy of the Comoros (that's the landmark for taxi drivers). It was originally built as the Lutherans' administrative center and provided accommodation for missionaries visiting the capital. Today, its guest houses are open to all, but you won't find it advertised on the hotel or backpackers' travel websites. Luke, who had stayed there on previous visits, recommended it. A group of two-story buildings around a garden, it's an oasis from the traffic and bustle of the city. Each building has a memorial plaque to a noted missionary or church leader. History is even celebrated in the Wi-Fi code. No boring "guest 123" login, but a real name, Andrianarijaona (difficult to type, especially if you're in a hurry). It celebrates Rakoto Andrianarijaona, whose father and grandfather were both prominent revivalist pastors; in 1960, he became the first native Malagasy to be named leader of the national church.

For about $18 a night, you get a simple, clean room with bathroom, and a shower (the water was always hot). The so-called Norwegian breakfast (rolls, butter, jam, cheese, ham, tomatoes, cucumbers, juice, and coffee) sets you back 8,000 *ariary* ($2.50); for $2.00 you can have the Malagasy breakfast of rice with leaves (rice and leaves in a broth), juice, and coffee. There's no bar, of course, but you are within a few minutes' walk of three excellent, modestly priced French restaurants and a Vietnamese one. Or you can always join the mission congregation to sing "Abide with Me."

Route Nationale 7—The Long Road South

I had arrived at Ivato Airport from Johannesburg late on a Saturday afternoon and was scheduled to lead a workshop for UA faculty and postgraduate students in Toliara (Tuléar), the main port on the southwest coast, starting Monday morning. Air Maybe was on strike again, so the only way to reach Toliara was by road on RN7. The UNICEF Nissan Patrol, with a driver and two staff members, was waiting at the airport.

"How long will the trip take?" I asked as I stashed my bag. I guessed we would reach Toliara on Sunday afternoon, giving me time to rest before the workshop began. There was an awkward silence. "*Alors, ça dépend* (Well, that depends)," the driver eventually said. I wanted to ask "*Sur quoi?* (On what?)" but thought better of it. I resolved to enjoy the trip, however long it took.

It's officially 577 miles from Tana to Toliara. All the guidebooks (and every Malagasy I've met) say that RN7 is the best road in the country. It's all relative. I'd classify RN7, a two-lane highway with many one-lane bridges, as a superior county road in Ohio or West Virginia, or maybe a lesser state route in need of maintenance. For better or worse, this is the main route to the south. And it doesn't even go all the way. The southernmost port and city, Fort Dauphin, administrative center of the region of Anosy, is another two days' travel from Toliara on dirt roads (which also have the status of RNs), bone shaking in the dry season and impassable during the monsoon.

To reach Fort Dauphin and other southern destinations, you need a vehicle that sits high off the ground so that it does not get stuck in the holes and ruts. Traveling south from Tana, we passed a boxy, high-riding bus, lumbering up a hill. "Fort Dauphin," remarked our driver. The bus was packed with passengers squeezed onto narrow bench seats, luggage piled high on the roof. I asked how long the trip would take. "Four days," said the driver. That's four days and four nights. The bus makes rest and meal stops but travels through the night, the two drivers taking shifts. I was happy our workshop had not been scheduled for Fort Dauphin.

This close to the Equator, night comes early (around 6:00 p.m.). UNICEF vehicles are not allowed to drive after dark, mostly because of the hazards—people, animals, and bicycles without lights are still on the road. There are few hotels outside the main towns, so we called in for clearance to drive thirty more minutes to reach Antsirabe, about one hundred miles south of the capital. You would expect the third-largest city in the country with a population of more than two hundred thousand to have at least a minor rush hour, but we saw few cars. Most people were traveling by *pousse-pousse*. Our hotel was in the center of town, but the sound of traffic was strangely absent—just the occasional car or motorbike. After 9:00 p.m., the only sound came from barking dogs.

We left at 7:00 a.m. and in late afternoon, 250 miles on, passed the Fort Dauphin bus as it struggled up another hill. Its passengers faced another fifty to sixty hours of travel, most of it on dirt roads. At least the bus had suspension to soften the ride. Throughout the south, the standard (and cheapest) mode of long-distance transport is the *camion-brousse* (literally "bush truck"). It's a military transport or freight truck with a rigid frame outfitted with bench seats; passengers are exposed to wind and dust, are bounced around violently, and are frequently sick. Public transport at its roughest.

Driving on RN7, it sometimes seemed that half the country was on the move: by *taxi-brousse* (bush taxi), the minivans with luggage, bicycles, and yellow *bidons* (jerry cans used for carrying water) piled so high that they look as if they will tip over on a curve, which they sometimes do; by auto and bicycle *pousse-pousse*; by bicycle; or by carts pulled by zebu. Every hour or so we stopped to let zebu cross the road, the boy herders shouting and waving their sticks. Outside the towns and villages, there were always people walking along the road. Rice farmers going to and from their fields. Men walking with axes and long sticks with curved blades, cutting eucalyptus trees for firewood and charcoal. Children returning from the river with *bidons,* lashed onto wooden pushcarts, the day's supply of water for cooking and washing. Families walking home from church.

If you've got something to sell—fruits, vegetables, motor oil, bicycle tires—your best storefront is along RN7, preferably on one of the few straight stretches. There are small retail clusters. If you're in the market for a garishly colored Jesus or Madonna statue or one of the animals from the Ark (in Madagascar, Noah did not forget to save a place for the zebu), your destination is a stretch south of Antsirabe; further south, a line of stalls sell wooden cooking utensils; south of Fianarantsoa, the second-largest city and the commercial center of the southern highlands, you can find musical instruments including drums and the Malagasy ukulele, and brightly painted tin models of trucks and cars.

Of course, most people in central and southern Madagascar were not on the move or hawking their wares along RN7. It's just that many of those who were traveling were squeezed onto its narrow ribbon. Outside the towns, I saw only a few east–west roads leading off RN7 with a tarmac surface, and who knows how far the tarmac went? Poor infrastructure—primarily the roads, but also lack of electricity supply in rural areas—is the major barrier to economic development. In the rainy season (January through March), landslides block the road, and sections wash away or develop huge potholes. In places, work crews were building ditches and culverts to divert the water, but many stretches had not been repaired. Our driver engaged low gear and zigzagged, expertly avoiding the largest holes. It was uncomfortable enough in a high-riding vehicle; it must feel much worse in a bus or *taxi-brousse.* Every government since independence has promised to fix the roads and extend the network, but, faced with poverty, hunger, and pressing social problems, the promises are soon forgotten. "You can't eat roads," remarked our driver drily.

The bridges, mostly one-lane, are in serious need of maintenance. That's except for one newish structure crossing a river north of Fianarantsoa. The old bridge, one UNICEF colleague explained, did not fall into the river through lack of repair; in 2002, during the six-month presidential standoff, forces loyal to Ratsiraka seized the government buildings in Fianarantsoa and blew up the bridge to stop troops from Tana from reaching the city. After the conflict ended, a new bridge was built with French aid. Communities up and down RN7 were left wondering whether the easiest way to get their bridges repaired was to blow them up and wait for donors to build new ones.

South of Fianarantsoa, RN7 turns southwest, dipping down out of the highlands to the treeless savannah grasslands. This is Madagascar's high plains country, where herders drive their zebu and sleep out under the stars. The grasslands stretch for almost two-thirds of the length of the country, west of the highlands, and have a dry season of seven to eight months. If it wasn't for the distinctive red-and-white kilometer posts and the absence of pickup trucks, it could have been Montana or Wyoming, the long grass blowing in the wind, the mountain ranges on the horizon. The grasslands gradually give way to a desert landscape of canyons, steep cliffs, and buttes dotted with scrubby trees and cactus; in the late afternoon, with the sun casting long shadows off the striking rock formations, we could have been in Arizona or New Mexico. We stopped for the second night in Ranohiro, gateway to the huge L'Isalo national park. Chez Alice, with its cactus fence and corral boasting Malagasy rodeo (presumably bareback zebu riding), was full, so we found a hotel in the town center, eating dinner alongside long tables of European tourists on their "Madagascar Adventure" tour. We were on the road again at 6:00 the next morning, as the sun rose over the bluffs and canyons, bathing them in the warm morning light.

Desert Treasures

The wealth in this beautiful but desolate landscape is not in them thar hills, but in the ground. And it's not gold, but sapphires. Gemstones were first discovered in the forests of northern Madagascar in the early 1990s, drawing migrants to seek their fortunes. In the south, prospectors were collecting garnets to sell to foreign dealers; in 1998, a batch mined near Ilakaka, a wide place in the road along RN7, turned out to be pink sapphires. The discovery transformed Ilakaka from a few ramshackle huts into a boom town. The field, which stretches southwest across the desert from Ilakaka, is reportedly the largest deposit in the world, yielding high-priced deep blue sapphires along with pinks, yellows, and rubies. Other mining towns sprouted up along RN7. Their streets are lined with ramshackle stores selling provisions and tools, and rough, single-story shacks where miners rent small rooms at high prices. These are wild towns, with high rates of crime and prostitution, where the lucky miner who has just sold his sapphires blows it all on sugarcane moonshine and the slots at Les Jokers Hotel and Karaoke Bar.

With such riches to be uncovered, no machinery is used; miners use pickaxes and shovels to break the rocky ground and dig shafts, using buckets to haul the earth to the surface. It's dirty, dangerous work; in the rainy season, shaft walls can collapse, trapping the miners underground. Most mines are individual or family operations. A few commercial mines, with optimistic names such as African Bank, Swiss Bank, and World Bank, are financed by investors who hire day laborers. The landscape is pockmarked with mine workings, but the deposits closest to RN7 and the towns have been exhausted, and miners must walk miles into the desert to work their claims.[3]

The real wealth is controlled by foreign traders—mostly from Sri Lanka, Pakistan, and Thailand—who buy the rough sapphires and sell them on Asian markets. The names on the gem stores—Fayez, Najeem, Iqbal, Farook—tell the story. The government, with support from donors, is training Malagasy miners and small traders in gemology and stonecutting and trying to collect export taxes. Regulating the industry and stamping out corruption is challenging. Rough sapphires are routinely smuggled out of the country, with a wink and a $100 bill slipped into the passport at customs.

The final sixty miles to Toliara are desolate, and the people poor. In contrast to the rough but functional two-story brick *trano gasy* houses of the highlands, the homes are single-room wood-and-mud huts with roofs of thatched reeds or palm leaves and a dirt floor, surrounded by fences of branches and cactus. Average rainfall in this region is just twelve to fourteen inches a year; the population depends primarily on zebu herding, raising meagre crops of maize, sorghum, and sweet potato in the sandy soil and along river banks.

Finally, we glimpsed the sea and the table mountain (a modest version of Cape Town's landmark) that marked the final descent to Toliara. We crossed the low sandy hills into the city and reached the chamber of commerce in time for midmorning coffee. Just in time—my first presentation was scheduled for right after the break.

The "Champaign Country"

In June 1630, ships of the East India Company anchored in St. Augustine's Bay at the mouth of the Onilahy River, about twenty miles south of present-day Toliara, to take on provisions before sailing up the Mozambique Channel. It was, by the standards of southern Madagascar, a cool winter, allowing the merchant Richard Boothby to feel comfortable in his suit of English cloth. During the three-month stay, not a single crew member died and there were few cases of sickness. "The country about the bay," wrote Boothby, "is pleasant to view, replenished with brave woods, rocky hills of white marble, and low fertile grounds." Crew members told him that away from the coast the land "abounds with mines of gold and silver and other minerals" and "a large plain, or champaign country, of meadow or pasture land as big as all of England," with ample fish and game. "It is very probable," Boothby wrote, "by the quantity of brown fat oxen, cows, sheep and goats brought down and sold unto us by the natives, that the country is very fertile."

Boothby was intoxicated by what he saw and heard, as was his colleague, the surgeon Walter Hammond, who later published a pamphlet, *Madagascar, the Richest and Most Fruitfull Island in the World*. You must wonder if they were intoxicated by something else when they recorded their impressions. Compared with the east coast of Madagascar, with its tropical rainforest and lush vegetation, the land beyond St. Augustine's Bay is among the most barren and infertile in the island.

Such enthusiastic accounts fell on eager ears in London, where city merchants, supported by King Charles I, were ready to invest in expeditions they hoped would make them wealthy. The East India Company was already engaged in a trading war with the Dutch and Portuguese in the Spice Islands and other parts of the Indian Ocean but had failed to establish settlements and forts. In 1635, a rival company, the Courteen's Association, was granted a royal charter to trade in the East. Boothby and Hammond encouraged Courteen's to sponsor a colony in

Madagascar. Several attempts failed because of lack of funds and opposition from the East India Company, but eventually in August 1644 three ships with 140 men, women, and children, under the command of John Smart, set sail. They arrived in St. Augustine's Bay in March 1645 and built a fortified settlement.

It was not the green and pleasant land Boothby and Hammond had promised. The settlers arrived at the end of the short rainy season, and the crops they planted perished for lack of water. The sparse cattle pasture soon dried up. There were no minerals. Smart sent out ships to seek trading opportunities, but they returned with discouraging news; the French and Dutch had established settlements on the east coast and threatened hostile action if the English tried to trade. By August, the St. Augustine colony was running out of supplies. The locals, writes Mervyn Brown, "who were usually friendly and ready to trade . . . became either non-cooperative or openly hostile when they realized that the visitors intended to settle and take some of their land." The settlers got into disputes over cattle and rashly joined local clans in raids on their enemies. Dysentery and fever took their toll. When the colony was abandoned in May 1646, only sixty-three of the original settlers had survived. "I could not but endeavour to dissuade others from undergoing the miseries that will follow the persons of such as adventure themselves for Madagascar," wrote one of the survivors, Powle Waldegrave.[4]

So ended, after little more than a year, the first English attempt to establish a colony. French trading settlements lasted longer, but none of the European trading powers succeeded in establishing a permanent commercial foothold on the island until French colonization in the late nineteenth century. English ships continued to call at St. Augustine, and some locals adopted English names, but no attempts were made to reestablish a settlement. After the French abandoned Fort Dauphin in 1674, trading contacts were mostly with pirates who preyed on European ships bound from the Cape to India and the Far East, and Arab vessels trading with East Africa. Pirate ships called in at St. Augustine and other west coast anchorages for provisions but did not establish settlements because of opposition from the powerful Sakalava kings and the danger of encountering warships on the main route to India. Although the south became part of the Merina Empire, its clans were never fully subdued. The French colonial government imposed nominal control, but historically this has been a region that has always resisted central authority.

You'd expect a place that claims (along with New York City and other cities) to be the "city that never sleeps" to be noisy at night. Toliara, capital of the region of Atsimo Andrefana, is almost eerily quiet. On first impression, it's a place where the sidewalks (such as they are) are rolled up at 6:00 p.m. when it gets dark. That would be misleading. There's certainly noise down on the seafront, where the discotheques at two nightclubs—Tam Tam and Zaza—keep everyone (including those who want to sleep) awake into the early hours. But even in the commercial district and along the broad Boulevard Gallieni outside my hotel, people are moving. They're just doing it quietly. There are few private cars in Toliara, with most people walking, cycling, or traveling by *pousse-pousse*. They're hanging out in the small *hotelys* (roadside diners with a few tables, serving fish and rice) and bars, at the communal water points, or just on the roadside. Occasionally, a motorbike or four-wheeler revs up and down the boulevard, but most of the time it's quiet at night. That does not mean the city is sleeping.

The goal of the Toliara workshop was to prepare UA faculty and postgraduate students to undertake field research in communities. We covered research tools—social mapping, transect walks, participant observation, interviews, focus groups—then sent teams to districts of the city to practice and report back. They encountered the usual problems, including getting lost, being misled by self-appointed community leaders with axes to grind, and making themselves understood. Most Toliara residents are *côtiers* of African descent; although the teams were ethnically mixed, most members were highland Merina, and it took them a few days to grasp the local dialect. To their credit, they decided to compile a glossary of unfamiliar words and phrases that they could use for reference in communities. All the same, they found that some local people were wary of them.

The fieldwork was complicated by politics. Mayoral elections were scheduled for the end of the week, and the campaigns were in full swing—or rather full voice. The main vehicle (and the word fits well in this context) is the *propogon* (a slang word derived from propaganda), variations of which are found in many countries with low-literacy populations and limited mass media. It's a minivan with a large poster of the candidate on the front and high-powered speakers blasting out music—Malagasy hip-hop and reggae seemed to be the favorites—and short slogans. Sometimes it's a truck with flag-waving campaign staffers dancing on the bed. It is usually followed by a parade of chanting supporters, on foot, on bicycles or *pousse-pousse*. The caravan makes stops around the city to allow the candidate to make short stump speeches, promising to restore water supplies or have the garbage picked up. Supporters hand out a few thousand *ariary* or T-shirts to everyone in the crowd to thank them for showing up at the event and to remind them who to vote for on election day. In Mahavatse, a sprawling *bidonville* (shanty town) of fishermen and *pousse-pousse* pullers, one of our teams was mistaken for the entourage of a candidate, probably because they were better dressed than most people. (I'll make one exception to this statement—the postgraduate student wearing a T-shirt with the slogan "Elect Larry Burns Sheriff, Clark County—A Lifetime of Leadership." It's one of the minor mysteries of globalization how campaign T-shirts for Burns, who lost a close race for sheriff of Nevada's largest county, which includes Las Vegas, in 2014, ended up at a market in Madagascar). When the crowd learned that they were not getting T-shirts (not even ones for Larry Burns) or enough money to buy a couple of beers, they dispersed quickly. We decided to postpone the actual research until after election day.

The workshop was held at the Toliara Chamber of Commerce. I'm no business expert, but I could tell that there wasn't much commerce going on there. The 1970s-style block building was showing its age. Whitewash was peeling from the outer walls, the toilets had no running water (a bucket was used to flush), and the ceilings had large brown patches from roof leaks during monsoon season. On the staircase, a faded bas-relief depicted the economy of Atsimo Andrefana—herders with zebu and goats, a woman pounding manioc, groves of spiny cactus forest. Most offices were locked and apparently unoccupied. The only going concern was the office representing civil society groups. Outside in the dirt yard, washing hung from the line, and dogs scavenged among the trash; one homeless person had camped out behind the kitchen. Fortunately, the electricity was on and the staff provided coffee, tea, and snacks for the morning break, and a basic lunch of fish, chicken, or zebu stew and rice. I'm sure they were glad to have our commerce for the week.

Four-Wheeler Prestige

It was a short walk from my hotel, the Mahayana, along Boulevard Gallieni to the chamber of commerce. I felt slightly ridiculous doing the three-minute drive in the UNICEF Nissan Patrol with its tinted windows and radio aerial.

Our vehicle, along with a few SUVs, was at the top of the transportation hierarchy in Toliara. Next down was the four-wheeler or all-terrain vehicle (ATV). Having lived in Appalachia for almost forty years, I know all about ATVs. They are the workhorses for farmers and hunters. Teenagers race them on trails in the woods and, illegally, on the roads. Toliara's ATVs were like nothing I'd seen before; most were in mint condition and looked as if they had never encountered a muddy road or a sand dune. Their drivers preferred business suits (or in the case of the women, bright clothing and lots of jewelry) to jeans and T-shirts; clearly this was the prestige vehicle for Toliara's nouveaux riches.

Next came the aging, battered French cars—the Peugeots, Citroëns, and Renaults. Most had a dodgy electrical system that required wire twisting to start the motor and turn on the headlights. One taxi driver, who went by the name Mr. Eugene, proudly showed me how he could pull the key out of the ignition of his 1990 red Peugeot 404 (as featured on his laminated business card) without any effect on rpm. There were a few motorbikes, some old, some new, and the occasional auto rickshaw.

By far the most common thing on the road was the brightly colored bicycle *pousse-pousse,* carrying one or two passengers, bags of rice, or crates of soda and beer. Most sported Malagasy names on the rear panels, but a few drivers had adopted more eclectic names. There were the geographically and culturally irrelevant—New York, Chicago, and Miami, or Billabong. Word plays—the Poussy Cat. Optimistic claims—Service Rapide. Statements of faith—Jesus is Lord, God reigns, Jehovah. And, curiously, some English first names—Sharon, Larry (Las Vegas Larry Burns?) It's tough going on the bumpy roads and the *pousse-pousse* has no suspension for driver or passengers. All along the wide median of Boulevard Gallieni and on the side streets, people were fixing punctures, straightening frames, or welding new parts. If you had your own bicycle—next on the hierarchy—it was never too far to the nearest repair shop. Then there were the wooden carts pulled by zebu, and a few human-powered rickshaws with their barefoot *tireurs* (pullers).

For a city of its size (about 150,000), Toliara has many good, reasonably priced restaurants. The fishing fleet lands its catch every day, so the seafood—tilapia, grouper, perch, tuna, and shrimp—is fresh. There are a few uninviting menu items (I decided to pass on the snail pizza), but I was never disappointed in a meal. Most hotels, restaurants, and bars had French owners. Indeed, the city, with its gently decaying colonial architecture and coconut palms waving in the sea breeze, had the air of an outpost of empire. Many French expats have married Malagasy and are settled members of the community. Most of the bars and restaurants had a full menu of French TV channels by satellite, relayed from Réunion. One night at Blu, a restaurant on the seafront, I met the owner, a German who had joined the French Foreign Legion and served all over Africa. He decided he wanted to stay in Toliara. He opened the restaurant, married a Malagasy woman, and during dinner was having their six-month old son named Hank practice baby steps along the bar. I wish I'd had longer to talk. I knew he had a story to tell.

By the end of the week, President Rajaonarimampianina had replaced the director of Air Madagascar and promised to address the strikers' grievances. Air Maybe was flying again. Mr. Eugene drove me to Toliara's small airport in his Peugeot, the ignition key sitting in the cup holder. At the airport, there was no luggage scanner or metal detector, just an amiable security guard who gave my backpack a cursory glance and asked why my wife was not traveling with me. In the waiting area, I had a late breakfast at the Snack Bar Moramora. It may be the only airport catering establishment anywhere in the world without airport pricing; the prices ($1 for an espresso, 75¢ for a croissant) were what I would have paid in Toliara.

I was expecting a forty-seat puddle jumper with propellers but instead boarded an aging Boeing 737 (probably purchased from another airline that was upgrading its fleet). The standard instruction to "fasten your seatbelt and return your seatback to the upright and locked position" was irrelevant because my seatback had only one position (slightly sagging). The announcements were almost unintelligible; I thought the crew member was speaking in Malagasy until she ended in French with "Thank you for your attention—have a nice flight." But the flight was smooth. What had taken almost two days by car took just seventy-five minutes by air. But I was glad I had seen Madagascar from RN7.

five

Inexplicable India

"How is the Taj Mahal? Is it really as beautiful as in the pictures?" A Brazilian journalist with one of those lovely, long, lilting Latin American names—Demétrio Pires Weber Candiota da Rosa—buttonholed me during the tea break at my workshop in Delhi in 2005.

"Well, actually, I've never been there," I admitted. Demétrio looked at me in disbelief. "You said this was your fifth visit to India, and third to Delhi. You've *never* been there? How can you come to India and not see the Taj Mahal? It's really just down the road."

It's not exactly down the road. It's a 125-mile drive southeast from Delhi through Uttar Pradesh to the city of Agra and the palace. But Demétrio had a point. On my visits to Delhi, I'd always been on a tight schedule, allowing myself a single day to rest before my workshop began and flying out soon after it was over. On weekends, I'd taken time to explore Delhi but had not ventured outside the city.

"I'm going there on Friday—I'll miss the last day of the workshop." Demétrio was not asking permission. After all, he had flown halfway around the world for a five-day workshop on education reporting sponsored by UNESCO. In Delhi, he might manage an evening trip to the Old City or Red Fort, but most of what he saw would be through the window of the minibus from the hotel to the workshop venue, the Indian Institute of Mass Communication—a few random images from the great pageant that is India. This was his first trip to India, and he knew it might be his last. He wasn't going to miss the Taj Mahal.

"Let me know if it's as beautiful as it is in the pictures." I said. "Maybe I'll see it someday." A decade later, I did.

Can You Take India?

As a Westerner visiting India for the first time, it's easy to feel overwhelmed. Of course, you have read guidebooks and watched TV travel shows to prepare for the trip. You know the basic facts—that India is the second-most-populous country in the world, diverse in topography, ethnicity, language, religion, culture, and cuisine. Nevertheless, after you have pushed your way past the hotel and taxi touts at the airport, shooed away the gaggle of barefoot young boys fighting to carry your bags, and settled into the air-conditioned comfort of the official car or the hotel shuttle, India still assails your senses.

There's no travel show that can prepare you for the crush of people, cars, auto rickshaws, hand carts, bicycles, and people on the city streets. Your driver is nonchalant about the traffic snarls. "Much worse in monsoon season," he says matter-of-factly. Street vendors, hawking snacks, newspapers, cheap toys, sunglasses, pens, pencils, balloons, coconut slices, and mobile phone car chargers, move among the stalled or slow-moving vehicles.

When I'm stuck in traffic in Delhi or Mumbai, it's easy to think that the city's jams are the worst I've ever experienced. On reflection I realize that the traffic can be just as bad in most other south and southeast Asian cities; the *New York Times* once described Dhaka as the "Bangladesh traffic jam that never ends." The difference is that in India stalled traffic offers a front-seat view of urban poverty. Beggars with long straggly greying hair, sad-eyed children, and women with babies bundled on their backs knock on the car windows, holding open their hands. At one intersection, children perform tumbling tricks on the road. "Look away and don't open the window," your driver instructs, hitting the automatic door lock. You feel a little guilty about ignoring suffering, but at the same time you check your billfold or purse to make sure nothing is missing after the jostling at the airport. The guidebook warned you about pickpockets.

Statistically, the wealth gap in urban India may be no greater than it is in Madagascar, Bangladesh, and Indonesia, but to me the poverty of Delhi or Mumbai always seems more apparent, more emotionally draining. Of course, panhandlers work the streets of Tana, Dhaka, and Jakarta, but somehow they seem less persistent or desperate. In urban India, the poor are often right in your face or following you down the street. Do you hand over that 20 rupee note (about 30¢) with its image of that champion of the poor, Mahatma Gandhi, to make the woman with her baby go away? How do you know that she's not part of an organized begging ring? In India, moral dilemmas await you around almost every corner.

Your car passes rows of dilapidated concrete apartment blocks, their courtyards strewn with trash. Along the roadside and the railroad tracks are rough, single-room shanties, bamboo poles framing rusting sheets of metal, cardboard, tarpaulin, and plastic; outside, literally on the street, women are bathing children and cooking on stoves or open fires. In parks, alleys, and under bridges, those who do not have a shanty claim a few feet of grass or dirt for a sleeping space, laying out a blanket and a few possessions. Yet, a few hundred yards further on is a residential compound of smart, high-rent apartments, with an electronic security gate, a guard post, and security cameras. Your car passes modern office towers, ornate wedding palaces, brightly colored Hindu temples, somber mosques, and a moving window display of commercial signage, some in comic English. The malls are packed with shoppers; at the food court, they go for traditional north or south Indian fare or sample KFC and Subway, before shopping or heading to the multiplex for the latest Bollywood blockbuster.

You arrive at your hotel, surrounded by high brick walls topped with barbed wire and spikes. At the security checkpoint, one guard opens the trunk to inspect the luggage; another slowly circles the vehicle holding a pole with a mirror, checking the underside for suspicious attachments. At the entrance, one hotel staff member opens the car door and two more carry your bags to the metal detector. The doorman looks as if he just stepped out of the military parade ground or a TV period drama. Six feet tall and well built, with a dark beard, he is resplendent in his yellow turban and tailored white suit with a red sash and ornamental sword. He salutes smartly. Standing nearby, two less well tailored security guards armed with semiautomatic rifles and perspiring in their flak jackets acknowledge your arrival, although their salutes are more perfunctory. There's more saluting and door opening as you enter the lobby and approach the reception desk, where a waiter offers you a welcome drink of watermelon juice. For an instant, you imagine you're back in the time of the Raj, that you're a British colonial officer with a small army of staff at your bidding. Then reality returns. You're in a modern hotel with air-conditioning, Wi-Fi, and room service. BBC World is on the TV monitor, the sound muted. The low-level Muzak sounds familiar, but somehow out of place. Then you catch the tune. "Let it snow, let it snow, let it snow." Surreal. The dark-suited desk clerk smiles and gives you your key. "Welcome to the Taj, sir. I hope you have a pleasant stay."

The wealth gap in urban India, perhaps more than in any other country I've visited, is striking and ever-present, sometimes within the same field of view. In some countries, most poor people are geographically segregated, confined to the outer limits of cities in shanty towns or informal settlements. In urban India, outside the oases of hotels and offices, the poor are with you all the time. In rural India, the wealth gap is less apparent, and in some villages, everyone seems to be living at about the same basic level. Appearances are deceptive. Even in the poorest areas, there are those who own the land and those who do not, those who operate shops and small businesses and those who work as day laborers. Because it's all palm and mango trees and rice paddies, it looks (at least from the car window) picturesque, even idyllic, but the reality of daily life is different.

Faced with crowds, poverty, pollution, trash, traffic congestion, and crime, some people find India too much to bear. There's always a danger of getting sick—from tap water at a budget hotel or restaurant, or from street food. Except in the foothills of the Himalayas, it's usually hot—in some months, almost unbearably so. If you're looking for a beach with palm trees, cheap Asian cuisine, bars, and nightclubs, India has a few destinations—the best known is Goa—but you're better off going to Thailand. If you're prepared to take India for what it is—often messy and disorganized, occasionally dangerous and always unpredictable—and put up with unanticipated inconveniences and hardships, including the occasional case of Delhi Belly (traveler's diarrhea), you will be well rewarded and relish its smells, sounds, sights, culture, and people.

Incredible, Inexplicable

You may also feel humble, as I do when Indian friends and colleagues start talking about history, religion, and culture. India is an epic of epics, spanning thousands of years—of war and conquest, of the rise and fall of great civilizations, of architecture, literature, and art, of migration and settlement, of commerce with Asia, Europe, and Africa. I know some of this but have much more to learn.

If there's one constant about India, it's that everything—politics, the caste system and social structure, history, literature, art, and culture—is permeated by religion. Hinduism, with its panoply of gods, demigods, ceremonies, festivals, and icons, is the largest faith; more than 80 percent of the population (that's close to one billion) identify themselves as Hindus. Hinduism is not a monolithic creed but comes in many strains, from hardcore fundamentalism with its nationalistic and even xenophobic tendencies, to secular, liberal, and cosmopolitan, where it is more of a personal value system and way of life than a religion. India has the world's third-largest Muslim population (after Indonesia and Pakistan), making it the country with the largest Muslim-minority population; in the 2011 census, 172 million people (more than 14 percent of the population) identified as Muslims. There are Buddhists, Sikhs, and Christians of all denominations, with Christianity strongest in the southwestern state of Kerala and the northeast. Among indigenous peoples, animist beliefs mix seamlessly with mainstream religions. Religion is easily harnessed to serve political and economic goals—to justify the free market, deregulatory policies of the Hindu nationalist Bharatiya Janata Party (Indian People's Party, abbreviated as BJP) of Prime Minister Narendra Modi or the state interventionist policies of communist-leaning parties in Kerala and West Bengal.

If India is an economic giant, as most economists say it is, it's a giant with arthritis in its joints that has had trouble getting up the steps to meet targets for GDP growth. The agricultural sector still consists mostly of subsistence farmers, contributing little to exports; India's rustbelt, its carbon-spewing industrial plants, look as if they were packed up in Akron or Allentown in the early 1970s and shipped—lock, stock, and leaking barrels—to Bihar and Madhya Pradesh. It is also a country of gleaming, manicured, ecofriendly IT campuses and modern manufacturing plants. The Mumbai stock exchange is a barometer of an economy that, after years of state regulation, has been freed to grow. Yet far away from the high rises, the red hammer and sickle flag flutters over rice fields; at night, communist guerrillas (the so-called Naxalites) sneak into villages to murder local officials and wealthy landowners and redistribute land to landless peasants.

Most citizens and visitors to India long ago accepted that any generalizations are at best tentative, at worst misleading. There is not one but many Indias. India is not only, as its tourism slogan goes, "incredible." It's inexplicable.

What If Uttar Pradesh Declared Independence?

I've always loved reading maps, speculating about place names, coastlines, and mountain ranges, rivers, roads, and canals, national and provincial boundaries, and what they tell us about the economy, politics, ethnic groups, and culture. In June 2011, the *Economist* presented me with a gift from cartographic heaven, modestly titled "An Indian summary." In an interactive map, it compared Indian states and territories to countries in terms of population, GDP, and GDP per person PPP (purchasing power parity). "How big is Uttar Pradesh, India's most populous state?" asked the *Economist*. "One way of answering the question is to look at its total area: 95,000 square miles (246,000 sq. km)." (That would make it a little larger than the UK.) "Another way is to think of it as a country. So if Uttar Pradesh were to declare independence, it would be the world's fifth-most-populous country, with the same population as Brazil [195 million in 2008]. Yet its economy would only be the size of Qatar, a tiny oil-rich state of fewer than 2 million people. That makes it poor on a per person basis. Despite India's two decades of rapid growth, Uttar Pradesh's GDP per head is close to that of Kenya."[1]

The maps graphically illustrate India's demographic and economic challenges. Over the last quarter century, owing partly to rising female literacy, India's birth rate has steadily declined—from 3.6 children in 1991 to 2.3 in 2014. Currently, its population is growing by 1.2 percent per year—less than it used to be, but still well above the annual rates for China (0.5 percent) and the United States (0.7 percent). India has made significant economic strides, but some states, especially in the north, remain poor and largely agricultural.

In 2011, the second-most-populous state, Maharashtra, with 110 million (similar to Mexico), topped the *Economist* GDP table. It was more prosperous than Uttar Pradesh, which had 85 million more people, partly because it includes Mumbai, India's commercial capital, but its GDP was still less than Singapore's and per person close to Sri Lanka. Bihar's population of 96 million was close to the Philippines, but its GDP was

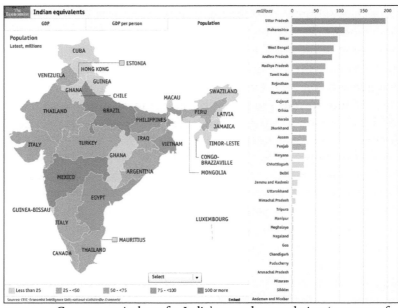

MAP 5.1   Country equivalents for India's states by population (courtesy of the *Economist*)

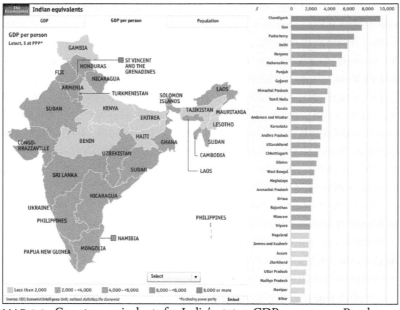

MAP 5.2   Country equivalents for India's states, GDP per person, Purchasing Power Parity, (courtesy of the *Economist*)

that of Uzbekistan (a post-Soviet basket case study in economic mismanagement and corruption) and per person equivalent to conflict-torn Eritrea, one of the poorest countries in the Horn of Africa. In 2011 only three small Union Territories—Chandigarh in the north, the former Portuguese colony and tourist hotspot Goa, and Puducherry, a hodgepodge of tiny former French outposts spread across three states—had a GDP per person of more than $6,000 per year. The rest of the GDP per person map consisted of countries from the lower tiers of the UN Human Development Index—Benin, Congo-Brazzaville, Gambia, Lesotho, Mauritania, Sudan, Haiti, Honduras, Nicaragua, Tajikistan, Laos, Papua New Guinea. We should be happy that these states do not—like Uttar Pradesh in the *Economist* scenario—declare independence. If they did, the international community would see its foreign aid burden increase dramatically.

If the *Economist* was to update its summary based on recent economic statistics, some states would have made major economic strides. In 2011, the economic table was led by Maharashtra with a 2009 GDP of $175.3 billion; it's still the leader, and in 2017 its GDP was expected to reach $380 billion, making its economy as large as Iran's. The major movers in the GDP table are two southern states. In 2011, Tamil Nadu ranked fifth with $80 billion; by 2017, it ranked second with $290 billion, making its economy comparable in size to Pakistan's. In 2011, Karnataka ranked seventh with $62.9 billion; now it's third with $190 million. Andhra Pradesh dropped from 3rd to 11th, but that's mainly because the northern part of the state, including Hyderabad, was lopped off in June 2014 to form the new state of Telangana; if combined, the GDP of both states would put it in third place, ahead of Karnataka. In the northwest, Modi's political ascendancy rested partly on his management, as chief minister, of the economy of his home state of Gujarat, whose economy doubled in size to $167 billion from 2009 to 2016.

The GDP of northern states such as Uttar Pradesh, Bihar, Rajasthan, and Madhya Pradesh has also increased, but not at nearly the same rate as the southern states or economic hotspots. The jumble of small states in India's northeast—the "chicken neck" or the "Seven Sisters" described in chapter 7—continue to lag behind on most development indicators.

Because the most recent census was done in 2011, there is no reliable recent state population data on which to calculate GDP per person PPP. However, the birth rate in northern, rural states remains higher than in southern states. Unofficial estimates put Uttar Pradesh's 2017 population at 223.8 million, an increase of 4 million from the previous year. If it was to declare independence, it would actually replace Brazil as the fifth-most-populous country in the world.

How do the countries of *Monsoon Postcards* compare with Indian states for population? Using 2011 data, Indonesia, the fourth-most-populous country in the world, would be roughly equivalent to Uttar Pradesh plus Telangana, India's newest state and its twelfth most populous. Take Bihar's 104 million and Assam's 31 million and you have Bangladesh. Madagascar's 2011 population of 21 million was a couple of million less than that of Haryana in the northeast, one of India's smallest states.

Such maps and comparative tables invite demographic doodling. Yes, the whole 2011 population of Mongolia of 2.6 million could move to the northeast state of Meghalaya, but the herders would need to leave their yaks, horses, and sheep back on the steppe, and they would probably not survive in the misty hills. Would the population of Latvia consent to move to the border state of Nagaland, where armed resistance to the central government continues and Internet connections are flakey? The population of Swaziland would find the high plateaus of Arunachal Pradesh cold and inhospitable, while Canadians would find Kerala on the hot side. And what would the casino-hustlers of Macau find to do in Buddhist Sikkim?

Such maps and tables are illustrative. Because India's total population of 1.3 billion is an abstract number, we need an analogy to grasp the demographic reality. I suppose that if we asked all Indians to stand in an orderly line (which, of course, they never would) along the Equator, we could figure out how many times they would ring the earth, but that doesn't tell us much. Comparing state populations, GDP, and GDP per person PPP is a more tangible way to describe the size and economy of the country, but it's still difficult to get a sense of scale. I needed a more concrete example.

In June 2015, while stuck in a traffic jam in Hyderabad, my traveling companion Mario Mosquera, head of communication for development at UNICEF India, gave me such an example as he talked about a shift in the agency's strategy. For many years, UNICEF, working with government and NGO partners, has undertaken projects in maternal and child health, nutrition, education, child protection, and water, hygiene, and sanitation. "With a large project, maybe you can make a difference in the lives of a few hundred thousand people," said Mario. "It's worth it, of course, but it's a drop in the bucket. What about the millions of others whose lives remain unchanged?" He said UNICEF was now concentrating on advocacy and policy change with national and state governments. According to the World Bank, India is now a lower-middle income country. The government has more money to spend, is less dependent on donors, and is not shy about saying so. Increasing budget allocations for maternal and child health or primary education by 1 or 2 percent can make more difference than a hundred UNICEF-funded projects.

The "Smart City"

The city of Ahmedabad sprawls across the scrubby coastal plain of the northwestern state of Gujarat for what seems like an eternity. And perhaps it is an eternity, because it is reportedly the fastest-growing city in India. The 2011 census put its population at 5.6 million; it's now well over 7 million, with a million or so more in the metropolitan area, making it either the fifth- or sixth-largest city in India, and the seventh-largest metropolitan area. By the next census in 2021, sixty years after it first passed the million mark, it could have 9 million.

Ahmedabad was not on my radar until June 2015 when I visited with Mario to check out the Mudra Institute for Communication (MICA), which had bid to host the 2016 workshop on communication for development for UNICEF staff. I had no idea the city was as large as it was, nestled in the population table just below Bangalore and Hyderabad. Flying in from Delhi, I assumed the terminal where we arrived was the airport itself and thought it looked rather empty. I soon saw signs pointing to three more terminals. Ahmedabad was building for future growth.

Ahmedabad was originally a city of textile mills—some called it the "Manchester of India." It's in the cotton-growing region of Gujarat and also imports raw cotton through the ports of Mumbai and Kandla. Climatic conditions are suitable for spinning, and water from the Sabarmati River for dyeing. The city had a large pool of skilled labor, investment capital, and good road and rail connections to Mumbai and other cities. The textile industry remains an important part of the economy, but Ahmedabad has diversified. Over the last decade, the main growth has been in sectors such as auto parts and pharmaceuticals, with a business-friendly state government offering cheap land and tax breaks to industry. It was the "Gujarat economic miracle" that helped propel the state's chief minister, Narendra Modi, to the national stage and to leadership of the Hindu Nationalist Party, the BJP.

From the airport, Mario and I drove for almost an hour on a freshly tarmacked four-lane ring road across a construction site landscape. Workers were laying water and utility lines on both sides of the highway and planting shrubs on the median. Large areas of former farmland were dotted with signs and surveyors' stakes announcing future industrial and technology parks. In the sweltering heat of the early afternoon— late June is the start of the monsoon season—workers with scarves tied around their heads clambered between the steel and concrete pillars of half-finished factories and office buildings, hoisted bamboo scaffolding poles into position, mixed cement, and carried bricks, effortlessly balancing them in baskets on their heads. Billboards marked the designation of economic zones, often expressed as acronyms, such as the Gujarat International Finance Tech (GIFT) City, a "smart city" initiative.

Ahmedabad is one of more than one hundred urban areas across India designated by the national government to become a "smart city." It's a catchy, if vague, slogan. Officially, a smart city is an urban region with top-notch infrastructure, making it attractive to businesses and residents. That means wide roads, commercial and industrial real estate, modern apartments, schools, and medical facilities, all wired together with high-speed links. Ahmedabad was one of twenty cities selected in the first round in January 2016 for government funding.

Knowing the average connection speed of Indian bureaucracy, it may take some time for the money to arrive. The state and city governments were not waiting on Delhi but plowing ahead with infrastructure. Ahmedabad will likely always be a work-in-progress, because there are few geographical limits to expansion, although eventually the city planners will run up against the Char Desert, which covers a wide area of the northwest in the states of Rajasthan and Gujarat. In late afternoon, as we drove away from the MICA campus through the borderland between construction sites and cotton fields, we passed camels hauling carts of hay for animal feed. Somehow, it did not seem incongruous to see camels and herders on a modern highway among the yellow Tata trucks and SUVs. The line between the urban and rural in modern India is constantly shifting.

I began to wonder if Ahmedabad was anything more than highways and construction sites. I was happy to discover an older city on a one-hour sortie to have my suitcase repaired. One advantage of working in a developing country is that it's almost always cheaper to have something fixed than to buy a new one. Whether it's bricolage on a Renault 4L in a metal fabrication shop in Madagascar, a line of sewing machines poised to make running repairs at a market in Indonesia, or the cobbler in Dhaka who put new soles on my Birkenstocks, there are always people with the skills and materials to make repairs. In this instance, the screws securing the pull-out handle on my suitcase had fallen out. The hotel gave me the name of a shopping center where luggage was sold. My auto rickshaw driver had a better idea. He pulled up beside other drivers who rooted around under the seats in their vehicles for screws. After ten minutes, I signaled that I wasn't prepared to wait and we set off again. The next stop was a hole-in-the-wall hardware shop, but again nothing fit. We set off again through the maze of streets of the old city and eventually reached a roundabout. The luggage repair *wallah* sat under a canopy on the narrow sidewalk, his sewing machine in the road, piles of used luggage behind him. He inspected the suitcase, dipped into a bag, pulled out two bolts and nuts, screwed the suitcase together and fixed a torn zipper. "How much?" I asked. He shrugged. "Whatever you think is right." I gave him 150 rupees (about $2.25), got back into the auto rickshaw, thought about it again, and gave him another 100. I fear that his days are numbered. There's no place in the smart city for people who hang out a shingle at a busy roundabout and fix things. Maybe they'll give him a cubicle on the ring road and a website domain. And no one will come.

My Passage to India

In my school days in Britain in the 1950s and 1960s, I didn't know much about India. It was a pastel pink blob on the world map, the third-largest (after Canada and Australia) and most populous country in the pastel pink expanse of what was now called the British Commonwealth. The newspapers sometimes mentioned the 1947 partition of British India, but they made it sound like a neat and orderly transition, as if the captains of two cricket teams had agreed to a gentlemanly draw and then retired to the clubhouse for tea. I knew that India had a hot climate, and that it suffered from natural disasters such as floods and earthquakes. I knew that Indians were good at cricket and had some devilishly clever spin bowlers to match the fast pace of the English and Australians.

To the British, tea was India's best-known export, along with cotton, rice, and spices. It also exported people. Some worked in low-paying jobs on the London public transportation system as cleaners, porters, and laborers; I remember my surprise when I first encountered a turbaned Sikh conductor on a double-decker bus. Others worked in the restaurants and curry houses that were opening in the London suburbs. My family rarely went out to eat, and when we did we stuck to traditional British fare, which was conservative when it came to spices and seasoning. There were a few daring outings for Cantonese. But Indian? Certainly not. "You really don't know what's in it," my father would say, although he could have said the same thing about the steak and kidney pie or blood sausage we were having for dinner.

The history of India received superficial treatment in school history books. Traditional historians focused on military and political events, telling the story within the framework of the inexorable, divinely ordained march of empire. British merchants, missionaries, soldiers, and administrators brought order and civilization to a subcontinent of feuding maharajas and restless masses, yearning to be freed from slavery or serfdom. In this narrative, the British East India Company was the enlightened, entrepreneurial pioneer, helping India develop its economy through global trade, creating an educated professional class and investing in infrastructure. The company established the rule of law and administrative system, with an army of native clerks to do the busy work in courts and government offices. British engineers built the railroads and telegraph lines and improved port facilities. The army defended India from hostile forces—the Burmese in the east, the armies of Imperial Russia to the north.

Language was key to historical framing. In British textbooks, the rebellion of 1857, which resulted in the killing of at least one million Indians and in which atrocities were committed on both sides, was referred to as the "Indian Mutiny." The reference was to the first outbreak of violence, a revolt by Indian soldiers (sepoys), protesting at military discipline and living conditions at the garrison of Meerut near Delhi. The rebellion quickly spread, fueled by resentment against harsh land taxes, social reforms, and economic exploitation by princes and large landowners. In India and Pakistan, it has been called the "War of Independence of 1857" or the "First War of Indian Independence" or, more neutrally, "The Revolt of 1857."

Similarly, the history books acknowledged the twentieth-century nationalist movement, led by Mahatma Gandhi, but downplayed its role in achieving independence. The standard explanation was that Britain, its resources exhausted by World War II, simply could not afford to continue supporting its most populous colony or provide the administrators and soldiers to maintain control. It was a matter of financial and human resources. The British were leaving India better than they had found it. They had developed the economy, and built schools, libraries, museums, and railroads with their majestic Victorian stations; they had established an administrative and legal system and trained the staff to run it. The legacy of the British Raj was considerable.

I supposed that some Indian historians, even those educated at British universities, were offering a counternarrative to the glorious imperial parade, but if so their books were not on the reading list. British politicians and royalty continued to pay courtesy visits and were greeted with appropriate pomp and circumstance by Jawaharlal Nehru, the nationalist leader and India's postindependence prime minister. The British still drank tea from Darjeeling and Assam, not thinking about the conditions of the workers who picked it. Indian cuisine became more popular. Indian spin bowlers were still feared.

I discovered India after I left university in 1970 and moved to the city of Leeds in West Yorkshire to work as a newspaper reporter. Or rather I discovered Pakistan. One of my first assignments was in the textile city of Bradford, west of Leeds. The industry was already in decline, but many of Bradford's garment factories were still operating, at least at part-capacity. As I got off the bus and pulled out my city map, I looked up at a street sign. It was in English and an unfamiliar, Arabic-looking script. I walked past curry and tandoori houses—the Karachi Restaurant, the Taste of Punjab—and small corner shops owned by people called Khan, Rahman, Abdullah, Farook, Firdoz. Down a side street, I saw a crescent and star sign over a small building and a sign with the schedule for Friday prayers. Most of the migrants, I learned, were from West Pakistan, and the street signs were in Urdu, the national language. They had arrived after World War II to work in the woolen mills, massive nineteenth-century structures built of brick or sandstone or limestone blocks, with towering chimneys. They were economic migrants, huddling against the damp cold and trying to protect their families and culture in a strange land. I did not see any women on the streets.

As a reporter, I covered the challenges these immigrants faced—to learn English and obtain social benefits and medical care—and their desire to maintain a cultural and religious identity separate from their host country. They tended to keep to themselves and stay off the streets at night, especially when the pubs emptied and drunken youths were out looking for trouble. Every few months, we reported the latest incident of what became known as "Paki-bashing." The victims were usually reluctant to go to the police or courts. The major controversy was over schooling and the Muslims' insistence on the segregation of sexes. This came into conflict with public education laws that required mixed classes. After a few civil cases brought against Muslims for refusing to let their daughters attend public schools, the issue became moot when the community started establishing its own private schools.

I was also discovering cheap, nutritious South Asian food—chapati, roti, rice, dahl, and chicken curries—at hole-in-the-wall eateries in Bradford and Leeds, which had a smaller, mostly Indian population operating small grocery stores and take-out restaurants. And I started thinking about Britain's role in the Indian subcontinent. In 1971, I had read about the brief and bloody war in East Pakistan that ended in Bangladesh's declaration of independence. Why had the Indian subcontinent been divided between a majority Hindu and a majority Muslim state? And why were the two parts of Pakistan separated by almost fourteen hundred miles of India? I began to study a history that had been ignored, or at least underplayed, in the imperial narrative.

The Colonial Legacy

In a speech at the Oxford Union in August 2015, the Indian Congress politician, diplomat, and writer Shashi Tharoor made a controversial proposal: Britain should pay India reparations for the damage its empire had inflicted. Descendants of former slaves and other groups, such as Australia's aborigines and Canada's First Nations, who lost their land or freedoms, have also called for reparations and official government apologies, but Tharoor's appeal was on a grander scale. The speech went viral on social media and was the topic for TV talk shows, newspaper articles, and university classes. Tharoor's book, *An Era of Darkness,* which elaborated his arguments, was a bestseller in India; the British edition is titled *Inglorious Empire: What the British Did to India.*[2]

"The British," writes Tharoor, "seized one of the richest countries in the world—accounting for 27 per cent of global GDP in 1700—and over 200 years of colonial rule reduced it to one of the world's poorest. Britain destroyed India through looting, appropriation and outright theft—all conducted in a spirit of deep racism and amoral cynicism. The British justified their actions, carried out by brute force, with staggering hypocrisy and cant." Tharoor says Britain suffers from "a kind of historical amnesia about colonialism."

As William Dalrymple, perhaps the best-known British writer on India, notes, "much of the story of the empire is still absent from our history curriculum. My children learned the Tudors and the Nazis over and over again in history class but never came across a whiff of Indian or Caribbean history. This means that they, like most people who go through the British education system, are wholly ill equipped to judge either the good or the bad in what we did to the rest of the world."

As a product of that system, I plead guilty as charged, or at least no contest. "Many of the British," writes Tharoor, "are genuinely unaware of the atrocities their ancestors committed." They are well documented: the rebellion of 1857, and the Jallianwala Bagh (Amritsar) massacre of 1919, when troops commanded by Brigadier General Richard Dyer fired on unarmed protestors and pilgrims, leaving 379 dead and 1,200 injured. Some, write Tharoor, "live in the blissful illusion that the British Empire was some sort of civilizing mission to uplift the ignorant natives." This opens the way for "the manipulation of historical narratives" with popular histories extolling "the supposed virtues of empire" and TV soap operas "with their gauzy romanticization of the 'Raj,' providing a rose-tinted picture of the colonial era."[3]

Tharoor's interpretation has been challenged on several grounds. Critics say that the "India" plundered by the British was an imaginary construct; except for the period of the Mughal Empire, it was never united; rather, it was the British who forged a collection of feudal principalities into a country. Unlike the Hindu and Muslim elites and rulers, the British encouraged education, establishing universities, colleges, and scientific and medical institutes; the liberal intellectuals of the Bengal Renaissance opposed the 1857 rebellion, which they regarded as a power grab by conservative forces. Critics say that Tharoor fails to quantify the value of social reforms, infrastructure, and science and technology: Would India be a major player in the IT world today without British investment in math and science education?

However, there are few on either side of the argument who will deny what happened when it all ended in August 1947. Faced with the demand for a separate state for India's Muslims, Britain decided, with the support of both Hindu and Muslim political leaders, to partition the country, creating the separate countries of India and Pakistan. Partition was the tragic culmination of almost two centuries of divide-and-rule by the British. What followed is well summarized in a review of Yasmin Khan's *The Great Partition: The Making of India and Pakistan:*

> The break-up of Britain's Indian empire involved the movement of some 12m people, uprooted, ordered out, or fleeing their homes and seeking safety. Hundreds of thousands of people were killed, thousands of children disappeared, thousands of women were raped or abducted, forced conversions were commonplace. The violence polarised communities on the sub-continent as never before. The pogroms and killings were organized by gangs, vigilantes and militias across northern, western and eastern India. They were often backed by local leaders, politicians from Congress and the Muslim League, maharajahs and princes, and helped by willing or frightened civil servants. . . . Today the upheaval on both sides of the partition line would be described as ethnic cleansing on a gigantic scale. It left two traumatised, injured nations—suspicious and fearful of one another even to this day—where once there had been one country of loosely interwoven peoples.[4]

Tharoor writes that "large-scale conflicts between Hindus and Muslims (religiously defined) only began under colonial rule." That may be an overstatement; throughout the history of the subcontinent, invading armies have killed thousands of Hindus and Muslims, so the real question is how a conflict is framed—as conquest or crusade. However, there are clear examples of how colonial policy contributed to communal tensions, notably in Bengal. In 1905, the viceroy, Lord Curzon, announced that, on the pretext of administrative efficiency, Bengal would be split into separate Muslim-majority and Hindu-majority provinces. Bengalis, who shared a common language, protested at a policy that turned the native population against itself in order to govern. Widespread resistance followed, and Bengal was reunited in 1911, but the attempted partition led Hindus and Muslims to form their own organizations, and it inflamed communal tensions. Tharoor argues that "many other kinds of social strife were labelled as religious due to the colonists' orientalist assumption that religion was the fundamental division in Indian society. . . . [T]he creation and perpetuation of Hindu-Muslim antagonism was the most significant accomplishment of British imperial policy: the project of divide *et impera* would reach its culmination in the collapse of British authority in 1947."[5] Partition once again divided Bengal along religious lines, creating the eastern portion of Muslim-majority Pakistan.

The decision on partition had been taken hastily by the British government, with little sense of the consequences. The announcement was made in the House of Commons on June 3, 1947. Six weeks later the British administration had packed up and gone home. The troops left behind were not permitted to keep order or protect people. Only the shock of Gandhi's assassination in January 1948 by a Hindu extremist opposed to his cooperation with Muslim leaders helped stem the violence.

Khan challenges the notion that a common religion is enough to bind diverse ethnic groups together into a nation state. Five years after partition, the violent suppression of protests by university students in Dhaka over the imposition of the Urdu language gave East Pakistan, the Muslim-majority state created by the partition of Bengal, its first Bangla "language martyrs" and marked the start of a struggle for independence that ended in 1971; for the Bangla, ethnicity and language were more powerful motivators than religion. Khan, writes the reviewer, "nails the propaganda lie that the transfer of power in India was an example of peaceful decolonisation that the rest of the world could follow."

Tharoor is critical of his fellow Indians for their "equanimity about the past." Despite the horrors of partition, India chose to remain in the Commonwealth and maintain friendly relations with Britain. "Whether through national strength or civilizational weakness," he writes, "India has long refused to hold any grudge against Britain for 200 years of imperial enslavement, plunder and exploitation."[6] I find most of my Indian colleagues and friends genuinely ambivalent about the colonial legacy. Many have benefitted from a British university education and have relatives and friends who have settled in the UK. They agree that India was economically exploited but credit the colonizer with helping to develop the economy and transportation system, and for replacing the autocratic power of the maharajas with secular democracy.

Escape from Lyallpur

"We weren't allowed to utter the word 'Pakistan' in our household," my academic colleague Suruchi Sood recalls. "As far as my grandmother was concerned, partition never happened."

Partition shaped the lives of both of Suruchi's parents. Both were from Hindu families living in Punjab, but from different backgrounds. During British rule, Suruchi's mother's family were loyal civil servants. Her grandfather was posted to Wazirabad, an industrial city about sixty miles from Lahore, where her mother was born. At partition, the family moved to Delhi, where her grandfather worked for the Central Bureau of Investigation (CBI), India's domestic security agency, and the family lived comfortably in a government house.

Suruchi's father's family was from Lyallpur, a major industrial and transportation center that, renamed as Faisalabad, is today the third-most-populous city in Pakistan. Her grandfather was active in the independence movement, and in 1947 he and his six brothers were serving prison terms for anti-British activities. "When partition came, my grandmother decided to stay," said Suruchi. "She didn't know whether or not her husband was alive. She hoped a male member of the family would return with news." She knew she had to get her children to safety. "She took my uncle, who was twelve, and my father, who was eight, to the station and shoved them onto a train to Delhi. There was pandemonium—they left with just the clothes on their backs, nothing more. The train was crowded—my father was inside, my uncle on the roof." In the confusion, the brothers were separated. "My dad remembers it as a terrifying time. Suddenly, he's in a foreign country, he doesn't speak the language. He speaks Punjabi, not Hindi." Remarkably, the brothers were taken to the same refugee camp where they were reunited.

Suruchi's grandmother left Lyallpur on the last convoy the Indian army sent into Pakistan to escort Hindus. "They sent trucks with loudspeakers around the city. They said that if you don't leave now we will not be able to guarantee your safety because in two days this will not be the same country." She left carrying only her jewelry. In Delhi, she looked up a cousin whose husband, a well-connected doctor, managed to locate her children. She sold her jewelry and cleaned houses to make ends meet; her husband had died of TB in prison, so she was now a single parent. Suruchi's uncle left school at sixteen to work to support the family, but her father went on to college and became an engineer. At the age of twenty-seven, with a good job and career prospects, he married Suruchi's mother in an arranged match. The couple moved to Kolkata in the early 1960s.

Like other children and grandchildren of partition, Suruchi struggles with the "Where are you from?" question. "I've been to Punjab once and I speak the language. But I'm very much Bengali because I grew up there. However, my natal name, Sood, gives away the fact that I'm not Bengali. It's a Punjabi or Himachal name."

Suruchi paused for a moment. "That's a hard question. I've lived longest in the US."

Bengaluru or Bangalore?

One indicator of a country's relationship to its past is how it deals with the reminders of colonial rule—the statues and plaques honoring administrators and generals, the chapters in school textbooks, the names of cities, towns, and streets.

India has not been in a rush to remove reminders of its colonial past. Since independence, more than one hundred cities and towns have been renamed, but that leaves hundreds more that are still known by their colonial-era names. The changes have included Mumbai (formerly Bombay), Chennai (Madras), Kolkata (Calcutta), Guwahati (Gauhati), Kanpur (Cawnpore), Kochi (Cochin), Mysuru (Mysore), Pune (Poona), Puducherry (Pondicherry), Shimla (Simla), Tiruchiapalli (Trichinapoly), Thiruvananthapram (Trivandrum), and Varanasi (Benares). The most recent rash of official name changes came in 2014 when the government finally approved new names for twelve cities. As usual, there was no way to hurry up the bureaucracy; it had been almost a decade since the state government of Karnataka had approved changing the name of Bangalore to Bengaluru ahead of the city's five hundredth anniversary in 2006. A popular, although historically dodgy, story has it that the place owes its name to a local king who got lost in the forest on a hunting trip. After hours of aimless wandering, the hungry and exhausted king spotted a hut inhabited by an old woman who offered him boiled beans because that was all she had. Impressed by the hospitality, the king named that part of the forest Bendakaalooru in memory of the meal; in old Kannada, the local language, benda means boiled, kaalu beans, and ooru town or city, making it literally the "city of boiled beans." Or perhaps the name is derived from Benga-val-ooru (City of Guards), a reference to the city's military muscle from the sixteenth to the eighteenth centuries. When the British captured the fort in 1791, colonial administrators, perhaps struggling to get their tongues around the Kannada name, dubbed the city Bangalore, and that was how it was known for more than two centuries. During the public debate over reverting to the original name, some tourism and business officials fretted about what impact "the city of boiled beans" would have on the image of the country's leading IT hub, but most on both sides of the issue expected that the similar-sounding name would be quickly adopted.

It didn't happen. Although the official signs, airport monitors, and websites have been changed, some Indians, including Bengaluru natives, continue to use the old name. The same goes for Mumbai, Chennai, and Kolkata, although the latter (the Bengali name) is close enough in pronunciation to Calcutta that sometimes you can't tell which name is being used. Indeed, many colonial-era city and town names were what the locals called the place, or how the name sounded to the British administrators. There aren't many real English place names.

Street names are another matter. India's municipal governments have systematically erased the names of colonial officials from signs and maps. The streets of central Delhi were once a who's who of British monarchs, prime ministers, generals, viceroys, and colonial administrators—King Edward, King George, Allenby, Canning, Clive, Cornwallis, Curzon, Kitchener, Monto, Reading. They've all gone. Kingsway is now Rajpath, Queensway Janpath.

During visits, I try to be culturally sensitive and use the new names, but sometimes I get puzzled looks. "Oh, you must mean Bombay—why didn't you say so?" Suruchi, who returns to India at least once a year for work or family visits, reports a moment of panic when she took an internal flight to Madras. She arrived at the gate and saw that the destination listed was Chennai. For a moment, she thought she was on her way to another city.

It was Monday morning at the All India Radio (AIR) Staff Training Institute in Bhubaneshwar, in the western state of Odisha. At the beginning of the second week of my workshop on training techniques for broadcasters, I'd asked the participants—senior managers from the government-run national broadcasting service—to share ideas for their final presentations.

We went around the table. How to plan and record a concert of classic Indian music. How to produce a one-act radio play, a talk show, a live-event broadcast. And so on. Ashok Tripathi, director of programs for Doordarshan (DD), the national TV service, was last to speak. "I'd like to present a training module on how to prepare and maintain the administrative file," he said matter-of-factly.

I must have visibly gulped at what sounded to me like the dullest topic anyone had ever proposed. The participants sensed my reaction because they quickly piped up. "Please let him do it." "It's really important that we know." "Trust us on this—he's the expert."

I gave in, sensing more interest in this topic than in others proposed. On the final day, everyone listened intently and scribbled notes as Tripathi explained the complex process. Nothing in AIR or DD—not a program, a purchase, or a promotion—moved forward without an administrative file. The file had to be in proper order; if it was not correctly labeled and annotated, it simply would not move but sit in a stack beneath other improperly prepared files.

The file was a manila folder with pockets. There was a prescribed format for labeling it. Certain documents were to be placed in the left pocket, others in the right. There were places for attaching notes and for check-offs and signatures; if a note was in the wrong place, the file could not move to the next desk for review. There were protocols for handling the file if the manager responsible was on leave or ill. And many more details.

I had allowed twenty minutes for each presentation, and Tripathi kept to his time, but the question and answer session lasted another thirty minutes. When it was over, the room erupted in applause. "After twenty years, I finally know what to do," said one regional radio manager. Over tea, participants told me of their frustrations dealing with the bureaucracy. They were required to prepare files but had no instructions or templates. Program and equipment proposals languished for months at headquarters in Delhi. The manager would call and write polite memos. Eventually he might reach a clerk who would point out the error in the file and perhaps even correct it. It could take many hours of time and effort to move the file forward while the project remained stalled.

Prasar Bharati (the Broadcasting Corporation of India) is the largest public broadcaster in the world with about thirty-five thousand staff. Its radio division, officially known since 1956 as Akashvani (literally, "voice from the sky"), has 418 stations across the country, provides programming in 23 languages and 146 dialects, and reaches 99 percent of the population; its external services broadcast in 27 languages to more than 100 countries. Doordarshan (literally, "seeing from afar") has two national TV channels, eleven regional language satellite channels, four state networks, an international channel, a sports channel, and two channels for live broadcast of parliamentary proceedings. There's a news division, departments for marketing, engineering, and research, and two staff training centers—in Delhi and Bhubaneshwar. That's a lot of physical plant, equipment, content, and people to manage, so you need administrative systems and files.

The problem is not that there's a bureaucracy. It's how well it functions and how long it takes to get things done. Even the most cursory review of AIR and DD organograms and staff rosters suggests that the Prasar Bharati bureaucracy long ago grew out of all proportion to its tasks. Like other bureaucracies in India—for ministries, state governments, railways, universities—it has become self-perpetuating, often viewed as a barrier rather than a facilitator.

In *English, August: An Indian Story,* a novel about a civil servant's frustrating year of service in a rural backwater, Upamanyu Chatterjee (himself a civil servant) wrote that administration "is largely a British creation, like the railways and the English language, another complex and unwieldy bequest of the Raj."[7] In the colonial era, the Indian Civil Service (ICS), headed by professional British officers, was responsible for all administrative and legal matters, and for maintaining law and order. Speaking in the House of Commons in 1935, former British prime minister David Lloyd George described the ICS as "the steel frame on which the whole structure of our government and of our administration in India rests." Not everyone wanted a steel frame. Nationalist leader Nehru, quoting a popular joke, liked to say that the ICS was "neither

Indian, nor civil, nor a service." Yet, as India's first prime minister, Nehru retained the organization and its leaders while changing its name to the Indian Administrative Service (IAS).

There's long been agreement among India's political parties and the business community on the need for civil service reform. National and state governments allocate vast sums for health, education, water, and sanitation, yet some is wasted because, as the *Economist* notes, it "is sponged up, or siphoned off, by a vast, tumorous bureaucracy." Successive governments have appointed committees, task forces, consultants, and other groups to study the problem and issue reports; on coming to power in 2004, Prime Minister Manmohan Singh said that administrative reform "at every level" was his priority. Yet he, like his predecessors, had little success in changing the way the bureaucracy does business. Its senior officials, including the members of the elite IAS, rule large fiefdoms and, like medieval nobles, are constantly battling each other for power and influence.

Meanwhile, the bureaucracy has grown by leaps and bounds. By 2010, it was estimated that the national government employed about 6.4 million staff, and the states another 7 million. In total, that's a couple of million more than the population of Belgium or Greece. Or, if you were to exchange them all for the residents of an Indian state, you would add more than a million to the population of Jammu and Kashmir. A lot of Indians would love to dispatch their *babus* to this remote and chilly northern outpost.

The title *babu,* also spelled *baboo* and derived from *bapu,* which means "father" or "grandfather," was traditionally used in South Asia as a sign of respect toward men. In the colonial era, *babu* became a common term for a literate Indian clerk in the ICS. From the early twentieth century, it began to take on negative connotations when used to refer to government bureaucrats and other officials. The Indian media have long been critical of individual *babus* and of the bureaucracy—the *babudom*—in general.

Although civil servants are hired through competitive examination, many complain that the quality of recruits has been falling. They blame lower education standards, competition from the private sector, political interference, and, above all, caste-based reservations, which set aside a percentage of positions for lower castes and members of tribal communities. Even the most competent senior civil servants find it difficult to develop expertise in a specific area because they are frequently shifted from one post to another. Bureaucracies such as diplomatic services, aid agencies, and UN organizations use a job rotation system to keep their staff honest. It's designed to ensure that a staff member does not develop business or political relationships that could influence decisions or be used for personal profit. The most common complaint from civil servants is that it usually takes a year to figure out what a new job involves, and another year to become good at it, at which point it's time to move on. Some studies have found that at least half those working for the IAS spend less than one year in a single position. "They can also end up working for India's vast number of state-run factories, hotels and airlines without much experience," noted BBC correspondent Soutik Biswas, "so an official administering a small northeastern state ends up running an ailing airline or a senior policeman can head up a liquor company."

Although the civil service is supposed to be legally protected from political interference, many bureaucrats, especially at the state level, are beholden to politicians who can promote, demote, or transfer them at will. Without transparency in appointments and fixed tenures, they have little job security. There are countless stories of honest bureaucrats who publicly challenge the way their political masters do business, only to find themselves abruptly shunted off to a remote rural area with few staff and little or no budget. The problem, claims the *Economist*, "is most grievous in north India, where civil servants tend to attach themselves to politicians for enrichment, advancement—or in despair of otherwise getting their job done."

For many years, the business community has lamented the costs of bureaucracy, and economists have constructed models to show what India's GDP growth would have been without the crippling costs of forms in triplicate and official stamps. Since the early 1990s, the economy has been opened to competition and freed of many regulations, leading to faster economic growth, but getting things done still requires dealing with the *babus*. "You cannot measure Indian red tape," notes the *Economist,* "but evidence of it is everywhere. One director of a 'new economy' company in Mumbai confides that he spends half his time with bureaucrats, who are generally looking for pay-offs."[8] In 2010, and again in 2012, the Hong Kong–based Political and Economic Risk Consultancy rated India's bureaucracy as "the worst in Asia." The report, based on a survey of more than thirteen hundred business executives in twelve Asian countries, ranks bureaucracies on a scale from 1 to 10, with 10 being the worst possible score. In 2012, India scored 9.21, an insignificant improvement on its 2010 score of 9.41, putting it behind Vietnam, Indonesia, the Philippines, and China. The consultancy noted the difficulties of starting a new business and of enforcing contracts, the links between bureaucracy and corruption, and the failure to hold *babus* accountable for poor decisions.[9]

As Sanjoy Bagchi, a retired senior civil servant, noted in his book, *The Changing Face of Bureaucracy*, inefficiency and apathy have diluted the efficiency of the civil service. Its leaders, often beholden to political interests, have abused their powers. "The diffident youngster of early idealistic years," he writes, "is transformed into an arrogant senior fond of throwing his weight around; he becomes a conceited prig."[10]

On the final day of the workshop in Bhubaneshwar, the chief executive officer of AIR flew in from Delhi to present certificates to participants. We assembled at the training center's administrative building, where staff had spent the day cleaning the foyer and rolled out a red carpet. A Hindu priest prepared to perform the *puja* prayer ritual to mark the event. The CEO arrived (late, of course) with his entourage and approached the makeshift shrine. Then his mobile phone rang. While we all waited, and the priest stood poised with incense sticks burning, the CEO spent ten minutes talking loudly to an accountant in Delhi about a problem with the transfer of funds. The certificate ceremony started forty-five minutes late. The CEO made a brief speech that made no reference to the training program. Afterward, he sat on a dais as staff approached with their petitions. "Esteemed sir, I greatly miss my family in Delhi. Will it be possible to approve my transfer? I would be eternally indebted to your honor if you would look favorably on my humble request." Most petitioners brought small gifts for the prince, who pretended to listen but most of the time looked as if he would have rather been somewhere else. After thirty minutes of scraping and bowing by commoners, he indicated that he was ready to leave. I pressed my business card into his hand, and he briefly acknowledged me. Then he was off to the next event, where another line of petitioners bearing gifts and false hopes was waiting for an audience.

Jokes about the excesses and absurdities of bureaucracy in India usually mention the colonial legacy. Three-quarters of a century after independence, it's a stretch to keep blaming the British. Today, India is a world power and lower-middle income country, quite capable of creating its own cumbersome bureaucracy without help from anyone else.

Delhi Dents

You can pretty much tell the age of a vehicle in Delhi by the number of dents, bumps, and scratches. Any vehicle that has survived the city traffic for more than six months has a few, and older vehicles such as the public buses look as if they've been battered many times from many angles. "We call them Delhi dents," said Ann Shoemake as her husband (and my former student) Khalid Syed negotiated the evening traffic with motorbikes passing left and right, cutting abruptly in front of their modestly dented Maruti Suzuki. Traffic regulations exist and are posted at police stations and public offices, but no one seems to pay attention. Buses, cars, auto rickshaws, and motorbikes take the fastest route, slipping in and out without signaling, squeezing into narrow gaps between other vehicles, missing collisions by important inches. Meanwhile, cyclists, bicycle rickshaws, pedestrians, and the occasional bullock- or horse-drawn cart try to hold their positions on the road. The concepts of "right of way" and "failure to yield" seem quaintly foreign in Delhi. Drivers eagerly embrace the "Please Use Horn" message painted on the rear of buses, trucks, and auto rickshaws but mysteriously have trouble reading the "Keep Distance" sign. I never saw a cop stop a vehicle for speeding or any other offense. There are police on the streets, but they're there to deal with crimes and demonstrations, not to prevent Delhi dents.

I would never drive in Delhi, and fortunately I don't have to because my workshop hosts always assign a driver who knows the urban jungle and how to survive. In September 2015, when I conducted another workshop on training techniques for AIR and DD, my driver was the intrepid Jair Bhagwan, who seemed to know instinctively which route to take from the hotel in central Delhi. Our destination on the north side of the city was the AIR Staff Training Institute on Rajpath (Kingsway), so-called because it was the route to the coronation grounds where in 1911 George V was declared Emperor of India. Depending on traffic, the trip took from thirty minutes to one and a half hours. One day, Jair skirted Old Delhi and the Red Fort to take the ring road to the east along the Yamuna River. On other days, he headed directly north, passing government buildings and Delhi University, or south past the India Gate before reaching the ring road, or west through a maze of small streets and alleys. Whichever route he took, it was a bumpy ride. There are speed bumps (apparently, the only deterrent to speeding) but also potholes that appear every year in monsoon season. The city will fix them, said Jair, but not until the rains end in early October.

The traffic would be worse if it were not for the Delhi Metro system, which now reaches many parts of the city, suburbs, satellite cities in the capital region, and the airport, with more lines under construction. Of course, tunneling and construction create new delays as roads are blocked off or traffic lanes reduced, but the system has already shortened the commute for many residents. It's also a source of pride. In a city notorious for littering, the Metro is clean. "People who would not think twice about throwing trash on the street don't litter the Metro," one workshop participant told me.

For a city with a population of fourteen million, Delhi is greener and cleaner than it used to be. Although there are few parks, the broad avenues of New Delhi are lined with trees. As the city has grown and traffic congestion increased, many companies, including most multinationals, moved to the new cities of Gurgaon and Noida, connected to the city by expressways and now the Metro. A few years ago, this was agricultural land—today, it's a landscape of apartment blocks, office buildings, and industrial parks, more like Dubai than Delhi. It's also almost treeless, but that will change—the target is to plant a million trees.

Delhi Smog

Delhi is heavily polluted, historically vying with Beijing for the unenviable distinction of being the world's most polluted major city. Its ranking depends on how pollution is measured. In studying air quality, scientists measure fine particles called atmospheric particulate matter (PM). The two standards are for $PM_{2.5}$ (particles two and one half microns or less in width, about three percent of the diameter of a human hair) and the larger and coarser (but still tiny) PM_{10}. Needless to say, both enter the lungs and blood tissue and cause health problems— eye, nose, throat, and lung irritation, coughing, sneezing, runny nose, and shortness of breath. Studies suggest that long-term exposure to fine particulate matter is associated with increased rates of asthma, chronic bronchitis, reduced lung function, and death from lung cancer and heart disease.

The World Health Organization (WHO) has set safe levels for $PM_{2.5}$ and PM_{10} as 60 and 100 respectively. For the period between December 2014 and January 2015, US embassy monitors registered an average $PM_{2.5}$ level of 226; the average in Beijing for the same period was 95, making Delhi's air twice as bad as Beijing's. In November 2016, during the so-called Great Smog of Delhi, air pollution spiked far beyond acceptable levels, with the PM_{10} level shooting up to a concentration that made even those with face masks gasp for breath—a staggering 999. The city government declared a health emergency, closed schools for three days, stopped construction and demolition work for five, and shut down the aging coal-burning Badarpur power plant for two months. The Supreme Court of India banned the sale of firecrackers in the city.

Delhi residents and the city government hoped the Great Smog was a pollution blip. It wasn't. Exactly one year later, the PM_{10} level reached 880 before dropping to a still unhealthy 470; $PM_{2.5}$ levels remained at an emergency level for several days. Delhi's chief minister said the toxic smog had turned the city into "a gas chamber." The American carrier, United Airlines, canceled flights to Delhi. Almost six thousand schools were closed for a week, construction projects halted, and only trucks carrying essential supplies were allowed into the city. Although vehicle emissions and dust from construction sites degrade air quality, the principal cause of Delhi's pollution was stubble burning. In the neighboring states of Punjab and Haryana, and the western part of Uttar Pradesh, farmers have about three weeks in Fall to clear their fields of rice paddy straw so that they can plant wheat, the winter crop. Most of the stubble is burned in the fields, creating huge clouds of smoke; without wind to disperse or rain to absorb it, the smog enshrouds the city. Until the federal government subsidizes alternatives, such as the conversion of straw to biofuels, farmers will continue to burn stubble. State laws banning crop burning are routinely ignored. According to an analysis by environmental scientists in the *Washington Post*, the challenge is political: "Politicians are wary of trying to prevent crop burning lest they antagonize the powerful farm lobby, lose electoral support and set off political turmoil among regional and ethnic interests." With India's emphasis on economic growth, "citizens have for the most part accepted the environmental costs."[11]

Air pollution in India is estimated to kill 1.5 million people every year. According to the WHO, the country has the world's highest death rate from chronic respiratory diseases and asthma. Crop burning, while a serious problem, is seasonal and restricted to certain regions. Nationwide, the main contributor to pollution is smoke produced by home cooking over stoves fueled by wood or cow dung. Even if you took cars off the road and closed industrial plants, India would still have a lot of pollution.

The government has tried to balance environmental controls with economic growth. In the early 2000s, it shut down some heavily polluting industries and power plants, banned the burning of rubbish, and required most buses, taxis, and auto rickshaws to convert to compressed natural gas (CNG). Some vehicle owners initially opposed the change because of the costs of conversion, but many now consider the investment worthwhile, and some private car owners have converted to CNG. However, at the same time as the government was pushing CNG for public transportation, the growing middle class was getting wheels; the number of vehicles on India's roads tripled between 2002 and 2013. The government was also subsidizing diesel fuel for farmers who used it to power water pumps and tractors. Cheap diesel fuel skewed the economics of the new car market; by 2013, almost half of new cars sold had diesel engines.

Delhi's government has acted to reduce vehicle emissions. It held a two-week experiment to restrict road use to odd- or even-numbered license plates on alternate days and placed restrictions on trucks entering the city. The Supreme Court ordered a citywide ban on the registration of luxury diesel cars. Meanwhile, the national government is trying to improve the quality of fuel and introduce stricter emission standards for new passenger cars.

Even with such measures, India's carbon emissions will grow as the economy expands. The *Economist* calls India "one of the big beasts of the climate arena." Currently the world's fourth-largest emitter of greenhouse gases, it is likely to be the largest single contributor to new emissions over the next fifteen years. Power generation is crucial to growth; almost half of rural households—perhaps as many as three hundred million people—have no electricity. Much of the new power capacity for homes and factories will come from coal-fired plants.

Western governments and environmental groups have criticized the government's refusal to set clear targets and dates to limit emissions;

instead, India has set a relative target—to limit the amount of carbon dioxide per unit of GDP. The *Economist* reports that with economic growth of 8 to 9 percent, government planners believe total emissions will reach 5.3 billion tons by 2030 (up from 1.7 billion in 2010). More significantly, per person emissions will increase from 1.6 to 3.6 tons. And therein lies the dilemma. As a country, India is a major contributor to greenhouse gases, but at an individual level each Indian contributes on average about one-tenth as much carbon dioxide as each US citizen. "To ask Indians for an ambitious cap on emissions risks them staying poor because of a problem mostly caused by other, richer people," notes the *Economist* in an editorial. Yet there are reasons to be optimistic because "the environment matters to Indians themselves." Besides the impact on public health,

> Climate change could do grave harm to India. Some two-thirds of its agriculture depends on the monsoon, which may become less reliable as a result of global warming. Some Himalayan glaciers are retreating, sending less water to rivers that feed hundreds of millions of people downstream. A quarter of Indians live near coasts that are vulnerable to sea-level rises. Many countries suffer one or more of these problems. Few have all of them. So while Indians need growth, they cannot ignore the consequences of it.[12]

Taj Mahal

"Would you like to see the Taj Mahal?" My former student Khalid Syed proposed a Sunday trip to North India's must-see destination, the showpiece palace of the Mughal emperors. A decade after my sheepish admission to Demétrio, I could not refuse. After all, said Khalid, his wife Ann also wanted to see it. It's like New Yorkers and the Empire State Building or Washington, DC, residents and the White House. You only go there when you have out-of-town visitors.

We left Delhi at 6:00 a.m. to avoid the worst of the traffic and were soon on an expressway heading southeast across Uttar Pradesh. It was flat farmland as far as the eye could see; if it hadn't been for the villages with rough brick houses and small temples and shrines, and rice paddies between the corn fields, we could have been on an interstate in the American Midwest. We arrived at the Taj Mahal before the Sunday crowds but not before the souvenir sellers with their postcards, guidebooks, miniature chess sets, and cheap wooden trinkets. Most bizarre were the Taj Mahal snow globes—a large version with a holder for the pens you bought from the kid when you were stuck in traffic, and the smaller version on a key ring. If there's snow Muzak at the Taj Hotel, there can be snow at the Taj Mahal.

To protect the structure from pollution, no cars are allowed near the palace. You arrive at the gate in an electric car or (in our case) a methane-producing horse-drawn carriage. The architecture is as dazzling as in the many pictures I'd seen, a testament to the power and wealth of the Mughal emperors, as impressive as the cathedrals of medieval Europe (and in better physical condition). We traveled next to Agra Fort, built from the same red sandstone as the Red Fort in Delhi. And finally, in late afternoon, to the lesser-known Fatephur Sikri, the capital of the Mughal emperor Akhbar from 1571 to 1585, when he left to campaign in the Punjab. The city itself lasted another quarter century before being abandoned during the reign of Akhbar's son, Jahangir. The hillside fort, well restored by the Archaeological Society of India, offers a commanding view of the plain. There were fewer souvenir sellers and "guides" than at the Taj Mahal or Agra Fort, although one enterprising young man offered to dive into the royal baths. "You take photo. Only one hundred rupees [under $2]," he said. I looked down at the green slime on top of the water and decided the feat wasn't worth one hundred rupees to anyone.

The Mughals needed to build alliances among the many principalities of India, and Akhbar practiced a form of religious soft diplomacy, taking three wives—a Muslim, a Hindu, and a Christian. However, he was no softie. Anyone convicted of a serious crime faced the standard Mughal capital punishment—being stomped to death by an elephant. Akhbar valued the services of one elephant so highly that he built a tower in his honor. Indeed, the Mughals were a ruthless bunch, without much sense of family loyalty; the typical route to the throne involved murdering or locking up your father and brothers.

Indian politicians may have learned a thing or two from the Mughals about ruthlessness, but at least politics today is less violent. There's the occasional political assassination, and some state politicians hire gangs to disrupt political rallies, but ambitious politicians—the modern

Mughals—prefer to dispose of opponents or rivals by more subtle means: charging them with corruption or cronyism, attacking them in the press and social media, or simply by buying more votes at election time. No need for heavy-footed elephants when you can tweet someone to death.

Reading India

India overwhelms you in so many ways—the history, the religion, the architecture, the food, the streets, the ethnic diversity, the labyrinthine politics. I'm an avid newspaper reader, but I find it difficult to get even a remote handle on the political, economic, and cultural landscape. Every day, journalists (or "scribes" as they are called) expose new scandals (and you're supposed to know the actors and their connections). The headline writers love cricketing metaphors; public figures who are in trouble are usually "on a sticky wicket."

One day, the Supreme Court canceled the All India Pre-Med and Dental Entrance Examination because of widespread cheating, and a former government minister got into trouble for buying faked college diplomas. Blood-feud murders merit a few paragraphs, unless the victims or perpetrators are politicians, cricketers, or Bollywood stars. A road accident in which seventeen members of one family riding on a jeep were killed when it plunged into a river made the inside page. One day, the top story was the deaths of over thirty people in a Mumbai slum after drinking "hooch" (Mumbai moonshine), but the next day it was pushed down the agenda when the monsoon hit the city, paralyzing the public transportation system and halting trading on the stock market. There are stories on simmering social rebellions in the forests of central India, the murders of landowners and officials by "Maoist guerrillas." In the northeast, I struggle to remember the acronyms of the assorted rebel groups in Nagaland. Was it the NKSN that absorbed the NPC, or was it the NSSC, and is China really smuggling arms across the border from Yunnan in retaliation of India's support for the Dalai Lama? And then there's Kashmir, and other long-running territorial disputes with Pakistan and China.

In a minor act of defiance (although I didn't know it at the time), I imported a copy of the *Economist* that included a story about plans to build a highway from a port on the Indian Ocean northeast through Pakistan and across the mountains to Kashgar in Xinjiang in western

China. It's one thread in the so-called New Silk Road, China's ambitious project to boost its economy by improving transportation links to Asia, Europe, and Africa; the trillion-dollar "Belt and Road Initiative," launched by President Xi-Jinping in 2013, includes the construction of railways, roads, and ports, with China providing billions of dollars in loans. The story featured a map with an inset noting that it would probably be cut out of copies imported to India: "Sadly, India censors maps that show the current effective border, insisting instead that only its full territorial claims be shown. It is more intolerant on this issue than either China or Pakistan."[13] Sure enough, the first item on the prohibited list on the customs declaration form (ahead of drugs, exotic flora and fauna, and counterfeit currency) was "maps and literature where Indian external boundaries have been shown incorrectly."

The paranoia over which country owns some desolate, uncultivable Himalayan mountain slope seems ironic, given the lively political scene and a thriving and often aggressive media sector. India is one of the few countries in the world where newspaper readership has been growing. And it is, to use the oft-quoted phrase, "the world's largest democracy." That seems an overstatement, given the wealth gap, the caste system, the dominance of local power elites, low literacy levels, and the intimidation and murders of politicians and journalists. In some shape or form, these factors are present in every so-called democracy; because of India's sheer size, they are just writ large. Inexplicable India.

SIX

A Tale of Three Cities

Counting Hyderabad

"What's the population of Hyderabad?" I asked Ruth Leano, as our car weaved through the city traffic. If anyone knew, I figured it would be Ruth, who headed UNICEF's regional office for the states of Telangana, Andhra Pradesh, and Karnataka. She leaned back and reflected, glancing out of the window at the rising tide of cars, battered city buses, overloaded trucks, and hand carts hauling furniture, vegetables, and building materials that seemed to threaten to engulf us. "I really don't know," she said. "It depends what you include."

She had a point. For any city, population is a fickle statistic. Do you count only the people who live within artificially defined city limits? Or the metropolitan area? And how is that defined? Boundaries are bureaucratic creations, dividing a population into manageable units to make it easier to count, govern, police, and tax them. That does not mean that people accept their residence in districts, blocks, zones, or wards. In greater Hyderabad, as in other urban areas, even those living on the rural borderlands feel as if they belong to the city. It's difficult to know where Hyderabad begins and ends, where to start and stop counting.

Hyderabad is really three cities. The old city, south of the Musi River, centers on the imposing sixteenth-century Charminar, its four towers facing in cardinal directions; around it are mosques and Islamic monuments and a maze of narrow, winding, dusty streets, with bazaars, hole-in-the-wall shops, and craftspeople forging pearl and silver jewelry, tools, and cookware. North of the Musi and the palaces of the Nizams, the hereditary rulers, lies new Hyderabad, its broad highways lined with commercial businesses, office towers, hotels, restaurants, and shopping malls. For almost two centuries, the heart-shaped artificial lake of

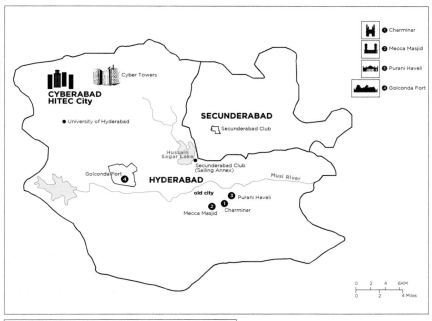

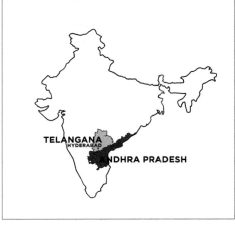

MAP 6.1 The three cities of Hyderabad (map by Belén Marco Crespo)

Hussain Sagar, built in 1563 to serve as a reservoir for the city, formed the boundary between Hyderabad and the British military cantonment of Secunderabad. Today the two cities merge untidily, with only street signs and lines on maps indicating the boundaries. Spreading out beyond both are upscale residential and commercial suburbs. Yet, a few blocks away from the hotels and malls are urban slums—blocks of dilapidated apartments with trash-strewn courtyards and, alongside railroad tracks or on unclaimed land between apartment blocks and highways, clusters of one- or two-room shanties with mud floors and sewage flowing along the narrow alleys. For the last twenty years, most expansion has been to the northwest, where the names—Cyberabad, HITEC City, and so on—symbolize Hyderabad's transition from its industrial past (steel, cement, and building materials) to a diversified economy with information technology, financial services, and pharmaceuticals leading the way. Three cities—old and new Hyderabad, Secunderabad, and, well, Cyberhitecinfosyslandia.

My colleague at the University of Hyderabad, Usha Raman, describes her city as a "soft landing" for first-time Western visitors to India. The traffic jams are annoying, but congestion eases at predictable times. While Delhi and Mumbai commuters spend hours snarled on multilane highways, most Hyderabad drivers have a pretty good idea how long a trip will take, depending on the time of day, often measured in ten-to-fifteen-minute intervals. "If you leave the hotel by 7:30, you'll be at the university by 8:15, no problem," another colleague advised me. "Leave at 8:00 and you'll make it by 10:00, if you're lucky." Traffic jams tend to breed reckless driving. Signs posted by the traffic police encourage caution, although the slogans verge on the corny: Don't Mix Drink & Drive, Speed Thrills but Kills, Don't Be Rash, Lest You Crash.

Pollution levels are high, but no higher than in other urban areas. There's poverty, but it's usually not the in-your-face variety of Delhi and Mumbai with panhandlers and organized begging, sometimes featuring blind or disabled people, at traffic intersections. In Hyderabad, homeless people sleep out in the parks, but you rarely see large groups under bridges and elevated highways. At Charminar and the other premier tourist stop—the medieval fortress of Golconda—you'll be approached by people offering to be your guide, but they don't argue when you say no. Most taxi drivers seem to have brothers or cousins with fabric and jewelry stores who will "give you a special discount because you are my friend," but if you say you're not interested, they will take you to your destination without a shopping detour. In a country that can easily overwhelm you, Hyderabad is a good place to get your bearings.

The 2011 national census put the population of the "twin cities" of Hyderabad and Secunderabad at 6.8 million; by 2014, demographers estimated it had risen to 8.7 million and was growing fast. That would make it the fourth-largest city after Mumbai (12.5 million), Delhi (11 million), and Kolkata (10 million), although its regional rival Bangalore is close at 8.5 million. Officially, India has eight "megacities" with a population of more than 5 million, and forty-eight others with over a million. Because the most recent census was in 2011, two things are certain—the population of all these cities has grown substantially, and Hyderabad's population has increased in the time it has taken me to write this paragraph. If Hyderabad were a country, it would be Austria or Serbia—or New Zealand times two.

Actually, the idea of Hyderabad as a country makes sense, because it once was.

The Long Reign of the Nizams

From the twelfth century, the Deccan plateau region of south-central India was ruled from the city and fortress of Golconda, built on a four-hundred-foot high granite hill, southwest of present-day Hyderabad. Golconda served as the capital of the Qutb Shahi dynasty. In the sixteenth and seventeenth centuries, the rulers expanded the fortifications; the inner wall has a circumference of more than three miles, the outer wall more than four. The massive gates are studded with large iron spikes to repel invaders, including the feared war elephants of the Mughal armies.

It's a brisk thirty-minute walk, with some steep ascents, from the outer gate and courtyard to the summit, to the living quarters of the sultans and the *durbar* hall where they held court. The ramparts provide commanding views over the plain. Golconda is massive, a city within a fortress, its walls and buttresses sprawling across the slope with paths leading off to underground chambers and tunnels. Because it was built from huge granite blocks, many structures are still standing. Golconda grew rich from the diamond mines of the Deccan and for hundreds of years served as a major trading center with secure vaults for the gems.

FIGURE 6.1 The medieval fortress of Golconda, capital of the Qutb Shahi dynasty; a city within a fortress, with secure vaults for the diamonds of the Deccan

In 1686, the Mughal emperor Aurangzeb from Delhi showed up with his army, complete with artillery and those feared war elephants, and besieged the fortress. Golconda held out for almost a year before the garrison was forced to surrender.

Golconda's history and impressive fortifications make it one of Hyderabad's premier attractions. The entrance area seethes with self-appointed guides and hawkers, brandishing postcard sets, Chinese-language guide books, and miniature plastic Golcondas. For 200 rupees ($3.50), you can pose in armor and try to look menacing, wielding a plastic sword. Golconda is the ideal location for shooting historical dramas, primarily for Tollywood, the Hyderabad-based Telugu-language film industry that has been producing movies for almost a century, and more recently TV soaps and action thrillers. When my colleague Andrew Carlson and I visited, actors and extras were suiting up in the lower courtyard, and a production assistant was checking out swords and daggers from the back of a Tata SUV. The 1686 siege—or perhaps a love triangle screenplay with the siege as the historical backdrop—was about to be reenacted. Apparently, the production budget did not include war elephants. They would have to be added in digital postproduction.

Like all great fortresses, Golconda was built for war, not for comfortable living. Supplies had to be hauled in from the countryside and up the hill by a small army of porters. By the end of the sixteenth century, the Qutb Shahi rulers had become tired of living in their vast fortress, with its dark chambers and long flights of stairs. In 1591, the fifth sultan, Muhammad Quli Qutb Shah, relocated the court and administration northeast to the banks of the Musi River, establishing a new city. It eventually became known as Hyderabad, from the Arabic word *haydar* (meaning "lion") and the Persian suffix *-abad,* meaning town or "cultivated place." Today, this is Hyderabad's Old City, with its majority Muslim population where families crowd into tenements and business spills out of the shops into the streets and alleys. Auto rickshaws weave around the potholes, made worse by the monsoon rains, dodging goats, women in full-length black burkas, and handcarts loaded with vegetables.

The Old City contains Hyderabad's most important Islamic monuments and its busiest bazaars. The iconic Charminar (four towers), traditionally the city's symbol, was built by order of the sultan to celebrate

FIGURE 6.2 Hyderabad's Old City viewed from the iconic Charminar (four towers)

FIGURE 6.3 Mecca Masjid, one of the world's largest mosques with room for ten thousand worshippers

the end of an epidemic in 1591. It stands more than 180 feet tall and almost 100 feet wide, each of its four arches facing cardinal points. Spiral staircases lead to the upper floors, offering panoramic views of the Old City. Adjacent to Charminar is the Mecca Masjid, one of the world's largest mosques with room for ten thousand worshippers; its middle arch is set with bricks from Mecca, hence the name. Like Charminar, it was commissioned by Muhammad Quli Qutb Shah, but took more than seventy years to complete. The builders were putting the finishing touches to it when Aurangzeb's Mughal army arrived at Golconda and conquered the sultanate.

The Mughals renamed the region *Deccan Suba* (Deccan province) and installed a local administration, headed by a governor. With Charminar and Mecca Masjid as its spiritual heart, Hyderabad grew into a thriving commercial center, an important source of tax revenue for the empire. In 1714, Asaf Jah was appointed governor with the official title of Nizam (administrator of the realm). A decade later, Jah took advantage of the declining power of the Mughals to declare an independent state and found the dynasty that was to last until Indian independence. Under his successors, Hyderabad became the most important Muslim city in southern India, a center for arts, culture, and education. Diamonds, other gems, and minerals made it prosperous and its rulers fabulously wealthy. The riches included pearls, drilled, cleaned, graded, and fashioned into jewelry in workshops in the Old City; Hyderabad earned the title of the "City of Pearls."

Throughout the eighteenth century, the British, French, and Portuguese vied for territory and trade in the subcontinent. They formed shifting alliances with local rulers who acted as their proxies, invading neighboring states. In 1768, the British East India Company forced the Nizam to surrender a coastal region; by 1798, the company's troops were literally on the Nizam's doorstep, camped around Hussain Sagar Lake. Faced with threats from the state of Mysore and the Maratha Empire, the third Nizam, Sikander Jah, accepted British protection. In 1806, he granted land north of the lake to the British to build a military barracks and paid an annual tribute to maintain the garrison. It turned out to be a sweet deal for the British; the base, named "Secunderabad" in honor of the Nizam, was exempted from customs duties on imported goods, making trade highly profitable.

The Nizams were reliable allies of the British, supporting the colonial power in suppressing internal uprisings, including the 1857 rebellion. The British trained the army and provided administrative support, but otherwise left the rulers to supervise Hyderabad's internal affairs. As long as the British stayed, the Nizams felt secure.

South Pakistan?

In June 1947, the seventh Nizam, Sir Mir Osman Ali Khan, found himself in a tough spot. In London, the parliament was about to pass the Indian Independence Act, ending more than two centuries of colonial rule and dividing British India on religious lines into India and Pakistan. Under the act, Britain abandoned its long-standing alliances with the traditional rulers, the princes and maharajas, leaving the future of their states uncertain. Most decided that trying to restore independence on a subcontinent dominated by two large, militarily powerful countries was impossible. One by one, they opted to accede to India or Pakistan, their decisions based primarily on whether their states had majority Hindu or Muslim populations.

The holdout was Osman Ali Khan, the Muslim ruler of a mostly Hindu state. He was, after all, the prince of princes, the highest-ranking ruler in British India, one of only five entitled to a twenty-one-gun salute at military parades. For more than two centuries, his ancestors had ruled a kingdom almost as large in land area as Britain itself. Hyderabad, with a population of more than sixteen million, was the largest and most prosperous of all princely states; its economy was the size of Belgium's, and its diamond mines had yielded some of the world's greatest gems, including the Koh-i-Noor and Hope diamonds. Osman Ali Khan had accomplished much during his thirty-six-year reign, developing the state's agriculture and irrigation systems, industry, health services, roads, and railroads. He founded libraries and museums, dedicated 10 percent of the government budget to education, and established the state's first university. Hyderabad had its own airline, radio broadcasting service, and central bank, and was the only state in British India allowed to issue its own currency.

According to *Time* magazine, which featured him on its front cover in 1937, Osman Ali Khan was also the richest man in the world. One contemporary estimate put his personal wealth at £100 million in gold and silver bullion and £400 million in jewels, and that did not include the royal real estate. He reportedly used a 185-carat diamond the size of a golf ball, valued at more than £100 million, as a paperweight. He had half a dozen palaces, owned a fleet of Rolls-Royces, and one of the Islamic world's greatest art collections. His loyalty to the British had been unwavering. The state made a large contribution to the tax coffers of the colonial administration. The Nizam's personal financial contributions to the imperial war effort in World War I earned him the titles of "His Exalted Highness" and "Faithful Ally of the British Crown." Queen Elizabeth's jewelry collection includes the thirty-eight-diamond "Nizam of Hyderabad" necklace he presented to her as a wedding gift in 1947.[1]

Osman Ali Khan saw no good reason why his kingdom should be forced to join either India or Pakistan. Why could it not become an independent constitutional monarchy within the British Commonwealth? The British turned down the proposal but the Nizam did not give up. The galleries of Purani Haveli, a former royal palace and now a city museum, display photographs from 1947 and 1948 of the Nizam posing with the political movers and shakers of the day, including Indian prime minister Jawaharlal Nehru and the British governor-general, Lord Mountbatten; he is pictured at government buildings, in official cars, shuffling between meetings, at state banquets and military parades. Meanwhile, out of the sight of the cameras, he was engaged in covert negotiations with Muhammad Ali Jinnah, leader of the All-India Muslim League, and other Muslim leaders. The architects of partition had already carved out the Muslim-majority states of West and East Pakistan. Although 80 percent of Hyderabad's population was Hindu, Muslims were dominant in the army, police, and government. There was talk of making Hyderabad Pakistan's southern outpost.

For a year, Hyderabad maintained a semiautonomous status, while political pressure to join the Indian Union grew stronger. The Delhi government accused Hyderabad of importing arms from Pakistan, and of raising and arming a Muslim militia, the *razakars* (an Arabic word meaning "volunteers"), that went on an anti-Hindu rampage of murder, kidnapping, and rape, destroying crops and houses and forcing thousands to flee. Hyderabad accused India of setting up armed blockades on land routes to stop trade. Nehru favored negotiations, but stronger voices argued that Hyderabad's continued resistance could encourage other states to rebel and lead to the disintegration of the new country. On September 13, 1948, India invaded.

Anyone for Polo, Chaps?

It's not only modern American military campaigns that are given silly, sanitized code names such as Just Cause, Provide Comfort, Enduring Freedom, and Restore Hope. When Indian troops launched their attack on Hyderabad, the operation was named for the favorite sport of British military and colonial officers, polo. It was as if the Indian officers were going to ride into town, play a few chukkas against the Nizam's cavalry captains at the Secunderabad polo ground, and then retire to the club veranda for tea. Instead, the Indian Army launched a two-pronged attack from the east and west with infantry, cavalry, artillery, tanks, and air strikes.

Operation Polo was over in five days. The Nizam's army, composed mostly of north Indian Muslims, Arabs, and Pathans, numbered only twenty-four thousand, only a quarter of whom were fully trained and equipped. The Muslim militia, the *razakars*, claimed to have two hundred thousand men, but they had little military training; only a quarter had modern small firearms, and the rest were armed with muzzle-loaders and swords. The fast-moving Indian army columns, advancing on both fronts, quickly secured major towns and bridges, inflicting heavy casualties. With his forces routed and the Indian army within forty miles of Hyderabad, the Nizam announced a ceasefire and condemned the *razakars* for terrorist tactics. At Secunderabad on September 18, the Hyderabad army commander formally surrendered to his Indian counterpart.

Communal violence followed as Hindu villagers took revenge for the terror campaign waged by the *razakars*. An investigative committee concluded that although Muslims were disarmed by the Indian Army, Hindus were often left with their weapons; the army ignored looting, mass murder, and rape, and in some cases participated in the violence. The official estimate was that between twenty-seven thousand and forty thousand Hindus and Muslims died in what the Indian government euphemistically termed a "police action." Some scholars put the figure at two hundred thousand or higher. The findings of the committee were not made public until 2013 when scholars started accessing reports in the archives of Nehru's library in Delhi.

Over the next decades, tensions between Hindus and Muslims often spilled over into violence. As the hereditary ruler, Osman Ali Khan stayed in his palaces, working to calm sectarian tensions and promote economic development. In 1956, the states of India were reorganized along linguistic lines, with Hyderabad divided between the new states of Maharashtra, Karnataka, and Andhra Pradesh. The nine Telugu- and Urdu-speaking districts of the Telangana region were merged with the Telugu-speaking Andhra state to form Andhra Pradesh, with Hyderabad as its capital, despite calls for a separate state of Telangana. The division further eroded the Nizam's influence, yet he remained a respected figure. When he died in 1967, more than a million attended his funeral in the Old City. In a traditional gesture of mourning, thousands of women broke their bangles, leaving the streets full of shattered glass.

Clothes Make the Man

Opulent palaces. Fleets of Rolls-Royces. A diamond paperweight. Chests bulging with gold, silver, and gemstones. It's difficult to conceive of the wealth and lifestyle of the Nizams, although there's no lack of jaw-dropping comparative statistics. Estimates from the early 1940s put the seventh Nizam's fortune as equivalent to 2 percent of the US economy, and twice India's annual tax revenue.

For those who have trouble getting our heads around such statistical abstractions, a visit to the wardrobe of the sixth Nizam, who died in 1911, will suffice. Mir Mahbub Ali Khan was famous for his lavish lifestyle and luxuries, his collection of cars and jewels. And he took the concept of an extensive wardrobe to a new dimension.

Beyond the second-floor galleries of Purani Haveli that display photographs and portraits of the Nizams and the gifts, souvenirs, and memorabilia presented by visiting dignitaries, there lies a long, dark hallway. "It's exactly 176 feet long," the museum guide proudly told me, as if he'd measured it himself. On either side, it is flanked by wooden doors opening to small cubicles, with windows looking out over the palace grounds; short flights of stairs lead to the upper level, with more cubicles on both sides. It took a small forest of Burmese teak, shipped across the Bay of Bengal, to build what may be the largest walk-in closet in the world. Mir Mahbub Ali Khan prided himself on his wardrobe, with shirts, coats, collars, socks, shoes, headgear, and walking sticks. His household staff were kept busy stocking the cubicles with clothes fit for a prince; if the Nizam did not like the outfit displayed in one cubicle, he would move on until he found the right clothes for the season, occasion, or his personal mood. Working alongside the wardrobe staff was a crew of strong-limbed men who operated a manual elevator, where ropes on pulleys were used to raise and lower the cabin with the Nizam and his valets. It was reported that the Nizam would never wear the same dress twice, and that most of his clothes were given away. In any case, he took the adage that "clothes make the man" seriously.

His son, Osman Ali Khan, the seventh Nizam, was less fastidious— sometimes wearing crumpled pajamas and a dirty fez cap—but maintained a large household and European-style palaces with gardens, fountains, and elaborate furnishings. At his death in 1967, his successor, his grandson Mukarram Jah, was saddled with a debt-laden operation in serious need of downsizing. As historian William Dalrymple notes:

> He had inherited a ridiculously inflated army of retainers: 14,718 staff and dependents, including 42 of his grandfather's concubines and their 100-plus offspring. The principal palace, the Chowmahalla, alone had 6,000 employees; there were about 3,000 Arab bodyguards, 28 people whose only job was to fetch drinking water and 38 more to dust chandeliers; several others were retained specifically to grind the Nizam's walnuts.

Everything was in disarray: the Nizam's garages, for example, cost £45,000 a year to keep in petrol and spare parts for 60 cars, yet only four were in working condition, and the limousine supposed to carry the new Nizam from his coronation broke down.[2]

Jah also inherited lawsuits brought by several thousand descendants of his grandfather and great-grandfather, each of whom claimed part of the inheritance. The legal assault was led by Jah's father, whom Osman Ali Khan had passed over to be the next Nizam, and his aunt. To make matters worse, the inheritance was distributed among fifty-four trusts, the control of which was disputed.

The legal and family wrangles proved too much for Jah. In 1973, he fired most of his staff, divorced his first wife, the Turkish princess Esra, and moved to a sheep station in Western Australia. He married four more times, each divorce adding to his legal and financial woes as each ex-wife demanded huge sums in alimony. In 1974, the Indian government abolished all hereditary titles and imposed heavy taxes, forcing princes to sell off their property. In Hyderabad, the palaces fell into disrepair and were plundered of furnishings, art, jewels, and manuscripts. Much of the sprawling Chowmahalla estate was gobbled up by developers who demolished the eighteenth-century buildings and put up apartment blocks. The disintegration of the Nizam legacy was finally halted by Jah's first wife, Esra, to whom he gave authority to save what she could. A team of conservation experts catalogued and restored thousands of artifacts, and in 2006 Chowmahalla opened to the public as a museum. The Falaknuma Palace was leased to the Taj hotel chain, which undertook restoration and opened it as a luxury hotel in 2010. Lawsuits were settled, and debts paid. Dalrymple credits Esra and her lawyer for selecting honest, competent people to manage affairs and undertake the restoration. She told him that she wished she had started earlier. "I was too young. At the time it all seemed impossible—the law suits, the huge taxes, debts accumulating, criminal cases, people abusing the trust we had put in them. We had no ready cash, and the palaces seemed like white elephants. So we fled, and then terrible things happened. So much just disappeared."[3]

Splendid Towers and Sorry Shanties

Hyderabad works hard to project the image its political leaders and business community want the rest of India and the world to see—that of a bustling modern city, with thriving retail, financial, and technology sectors and an educated workforce. The names of commercial buildings—Fantasy Square, Trendset Towers, Splendid Towers—help set the tone. A city-wide monorail is under construction, its concrete towers sprouting from the middle of the highways. Billboards and painted signs plaster the walls of commercial and office buildings, advertising concrete and steel supplies, mobile phones, dairy products, and consumer services from insurance to astrology.

As in most cities in south and southeast Asia, wealth and poverty exist side by side. A few blocks away from the commercial streets, where the lights and neon signs blaze long into the night, away from the five-star hotels and gated communities with their guard posts and artificial lakes, lies another Hyderabad. Rows of dilapidated apartments, their stucco exteriors peeling from the humidity and stained a dull gray from years of pollution. Rough, informal settlements of flimsy *kacca* (a Hindi word meaning raw or unripe), mud-floor one- and two-room shanties, constructed from salvaged sheets of metal and wood and framed by bamboo poles, with bricks or blocks weighing down the metal roofs and plastic trash bags plugging the holes to keep out the monsoon rains. Walking to meet colleagues at one of Hyderabad's popular *biryani* restaurants, I crossed an open area between apartment blocks. Chickens pecked in the dirt, and a horse in a tarpaulin-covered makeshift stall kicked up the straw. On the muddy strip between an apartment block and the street, a small SUV was jacked up, its rear driver's-side wheel missing. A camel was tethered to it. Was this a traditional form of

FIGURE 6.4 Can you call Uber for a camel?

transportation in a city where you can book an auto rickshaw by Uber? More likely an example of entrepreneurship. I'm told camel rides are popular at middle-class children's birthday parties.

With Hyderabad, it's difficult to avoid those "city of contrasts" clichés.

Cyberhitecinfosyslandia

To the northwest of old and new Hyderabad and Secunderabad lies the third city—the fast-growing region of Cyberabad or HITEC City, the acronym for the Hyderabad Information Technology and Engineering Consultancy City. Although such names were dreamed up by marketers or city planners, not by historians, the city's recent growth and prosperity owes much to the pharmaceutical, biomedical, and information technology sectors, and industries that support them. Hyderabad still has a traditional manufacturing sector—agricultural products, heavy engineering, steel, textiles, and construction materials. From the 1960s, Indian and global drug companies opened manufacturing plants and research facilities, earning the city the name of "Genome Valley." Hyderabad is a medical center, with specialized hospitals and clinics patronized by middle-class Indians. It's a destination for medical tourists with an estimated eight hundred to one thousand foreign patients—mostly from Asian and African countries—receiving treatment each month. If you need intestinal surgery, a hip replacement, hair transplant, or just some plastic surgery to take out a few wrinkles, Hyderabad has a place for you.

The city has used tax breaks and special economic zones to lure businesses, laying out new commercial and residential subdivisions, building roads, and providing technological infrastructure. The HITEC City development attracted global IT companies, including Microsoft, Apple, Amazon, Google, Yahoo!, Facebook, IBM, and Dell, and Indian firms including Infosys, Tata Consultancy Services, and Wipro. It's estimated there are more than thirteen hundred IT firms in the city, although that number (like the population) is a dodgy one. Cyberabad even has its own iconic structure to rival the Old City's Charminar—the ten-story Cyber Towers, the first high-rise purpose-built to house IT companies. When Microsoft set up shop there in 1998, other companies rushed to fill the office space. Just as Charminar has four towers, Cyber Towers is divided into four quadrants with a fountain in the middle, but its towers are topped with satellite and microwave dishes, not minarets.

Other office blocks, technology parks, and campuses followed, transforming what were once fields into a landscape of high-rises and gated compounds with manicured gardens. Private developers and public-private partnerships have built the Laxmi Cyber City, L&T Infocity, the HITEX Exhibition Centre, the Mindspace Tech Park, the Ascendas IT Park, the RMZ Futura IT Park, the Cyber Gateway, and campuses for Microsoft, Facebook, Tech Mahindra, and other companies. There's a growing financial district with banks, insurance companies, and law firms, and new hotels, apartment blocks, and shopping malls.

The five-thousand-seat Hyderabad International Convention Center (HICC) hosts major tech trade shows and conferences. Of course, big events don't happen every week, so the HICC needs to fill its cavernous spaces with other clients. I don't normally associate convention centers with weddings, but the HICC is in earnest competition with luxury hotels for the lucrative market. A poster showing a wedding party in traditional dress—all turbans, bangles, and multicolored saris—recommends the facility "for the biggest thematic weddings that reflect sheer grandeur" (translation: to show your guests how much money you can spend). I was visiting the HICC with colleagues from the University of Hyderabad on a more mundane mission, scouting locations for a workshop for UNICEF staff. We needed a large air-conditioned room with good audiovisual facilities and fast Internet. The HICC offered all that, and even had a three-hundred-room hotel next door, but it seemed remote from the historic city and its culture. It looked like convention centers I've visited in American cities, with its vast lobbies, coffee shops, and restaurants. We ended up selecting a downtown hotel. It had some inconveniences, but at least it was in India, not in Cyberhitecinfosyslandia.

Taxing Times

Whatever one may think of drug companies, facelift clinics, and IT campuses, at least they are legal businesses that usually pay their taxes, even if they hire lawyers and accountants to find breaks and loopholes. Many small businesses in India avoid paying taxes altogether. A study by Credit Suisse (CS) estimated that half of India's economy is informal. This below-the-radar economy is mostly urban; CS estimates that only 13 percent of industrial companies and 12 percent of materials businesses are formally registered. That's a quarter of all enterprises, so 75 percent of all businesses in India fall into the unlisted and informal category.[4] If you're in the informal economy—as an employer or worker—you do not pay taxes.

Understandably, India's government wants to change that. It will not be easy. One small step would be to simplify the tax system, which is confusing, even for those prepared to pay. After several visits to India, I knew that hotel taxes amount to a New York City–sized 29 percent. I wasn't prepared for the hotel meal taxes. After lunch on the first day of our workshop at the Taj Deccan Hotel, I was presented with a bill showing multiple charges on top of the menu price for the chicken korma. I asked my University of Hyderabad colleague Vasuki Belavadi to translate.

The first tax was the KCC. "That's for farmers' welfare," Vasuki explained. "It's on every transaction. If I have my mobile phone repaired, I pay the KCC." Next was the Swachh Bharat (Clean India) tax, introduced by the government of Prime Minister Modi to fund a nationwide environmental program. Then came VAT (Value Added Tax) on food, then VAT on beverages, then a service tax. And finally, in what I'll call the tax crescendo, the VAT on the service tax. Yes, a tax on the tax. Some might conclude that India is being governed by a bunch of tax-and-spend liberals. Far from it—the Bharatiya Janata (BJP) government is both fiscally and socially conservative. And it is committed to tax reform, having pushed through a national Goods and Services Tax (GST) to eliminate the host of overlapping state taxes and tariffs that were holding back interstate commerce. But at five-star hotels, you still pay 39 percent on top of the menu price for your food. "You should be glad we're not in a seven-star hotel," said Vasuki. "Then you'd also be paying the luxury tax." I didn't dare ask how much that would add to the bill.

Although both major political parties—the BJP and the Congress—supported the GST, it took several years, many studies, and intense lobbying before it was approved by both houses of parliament and the required 50 percent of state legislatures in August 2016. It replaces what the *Economist* called "a monstrous excrescence of taxes, duties, surcharges and cesses levied by the centre, the states and local authorities—a system that fragments the economy and gives huge scope for corruption by officials and politicians." In India, a commercial truck can take several days to make a journey that in another country would take a few hours. Poor roads are part of the problem; however, travel time and costs are increased because of the number of times a truck stops at checkpoints to pay the local "entry tax," the *octroi*, which may go straight into the pocket of the collector. Trade between states is subject to a 2 percent central sales tax, and some states also tax products entering from other states. Because of taxes and other barriers to internal trade, it's often cheaper to import than buy domestically. Delhi's markets, notes the *Economist*, "are as likely to stock apples from New Zealand or California as from Himachal Pradesh or Kashmir." A GST, even one with multiple rates for different goods and services, will boost the economy and encourage domestic trade, but making businesses pay up will be a challenge.[5] A year after its introduction, Reuters reported that many small textile workshops in Panipat, the "City of Weavers" near Delhi, had been forced out of business because their unschooled owners could not navigate the complex tax reporting system or afford to pay for accountants to do it for them. A survey by the All India Trade Union Congress (AITUC) found that a fifth of India's sixty-three million small businesses faced a 20 percent fall in profits since the introduction of GST and had to fire hundreds of thousands of workers.[6]

A Jolly Good Time at the Secunderabad Club

One business that has always enjoyed generous tax breaks is the Secunderabad Club. It was founded in 1878 to provide recreation and social activities for British military officers, colonial administrators, railway officials, traders, and their families. The main club facilities, with cricket and polo grounds, a library, shops stocked with booze and British comfort foods, and two eighteenth-century cannons symbolically guarding the entrance, occupy a twenty-two-acre campus several miles north of Hussain Sagar lake. In colonial times, members came to the club's Sailing Annexe on the lake to go boating, take high tea on the terrace, and grumble over cocktails about Indian nationalism and the bureaucrats in Whitehall. "That bounder Gandhi and his passive resistance. Damn annoying. And the Foreign and Commonwealth Office? Doing nothing about it. Hey boy, give me another gin and tonic."

You must wonder what the "boys" thought about stiff-upper-lipped, mustachioed colonial officers dissecting their country and national hero, but of course they remained silent, hovering in the background in their cleanly pressed suits, an almost-invisible army of servants. Except for members of the Nizam's family and a few high-ranking Indian civil servants, no Indians were permitted to join the club or accompany members as guests. The only exceptions were Anglo-Indians of mixed race, who formed a distinct subcommunity in Hyderabad. After independence, the Secunderabad Club opened its doors to the city's political, business, and academic elite. It is still highly selective; family memberships can be passed from father to son, but new applicants may wait up to fifteen years to be nominated and admitted. Today, the club says it has eight thousand members in ten categories. It also has "over 30,000 potential members," perhaps a reference to those who have been waiting for years to join. Voting rights are restricted to male members, although this provision is under court challenge. Members still cast votes using balls; if your nomination is refused, it will be because at least one member has cast a black ball. The Secunderabad Club is one of the few clubs in the world where you can still be black-balled.

Fortunately, the family of one of our University of Hyderabad colleagues had a membership, and he booked tables at the Sailing Annexe for dinner. I'd expected the food and drinks to be pricey, but they were not. The club inherited the colonial exemption from customs duties, so alcohol is cheap; food is subsidized by membership dues. We sat on the terrace and enjoyed an excellent meal topped off with the club's signature British dessert, trifle. A light breeze blew off the lake. In the distance, lights illuminated the huge Buddha statue built on a rock in the lake and the lakeshore road. One member of our group pulled out her mobile to take a photo of the team relaxing after a demanding work week. A waiter leaned over the table and said, ever-so-discreetly, "Club rules—no photos." Yes, in the free-for-all that is modern Hyderabad, there's still decorum at the Secunderabad Club.

Desperately Seeking SIM Card

In the city that spawned Cyberabad and prides itself on technological infrastructure, I thought it would be easy to buy a SIM card and have it activated. Far from it. My story begins at the reception desk of the Taj Deccan Hotel.

"Where's the nearest mall?" I asked the duty manager. "I need to buy a SIM card."

"Sir, the City Centre Mall is close by, but I deeply regret to inform you that you will not be able to buy a SIM card there. You must go to a mobile provider shop."

I didn't bother asking about the marketing logic of restricting SIM card sales to specific outlets, presumably with limited opening hours.

"OK, please give me the addresses," I said. The manager wrote down three. "You could walk but, in this heat, I'd advise taking an auto rickshaw."

I selected the closest one, Airtel, whose address was listed as Road No. 12, Banjara Hills. It seemed a bit imprecise, but I assumed the driver would know where to go.

The duty manager approached me again. "Do you have a copy of your passport face page and visa, also a passport picture?" he asked. "I really need all that?" I answered, but with almost rhetorical resignation. "Yes, and you will need a letter from the hotel stating that this is your local address. I'll be pleased to write it."

After assembling the paperwork, I set off in an auto rickshaw. We turned off the main road onto Road No. 12. After a few minutes, I remembered the manager's remark that I could have walked to the store if the weather had not been so hot. I would not have walked this far, even if the temperature had been twenty degrees lower. We were now moving out of the commercial area, passing a hospital, villas, and the gardens of the Income Tax Department guest house.

"I don't think it's this far," I told the driver.

"Where is it you want, sir? This is Road No. 12."

"The Airtel mobile shop."

"You can buy recharge at many places."

"No, I need a SIM card, not a recharge. Please turn around."

Eventually we did, then sat in a traffic jam for fifteen minutes as we edged slowly toward the main road. The Airtel store was near the junction, and the detour had cost me almost thirty minutes. I joined a line of customers. The sales assistant scrutinized my passport and visa page copies. I was half expecting him to ask for a notarized copy, but he didn't. His only comment was on the passport picture, which was too large for the box on the registration form. "Feel free to cut it down," I told him.

I asked when my SIM card would be activated. "Sir, tomorrow is a holiday. It will take three days." He could sense my displeasure. "But you can go to the Airtel head office and they can activate by this evening." I asked for the address. It was, at least, reasonably precise: Splendid Towers, near Begumpet police station.

"Yes, sir, I know it well," said my next auto rickshaw driver. It turned out that he didn't. We stopped several times on our way across the city so that he could ask for directions, and once so he could buy a coconut milk. We got there eventually. "I wait for you, sir?" he asked. I said no. I had no idea how long the transaction would take.

The application form for a SIM card is a page long with many boxes to complete. The sales assistant said he could fill out most of the questions from the information on my passport and visa but needed additional data. "What is the name of your father?" he asked. I wondered briefly about questioning the relevance of this question, considering that my father died thirty years ago, but thought better of it. The culture of the *babudom* had extended to the private sector. The assistant was simply following instructions.

"I also need the names, addresses, and mobile numbers for two people in Hyderabad." I listed the numbers of two colleagues from the University of Hyderabad, but this time felt justified in asking why their mobile numbers were needed.

"So we can notify them by text when your SIM card is activated."

"Why can't you text me on my number?"

"No, sir, we are not allowed to do this. Please inform them they will receive a text."

I was about to ask how I was supposed to do this if I did not have a working mobile phone but decided to go with the flow.

"Now you must sign," said the assistant. I signed in three places on the application form, and on the copies of the passport and visa.

"I'd like to buy some time while I'm here," I added.

"We cannot sell you time until your phone is activated," the assistant replied.

"Seriously?"

He did not see the irony. "You will go online to Airtel. There you will find some most attractive data packages," he said.

Half an hour later, I was back at the hotel. The expedition had taken more than two hours, and all I had to show for it was a 25-rupee (40¢) SIM card with no credit. I had spent almost 700 rupees ($10) on circuitous auto rickshaw rides, but at least I collected a few travel notes along the way.

Airtel would not accept my credit card. Over dinner, a colleague said he would add credit and I could pay him back. Later, I received a text saying that 500 rupees had been added, followed by another text saying my credit was under five rupees and I could not make any calls or

FIGURE 6.5 Two hours on the road and $10 in fares for a SIM card with no credit

send texts. I gave up and went to bed. The next morning, the credit had been activated. I felt newly empowered.

The Dry Side of Hyderabad

The tiny community of NBT Nagar is squeezed into a narrow strip of land, bounded by railroad tracks, a road, a government school, and the wall of a mosque. It has just twenty-nine families—twenty-five Muslim and four Hindu—living in simple one- and two-room single-story *kacca* with mud floors. Most have lived there all their lives. The men find casual work as day laborers and auto rickshaw drivers, and the women earn money selling vegetables or cleaning streets and apartments. The more substantial homes are built from mud bricks, with metal or asbestos roofs weighed down by rocks or bricks. Most consist of metal sheets nailed to a rough wooden frame with plastic sheets or tarpaulins covering the holes in the roof. The alleys between the houses are so narrow that you often have to step into a doorway to let another person pass. The community lies in a shallow depression created by the road and the railroad embankment; in the monsoon season, the houses are often

FIGURE 6.6 The narrow alleys of NBT Nagar, Hyderabad

flooded, and snakes emerge from the bushes along the lake shore on the other side of the railroad tracks to crawl under walls into homes.

In the middle of NBT Nagar, in what I'll call a wide place in the alley, is the single water tap serving the whole community. Water supply is always precarious. The line runs from the road to the mosque and then to the tap. During the month of Ramadan, pressure dropped because worshippers used most of the water to perform their ablutions. Sewage leaked into the line and the residents complained to the imam. In a thoroughly nondiscriminatory action (because it affected Muslims and well as Hindus), he had the water line cut, leaving the community with no water and forcing residents to carry water from another tap further along the road. The water board eventually fixed the line, but supply is still intermittent.

"We have water for about one hour in the morning, every other day," a woman told my UNICEF colleague Carol. "Sometimes 7:30, sometimes 8:30. We never know. We just have to wait." While we sat on a straw mat on the side of the road with women from the community, others passed carrying large plastic jugs of water on their shoulders. "They would like to join us but they're too busy fetching water," someone said. Everyone laughed.

The UNICEF team had joined staff from the community-based organization Basthi Vikas Manch (BVM; literally, Slum Development Platform), which campaigns for water rights in the slums of Hyderabad, on field visits to communities to try to understand why so many people in this densely populated metropolitan area lack safe, clean water. Predictably, the arrival of outsiders in NBT Nagar attracted a crowd. About a dozen women sat talking with us, with BVM organizer Sunny Rai (his real name, and most of the time he's smiling) translating from Telugu. A few children listened in from outside the circle. "Go to school," the women shouted, and we joined in the chorus. They ambled off in the general direction of the government school.

The gathering attracted people who sensed an opportunity. A man in his midtwenties squeezed onto the mat beside me. Speaking in English, he claimed to have given water to residents from the tap at his nearby house. He kept interrupting the women, sometimes to translate but more often to talk about himself. I asked him to write his name and mobile number in my notebook: K. Rakesh, M.S.W., trained social worker. "I have a degree in social work but cannot find a job," he said. "I would like to start my own NGO. Are you on Facebook? I would like you to help me."

I've seen this happen in other places where self-proclaimed community leaders with English-language skills push their way into the conversation. You have no idea whether they represent interests other than their own. Sometimes they have good intentions, but often they are simply networking, hoping you will be the person who opens the door to a job or a grant. Because they speak English (and the community members do not), they tend to dominate the exchanges. I've learned to be wary. "Another failed local politician," Sunny commented later.

Rakesh fell silent when an older woman joined the group. The other women shuffled aside to give her the most prominent position on the mat. She said she could speak for the community because she was the general secretary of the local branch of Telangana Rashtra Samithi (TRS), the ruling party in the state of Telangana. Meanwhile, an official from the human rights office of the state administration buttonholed me to give me her mobile number. I had no idea how they knew about our impromptu community meeting. Probably someone had called to tell them that foreigners and BVM organizers were holding a meeting about water in NBT Nagar. They sped to the scene to take over the agenda. What had begun as a meeting with community members had been shanghaied by the politicians.

In densely populated urban areas all over India, water and sanitation are high on the political agenda. According to Sunny and other water activists, local politicians make campaign promises to bring water and public toilets to communities, but as soon as the election is over the commitments are forgotten (at least until the next election). In Hyderabad, community members are left to complain to the officials and engineers of the Hyderabad Metropolitan Water Supply and Sewerage Board (HMWS&SB). Underfunded and stifled by bureaucracy, HMWS&SB is ill-equipped to maintain its existing infrastructure, let alone expand it to serve communities such as NBT Nagar.

Despite the claims of its local secretary, the TRS has done little to help NBT Nagar residents. After several appeals from BVM, water board officials visited the community. Residents pointed out that although their dwellings were modest, they all had electricity and paid their bills. Why not water too? The officials agreed to install lines and water meters but reneged a few weeks later when residents could not produce legal titles to their land and houses. BVM reminded officials that the board had provided taps to other slum communities where the legal titles were as iffy as in NBT Nagar. The HMWS&SB said it would review and respond.

No one holds out much hope that will happen. Indian *babus* are skilled at burying paperwork in the large and dark holes between management levels and functions or rejecting it on technical grounds—an illegible signature, the lack of an official stamp, an ambiguous reference to state or federal statute. Most people, says BVM, do not know their water rights, and even if they do, they lack the capacity to demand them from officials who fear they will lose their jobs if they take any initiative. BVM tries to help by drafting petitions and occasionally takes a case to court, but there's a limit to what a small community-based organization can do.

At the government school in NBT Nagar, the principal told us that her complaints about water supply had also been lost, this time in the labyrinthine education bureaucracy. The school installed a large plastic drum to store drinking water for the five hundred-plus primary and high school students. Two boreholes were sunk to supply water for washing and flushing toilets, but the school pays for maintenance and electricity for the pumps. "We try to find donors but often the principal has to pay from her own salary," one teacher told us.

Just inside the school gate near one of the boreholes is the "HMWS&SB Rain Water Harvesting Pit," a hole lined with concrete to direct rainwater into the ground, renewing the supply from the bore hole. The project stopped after the pit was dug. There are no gutters to collect water from the roof, no pipes to direct it into the pit. Most days it is completely dry.

City authorities estimate there are more than sixteen hundred slums—many of them larger than NBT Nagar—in the metropolitan area with about 12 percent of the population (more than a million people) living in them. Of course, it's tricky deciding what's a slum and what's not because agencies use different criteria—housing type and building material, population density, land ownership, availability of services. The slum designation provides a useful pretext for taking over land, especially when residents cannot prove legal title. Indeed, the authorities have little incentive to improve services to communities such as NBT Nagar. With property prices rising, private developers are eyeing slum areas. A few hundred yards from NBT Nagar is a modern apartment block with views of the lake. It's probably only a matter of time before the authorities evict the residents of NBT Nagar and demolish their homes in the interests of urban renewal. If the bulldozers move in, the residents will be homeless or forced to squat on land on the outskirts of the city. They will not have the money to travel into the city to work. And they probably won't have water.

NBT Nagar's water problems are mirrored in urban and rural areas all over India. At the macro level, India is not a dry country, at least compared with some African and other Asian countries; per person, India has twice as much water as arid northern China. The problem is that it receives most of it during the four-month monsoon season, beginning in June, and some areas have far less than others. In 2016, after two years of poor monsoons, India faced its worst water crisis since independence. Rivers ran dry, and wells were exhausted; destitute farmers migrated to cities, and some committed suicide. The central and state governments responded by dispatching water trains and tanker trucks to parched regions and announcing new irrigation and water diversion projects. One, priced at $165 billion, would involve thirty-seven links between rivers, most by canals—almost one thousand miles of artificial waterways.

Such big-ticket projects, touted by politicians, make headlines but fail to address basic problems. Underground aquifers, not rivers, lakes, or dams, supply two-thirds of the water used for irrigation and more than three-quarters of drinking water. With so many wells and pumps drawing water, groundwater levels have been falling. In a perverse effort to boost agricultural production, some states provide free or cheap electricity to farmers; this encourages them to pump groundwater to flood their fields and grow water-guzzling crops such as rice. In some states, rivers are dammed to provide hydroelectricity, while farmers downstream pray for rain. At the same time, half of India's villages have inadequate drinking water. Canals built to bring water to urban areas lose up to 70 percent of their supply.

A raft of confusing policies and regulations results in water wastage and disputes—between states, and between farmers, industry, and household consumers. Under India's constitution, water is mainly the business of the states, not the central government. Rivers and lakes do not respect state boundaries, so quarrels are bitter. Activists say that control of water resources should be given to organizations that span the river basins, but interstate agreements are difficult to reach because each state has different priorities for water resources. More progress has been made at the local level, with some states handing over control of irrigation canals to water users' associations, where farmers elect their own leaders. Hydrologists and water activists say more can be done to conserve water without the massive infrastructure projects. They call for simpler solutions—better treatment of urban sewage, rainwater harvesting, drip irrigation instead of wasteful flooding techniques, sensible regulation, and more realistic pricing.[7]

It's not as if the water problem is a new one. In the sixteenth century, the sultans of the Qutb Shahi dynasty built a network of artificial lakes, called tanks, in Hyderabad to hold water. Some, such as Hussain Sagar Lake and the small lake across the railroad tracks from NBT Nagar, remain. Others in prime residential and commercial districts have been filled in by developers and no longer serve as sources of water. At least one luxury hotel in the high-rent Banjara Hills district is built over a tank; all that remains today is a picturesque pond with manicured lawns. Hyderabad has to pump much of its water from rivers and reservoirs and try to maintain an aging supply system. Every day, the HMWS&SB's fleet of blue-and-yellow water tankers are on the streets, delivering water to paying customers and slum communities. Their slogan is "Water is precious—Every drop counts." There's no sign that many people, least of all the politicians, take that message to heart.

An Unhappy Union

In Telangana, as in other states, basic services such as water and sanitation have become politicized. The HMWS&SB is chaired by the state's political boss, Kalvakuntia Chandrashekhar Rao, popularly known as KCR. He founded the Telangana Rashtra Samithi (TRS) in 2001 as a regional political party with the single goal of breaking up the state of Andhra Pradesh to create a separate state of Telangana in the north with Hyderabad as its capital. Under the Nizams, Telangana had developed as the Telugu-speaking region of the state of Hyderabad. When the state was dissolved in 1956, the Telangana region was merged with the state of Andhra, where Telugu is also the primary language, to form Andhra Pradesh, with Hyderabad as its capital.

It was never a happy union. For more than half a century, politicians and activists campaigned to break away from Andhra Pradesh, citing injustices in the distribution of resources, budgets, and jobs. In Andhra Pradesh, two-thirds of the catchment areas of the Krishna and Godavari Rivers, flowing to the Bay of Bengal, are in the Deccan plateau region of Telangana. Telangana supporters claimed that three-quarters of irrigation water went to the Coastal Andhra region, while their region got less than 20 percent. Coastal Andhra also received the largest budget allocations for state services including higher education, forcing students from Hyderabad to travel hundreds of miles to attend college.

The campaign for a separate state began in earnest in 1969, with periodic strikes by public employees and students, demonstrations, political maneuvering by Telangana politicians, and sporadic violence. In 2009, the central government began the process of creating a separate state. Violent protests in other regions of Andhra Pradesh followed, with unions, lawyers, and students demanding Andhra Pradesh remain united. The government was rattled; it withdrew its plan, saying no action would be taken until a consensus was reached by all parties. In response, state legislators and ministers from Telangana submitted their resignations. Finally, in June 2014, the Indian Parliament passed a bill forming Telangana state out of ten districts in northwestern Andhra Pradesh. Hyderabad was to remain as the capital of both Telangana and Andhra Pradesh for a period of up to ten years. The TRS party that led the statehood campaign easily won the elections for the new state assembly, and its leader, KCR, became Telangana's first chief minister.

KCR enjoyed the spoils of victory. He poured millions of rupees into a three-day religious festival that elevated him to demigod status, with worshippers praying for his health and long life. He attempted to take credit for the development of the high-tech sector. Political power in Telangana and the wealth it brings are now a family affair. KCR's son is the minister for IT, local government, and urban development, and his nephew holds the portfolios for irrigation and water resources, legislative affairs, and marketing; in total, seventeen state ministries are held by Rao family members.

If voters are concerned about what appears to be blatant nepotism, they have not shown it. Nor do they seem concerned about KCR's beliefs in astrology, numerology, and Vastu, a traditional Hindu system of architecture with geometric patterns and directional alignments. KCR is reported to have fixed the precise time for his inauguration on June 2, 2014, on the advice of astrologers to suit his lucky number, six. More worryingly, in November 2016 he proposed demolishing the Saifabad Palace that houses the state governments of Telangana and Andhra Pradesh because it did not follow the architectural principles of Vastu. The European-style palace was built in 1888 during the reign of the sixth

Nizam, Mahbub Ali Khan, and had been renovated for official use, but KCR claimed Telangana would suffer for having a non-Vastu building house its government. A court halted the demolition plans. In 2016 KCR faced criticism when it emerged that the state had funded a $7.3 million official residence with bullet-proof offices and bathrooms and a movie theater. The next year, KCR fulfilled a campaign promise to thank the gods for Telangana's statehood by donating a gold lotus-shaped necklace and collar, valued at $750,000, to a Hindu temple. Social media users laid into KCR, accusing him of plundering the state treasury for personal needs.

Expensive religious rituals, astrology, and Vastu don't go down well with Hyderabad's educated urban elite, but the chief minister does not care because the TRS has a broad base of support in rural areas and among the urban poor, many of whom also blend traditional Hindu beliefs with lucky numbers and symbols. According to polls, KCR is one of the most popular chief ministers in India.

While KCR frets about Vastu compliance in public buildings and donates gold to temples, the government of the reduced state of Andhra Pradesh shares digs with the rascals who destroyed state unity. Andhra Pradesh's new capital, Amaravati, is under construction on the banks of the Krishna River near Vijayawada, the second-largest city in the state with a population of 1.5 million. The name comes from an earlier settlement upstream on the Krishna where Buddhist culture flourished for almost fifteen hundred years, attracting pilgrims from as far away as China. The capital site is massive, covering thirty villages and thirty-five thousand acres of agricultural land. The central government has invested heavily in the project, designating Amaravati as one of its "smart cities," where technological infrastructure will spur economic development. Unfortunately, the area is also prone to flooding when the northeastern monsoon surges across the Bay of Bengal to break river banks in low-lying areas. Almost every year, coastal areas of Andhra Pradesh and its southern neighbor, Tamil Nadu, are submerged, with crops ruined, city streets flooded, and bridges and roads destroyed.[8]

Andhra Pradesh state agencies have begun moving to temporary offices in Amaravati, but the schedule seems to depend as much on the religious and astrological calendar as on any plan for government efficiency. In the traditional Hindu Telugu calendar, Ashadam is the fourth month, starting in late June or early July. Traditionally, it's a time when people do not start on new projects; marriages, housewarmings, and other ceremonies are not held during Ashadam. In July 2016, officials asked Andhra Pradesh's technocratic chief minister Chandrababu Naidu to postpone the schedule for shifting their desks and filing cabinets to Amaravati to mid-August. They did not want to relocate during the "inauspicious" period of Ashadam.

Bureaucracy, technology, religion, and astrology. It's a classic Indian mix.

seven

The Seven Sisters

Are You Coming from India?

"The mangoes are from mainland India." Bhrigu Talukdar wanted to make sure I knew what I was buying. The comment puzzled me. Mainland India? We were not on one of the twelve hundred islands that dot India's coastline, but at a street market in Tezpur, a bustling commercial city in the northeast state of Assam. What did Bhrigu mean by "mainland India"?

The observation had as much to do with history as with geography. Bhrigu is from Assam but works at a research university in Delhi. Back in his home state for a two-week course I was teaching at Tezpur University for faculty and doctoral research students, he volunteered to accompany me on a shopping trip to the town, a thirty-minute ride by auto rickshaw from the campus. With a subtle reference to mangoes, Bhrigu wanted me to understand that Assam and the other northeastern states had always existed in what he called a "colonial relationship" to a dominant power. He wasn't talking only about two centuries of British rule, when India was a source of raw materials and cheap labor to be exported to other parts of the empire, but about more recent history.

The northeast has long suffered from lack of investment and infra-structural development. Cut off from the Bay of Bengal by the partition of British India, the region did not share in the economic boom of the mainland states; while other parts of India industrialized in the 1960s and 1970s, the northeast remained primarily agricultural. "We have oil, coal, and other mineral resources," another colleague from Assam told me. "They are always shipped outside the northeast for processing. We have little industry here. India is taking our wealth, and we see few benefits." Prime Minister Modi's government has been allocating more resources, and promising infrastructure and economic development, but there's also resistance to government projects. Barely a month goes by without an attack on contractors building a road or a bridge in a remote region. The same forces that drive people to leave rural areas in Madagascar, Bangladesh, and Indonesia—poverty, high rents, population pressure, and lack of opportunity—continue to undermine the economy of the northeast. Every day, young men board trains bound for mainland India, where they live in crowded conditions and save what money they can to send home to their families. The distinctive Assamese *gamosa,* a white scarf with a red border, is a common sight on the construction sites of Delhi and Mumbai.

Over dinner at the Tezpur University hostel, Bhrigu asked if I understood how one part of a country can exploit another. I said I knew all too well. I've lived in Appalachia—southeastern Ohio and now West Virginia—most of my adult life. I've seen the region's natu-ral resources—timber, coal, and natural gas—exploited by out-of-state companies, its young people forced to leave. I told Bhrigu that north-eastern India, in some ways such a foreign land, in other ways seemed quite familiar.

The northeast has always felt a long way away from the centers of power and wealth in India. Apart from Assam, six states that many Indian schoolchildren cannot name or place on the map border Tibet (Arunachal Pradesh), cluster around Bangladesh (Meghalaya, Tripura, Mizoram), and butt up against Myanmar (Manipur and Nagaland). My colleague Suruchi Sood recalls friends from the northeast at her college in Kolkata who talked about going to and coming back from "India." Another university colleague, Sonia Wahengbam, told me that when visitors from Delhi or Mumbai arrive in her hometown in Manipur, peo-ple ask them, "Are you coming from India?"

MAP 7.1 The Seven Sisters—the northeast states of India (map by Belén Marco Crespo)

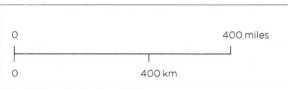

The Chicken's Neck

Although the Himalayan plateau region south of Tibet and the densely forested hill country bordering Myanmar were always on the borderlands of British India, the isolation of the northeast was formalized by the borders drawn at partition in 1947. The province of Bengal, which the British had first attempted to divide along religious lines in 1905, was carved up between Pakistan and India. In the scramble for land before boundaries were drawn, the Muslim League encouraged Bengali

Muslims to move north to Assam, hoping a Muslim majority in its southern districts would expand East Pakistan's frontiers; ultimately, only one, Sylhet, became part of Pakistan. The new borders left northeastern India—the large state of Assam and the small princely states of Manipur and Tripura—literally hanging out there, encircled by East Pakistan, Myanmar, and China. The creation of East Pakistan cut off road, rail, and river routes to the Bay of Bengal, leaving the region landlocked.

To connect the northeast to mainland India, the partition agreement created the Siliguri Corridor, a narrow strip of West Bengal between East Pakistan and Bhutan. At its widest, the corridor—the only land and rail route—is twenty-five miles, at its narrowest only fourteen. "The Siliguri corridor," one Indian analyst wrote, "is a terrifyingly vulnerable artery in India's geography. For Indians in the northeast, every look at a map is a sobering reminder of just how fragile their physical and economic tether to the rest of the country remains."[1] No wonder it's called the chicken's neck.

It's not difficult to imagine the chicken's neck being wrung by the forces of nature or geopolitics. Every year, monsoon rains cause flooding and mudslides that threaten to sever the rail and road link; the region is also prone to earthquakes. Since the 1962 war with China, Indian military strategists have fretted over what they can do if Chinese troops made the short hop across Bhutan or Sikkim, closed the corridor, and cut off the northeast. The answer is: probably not much, although the Indian Army maintains a heavy presence in the corridor. Because of its strategic location, the corridor has long served as a refuge and supply route for an assortment of rebels and criminal groups, some of them toting Kalashnikovs and bags of stolen cash—ethnic insurgent groups, Maoist cadres from Nepal, drug traffickers, and weapons dealers. Enough to choke a chicken.

Son of Brahma

East of the Siliguri Corridor, northeastern India broadens out into western Assam. Here, one of Asia's great rivers, the Brahmaputra, begins a slow arc to the south to flow into northwestern Bangladesh. The headwaters of the Brahmaputra lie on the northern side of the Himalayas on the Angsi glacier in Tibet, where it is called the Tsangpo, the "purifier," or by its Chinese name, Yarlung Zangbo. It flows east for almost 680 miles before cutting a course north through a series of narrow gorges and then flowing south across the eastern Himalayas through a deep canyon whose walls in places rise to sixteen thousand feet on each side. The river enters India in the state of Arunachal Pradesh, where it is called the Dihang (or Siang). Near Sadiya in northeastern Assam, it is joined by two major tributaries, the Lohit and the Dibang; beyond this confluence, it is known as the Brahmaputra. Throughout its 450-mile course southwest across Assam, it is fed by tributaries from the north and south. In western Assam, the river turns south around the Garo Hills to flow into Bangladesh, where it is called the Jamuna. Downstream, it joins India's other great river, the Ganges (Padma), and the Meghna, ending its 1,800-mile course and emptying into the Bay of Bengal.

Even during the dry season, the Brahmaputra is a massive, untamed river with its banks often several miles apart. It has two high-water seasons—in early summer when the Himalayan snows melt, and during the monsoon season from June to October. Swollen waters submerge river islands, erode the banks, and flood farmland. Over the past 250 years, the river's course has shifted dramatically, as water levels and seismic activity created new channels. Each year, the riverscape changes—new islands, sandbars, and levees appear, while older ones are washed downstream.

Millions of people in India and Bangladesh live in the river valley and depend on its waters for survival. The Brahmaputra provides fertile farmland and irrigation, vital for the three annual rice crops; fish caught in the river or harvested from ponds fed by it are a major source of protein. The river is awe inspiring, and often terrifying; to some, it is sacred. In Hindu mythology, Brahmaputra is the son of the god Brahma, rising from a sacred pool known as the Brahmakund; in its lower reaches in Assam, the river is worshipped by Hindus, and temples and monasteries were built on its banks and on river islands.

The Brahmaputra valley is at its narrowest, bank to bank, in western Assam, where it cuts through a low range of hills before turning south toward Bangladesh. For centuries, this was the gateway to the region; whoever controlled it would be able to rule the upper Brahmaputra valley. In 1671, at the village of Saraighat, the Ahom king, Lachit Borphukan, defeated an invading Mughal army, effectively ending the Mughals' last attempt to extend their empire into Assam. The first road and rail bridge across the Brahmaputra was opened in 1962 at Saraighat, now a district of the industrial city of Guwahati. For many years, it was the *only* bridge crossing the river. Today, a second Saraighat bridge relieves traffic congestion, and four other road and rail bridges cross the Brahmaputra upstream. It's still a long haul between them. The Brahmaputra, navigable for most of its length, is a major transportation highway, but also a barrier to north–south commerce. Local people still rely on ferries for travel and trade.

I didn't see much of the Brahmaputra valley on my first road trip from Guwahati Airport to Tezpur. By road, it's about 125 miles, but the journey takes at least three hours. At night, the trip is hair-raising, the kind of journey where you tighten your white-knuckle grip on the seat handles, brace your feet, grit your teeth, and close your eyes, all at the same time if you have the coordination. Trucks surged toward us with headlights blazing; those ahead of us often had their back lights out, so you didn't realize how close you were until the car's headlights illuminated the ubiquitous hand-painted signs, "Slow drive, long live" [*sic*], "Blow horn," "Good luck," or "Thanks." Fortunately, most of the cows and goats that graze on the roadside and wander into traffic during the day had gone home for the night, but there were other hazards—bicycles (with no reflectors), hand carts, and, on the final stretch south of the river, potholes.

East of the airport, the highway leaves the city and winds through the low hills south of the Saraighat bridge before descending into the broad river valley. At Jorabat, National Highway (NH) 37 joins Asian Highway (AH) 1—one link in a 12,700-mile cross-country network that technically starts in Japan and passes through both Koreas, China, Vietnam, Cambodia, Thailand, and Myanmar to northeast India and the Brahmaputra valley, then through Bangladesh, mainland India, Pakistan, Afghanistan, Iran, and Turkey to eventually link up with the European motorway system at the Bulgarian border. In other words, it's the mother of all road trips, although I'd guess the total driving time is less than the months it would take to obtain all the visas.

Two weeks later, traveling during the day with my wife, Stephanie Hysmith, I began to appreciate why the valley is the most densely populated region of Assam. To the south the densely forested hills of the state of Meghalaya, once part of Assam, rose steeply from the valley; to the north, another line of hills was a hazy outline in the distance. Between them, the valley lay flat and fertile. We passed rice paddies and fields of corn, soya, and sugar cane; other crops include rapeseed, mustard seed, and jute, used for making rope and baskets. Tall brick kilns with gently curving angles rose from the fields, looking (at least from the distance) like ancient temples. Every mile or so, we passed a *dhaba*, the Punjabi word for a roadside restaurant now widely used across India; most had short, easy-to-remember English names—Delight Dhaba, Happy Dhaba, Lovely Dhaba, U Like Dhaba, even Deluge Dhaba. Other roadside establishments are called "hotels," although only those such as the Dream City Hotel, which offered "fooding and lodging," appeared to have rooms to rent. Some looked as if they were a couple of steps down from the *dhabas* in terms of food and cleanliness, so we opted for the Highway City Dhaba for a lunch of "fish fry" (tiny fish fried whole), vegetable and paneer *pakoras*, and roti, with lime and raw onions.

For the first sixty miles or so, AH1/NH37 is a divided (although unfenced) highway, with the usual animal hazards. The occasional road sign with an image of a cow seems superfluous, because cattle are everywhere. At the town of Nagaon, AH1 branches off southeast toward Nagaland, and NH37 becomes a two-lane that meanders through villages and a green landscape of eucalyptus, palm and banana trees, and bamboo thickets. Roadside stalls sell bananas, potatoes, sweet potatoes, papayas, jackfruit, coconuts, and lychees. During the day, the bicycle and animal traffic is heavy, with chickens and ducks joining the cows and goats. Our driver skillfully braked and swerved, avoiding the trucks and buses hurtling toward us; a couple of times, we idled behind the rump of an elephant until the road ahead was clear.

Most people in these villages live in traditional Assamese houses, simple one- or two-room dwellings framed from bamboo or wood, with walls of reeds (locally called *ikara*) and clay-tile roofs. On some, the *ikara* is plastered with mud to form a rough stucco. Near streams, the houses are built on stilts. Studies have shown that this traditional design, using cheap, lightweight, and locally available materials, with flexible connections between walls and roof, stands up well to harsh weather and even earthquakes. Traditional homes stand side by side with houses and stores built from concrete blocks, with metal roofs. On this and other highways, cement companies are fighting their brand wars. Almost all the utility poles on NH37 were adorned with signs advertising the "state-of-the-art" and "global quality" Atibal Gold cement. A rival Guwahati concern, Prithvi Cement, had bought up all the bus shelters and painted them with its red-and-white logo, promising "solid settings for solid dreams."

Rural India is trending toward modern construction methods—reinforced concrete pillars, brick walls, and metal roofs. If there is a symbol of optimism—but also of stunted progress—in Assam, it is the concrete pillar with strands of rebar reaching upward, yearning to support a new story. Wherever we traveled, we saw dozens of half-finished concrete buildings. Often, the first floor was complete and occupied by stores or workshops. The second or third floor usually had no walls; bamboo poles had been inserted as braces; these would be removed when the walls were filled with rough, clay bricks. These semiopen areas provided makeshift living spaces for families and construction workers with beds, plastic garden chairs, and cook stoves. The top floor was open to the elements with washing lines strung between the concrete pillars, a large barrel to catch rainwater, and occasionally a satellite dish. Alongside the new construction, old brick buildings were being demolished. It was sometimes difficult to decide whether a building was going up or coming down.

Finally, we turned north off NH37 and headed toward the bridge linking Tezpur with southern Assam. The Kolia Bhomora Setu road bridge, named for one of the Ahom generals who sent the Mughals packing, was opened in 1987. It was the second bridge to span the river and at 1.87 miles is more than twice the length of the Saraighat bridge. We paid the 20-rupee (30¢) toll and the attendant pushed aside the rusty metal shelf that substituted for a tollbooth arm. And then we were over the Brahmaputra. A cargo boat, its deck stacked high with bricks, passed under the bridge spans. Small fishing boats seemed suspended in midstream as their crews pulled in the nets. Long, narrow boats with high prows, paddled by a single man standing at the stern, carried half a dozen passengers and a couple of bicycles along the shoreline. Smoke rose from cooking stoves in villages. The setting sun glimmered on the slow-moving water. It was a view worthy of a postcard or an image in an "Incredible India" TV commercial. You'd expect people to write poems and songs about the river. Indeed, they do.

Ol' Man Brahmaputra

As the city that claims to be the center of Assamese culture, Tezpur is underwhelming. You can cover most of the sights—a couple of temples and the picturesque Cole Park with its artificial lake—comfortably in half a day. The top tourist attraction is Agnigarh—in Sanskrit, the "fortress of fire"—on a hillock overlooking the Brahmaputra. Stories from Hindu mythology tend to be long and involved, with many characters and subplots, so I'll do the short, soapy version. Usha, daughter of Banasura, the thousand-armed king of central Assam, fell in love with Aniruddha, grandson of Lord Krishna. As relationships go, this was a nonstarter, because Banasura was a devotee of Krishna's sworn enemy, Shiva. Banasura tied up Aniruddha in a mess of snakes and packed Usha off to the Agnigarh fortress, which was surrounded by a ring of fire. A bloody war between the forces of Krishna and Shiva—a scene vividly depicted in stone sculptures along the pathway—followed. Wise Lord Brahma stepped in, told them both to behave, and brokered the deal that ended with Banasura agreeing to the marriage. From the legendary battle, Tezpur earned the name of "city of blood."

After a steep ascent on a hot, sticky day and a heavy dose of Hindu mythology, Stephanie and I needed lunch and a less taxing afternoon schedule. We decided on the city museum, housed in a British colonial-era bungalow, where we hoped to find AC along with sculptures, crafts, and Ahom-era cannons. There was no one on duty at the ticket office, so we entered the garden and looked for the entrance. On a covered stage near the gate, a small group of men had gathered for a ceremony around a makeshift altar with an offering bowl, incense sticks, and framed photographs. I approached them.

"Is this the entrance to the museum?"

"Sorry, it's closed today," one man replied. "We're celebrating the birthday of Bhupen Hazarika. Would you like to join us?"

This was not the first time I had heard the name of Hazarika, the much-revered artist and musician who literally put Assam on India's modern cultural map. He was a singer, composer, lyricist, poet, and filmmaker, widely credited with introducing the culture and folk music of Assam and northeast India to Hindi cinema at the national level. He was also a tireless campaigner for social justice.

In 1935, nine-year-old Hazarika moved to Tezpur with his family. His public rendition of a classical Assamese devotional song, taught to him by his mother, caught the attention of the playwright and pioneer Assamese filmmaker Jyoti Prasad Agarwala and the artist and revolutionary poet Bishnu Prasad Rabha. Under their patronage, Hazarika recorded his first song at a Kolkata studio in 1936 and went on to sing in a 1939 Agarwala film. Meanwhile, he started writing his own songs.

In 1949, after earning an MA in political science and working briefly for All India Radio, Hazarika won a scholarship to Columbia University in New York. He completed his PhD in mass communication in 1952. In New York he became friends with the African American singer, actor, and civil rights activist Paul Robeson. The imagery, theme, and melody of one of Hazarika's most famous songs, "Bisitirno Paarore" (On your wide banks), was heavily influenced by Robeson's rendition of "Ol' Man River" in the 1936 movie version of the musical *Show Boat*. Oscar Hammerstein II's lyrics to "Ol' Man River" contrast the struggles of African Americans with the endless, uncaring flow of the Mississippi River. In Hazarika's version, the Mississippi becomes the Brahmaputra, flowing silently through a world of suffering and moral decay:

> Bistirna paarore (On your wide banks)
> Axonkhya jonre (That are home to countless people)
> Hahakar xuniu (In spite of hearing their anguished cries)
> Nixobde nirobe (So silently and unmindfully)
> Burha luit tumi (Oh you, Old Luit)[2]
> Burha luit buwa kiyo? (How can you flow?)

After a brief spell of university teaching, Hazarika established himself in Kolkata as a music director and singer. He made several award-winning Assamese films and composed scores for Bengali films and, in his later life, for Hindi films. As a singer, he was famous for his baritone voice and diction. As a lyricist, he was known for poetic compositions and social and political messages. His songs, including "Bisitirno Paarore," were translated into Bengali and Hindi. Hazarika dabbled in politics and for five years served as a representative to the Assam Legislative Assembly, but he always saw his music and films as the most effective forums for social action. By the time he died in November 2011 at age eighty-five, his fame had spread far beyond his native Assam. An estimated half a million mourners attended his funeral in Guwahati; a monument opened four years later is now a place of pilgrimage. Fittingly for the artist who composed an ode to a river, Hazarika's name is on India's longest bridge, opened in May 2017 by Prime Minister Modi. More than five miles long, it spans a major tributary of the Brahmaputra, the Lohit, linking Assam and

Arunachal Pradesh, saving one hundred miles and five hours in travel time between the states.

Stephanie and I joined the group, which included two writers and a filmmaker, on the stage, lit incense sticks, and scattered lotus petals on the altar. There were short tributes to Hazarika, then the group sang one of his songs. Afterward, we chatted and thanked them for making us part of the ceremony. "Please wait a few more minutes," one insisted. Soon, one member of the group who had slipped away entered through the gate carrying a *gamosa* he had bought. I stood, feeling humble, while two others draped it around my neck.

Seven Troublesome Sisters

Assam is the northeast's largest and most populous state; with more than thirty-one million (2011 census), it has more than twice the population of the other seven northeastern states combined. Outside India, Assam is known mostly for three things—wildlife, silk, and tea. Kaziranga National Park, a UNESCO World Heritage site upstream from the Tezpur bridge, is a refuge for the fast-disappearing Indian one-horned rhinoceros. Other threatened species at Kaziranga and the larger Manas Wildlife Sanctuary along the border with Bhutan are the Asian elephant, Bengal tiger, pygmy hog, wild water buffalo, and species of monkeys, birds, turtles, snakes, and fish. Silk production is concentrated in the town of Sualkuchi, on the north bank of the river twenty miles east of Guwahati; it has been a center of the handloom industry since the seventeenth century, with hundreds of small workshops producing silk and cotton textiles.

The first tea plantations were established by the British in the 1840s, growing a local variety called *camellia asamica*. By the end of the nineteenth century, as the industry became mechanized, tea became Assam's principal agricultural export, and today the state produces more than half of India's tea. Plantation owners, dissatisfied with imported Chinese laborers and unable to recruit native Assamese, brought in workers from central and eastern mainland India, contributing to both ethnic diversity and tensions. Tea workers are poorly paid and often live in rough metal shacks with limited access to education and medical services.

Eastern Assam is also oil and natural gas country. Mechanical drilling began in the late 1860s, and today the state accounts for about 15 percent of India's crude oil output. Exploration continues, and with it battles over how drilling licenses should be awarded, how oil revenue should be taxed, the environmental impact of drilling and refining, and whether the state receives its rightful benefits from the extraction of its natural resources. It's a familiar story—similar battles are fought out over natural resources in Madagascar, Indonesia, and other regions of India.

On the map, Assam is shaped roughly like a Y laid on its side. From east to west, it lies north and south of the Brahmaputra valley; South Assam, bordered by Nagaland and Manipur to the east and Meghalaya and Bangladesh to the west, is dissected by the Barak River, which flows into Bangladesh as part of the Surma River system, a major tributary of the Brahmaputra (Jamuna). Assam's shape suggests it was once larger in area than it is today, almost as if it was chewed around the edges by carnivorous cartographers.

In the colonial era, Assam was one of eight British provinces, occupying almost all of what today is northeast India, except for the two small princely states of Manipur and Tripura. In 1947, its southern Sylhet district became part of East Pakistan. Division along religious lines did not satisfy the tribal populations of the Himalayan region, the hill country south of the Brahmaputra, and the east near the border with Myanmar. There are more than two hundred ethnic groups in the northeast, and as many languages and dialects. From the 1960s onward, pressures from tribal groups, some of them backed by guerrilla armies, forced the central government to slice off some of Assam's hill regions to form new states.

In 1963, the Naga Hills region, bordering Myanmar, became Nagaland. The Naga tribes never liked outsiders much anyway, and for centuries displayed the heads of unwelcome visitors, including colonial officials and missionaries, outside their villages to deter other intruders. In 1972, the hill country south of the Brahmaputra became the state of Meghalaya, and two Union Territories (later to become states) were created: the sparsely populated northern region bordering Tibet became Arunachal Pradesh, and the southeastern panhandle between Bangladesh and Myanmar, Mizoram. In 1975, India's fears about Chinese troops closing off the Siliguri Corridor were partly eased when the kingdom of Sikkim, bordered on the north and east by Tibet, officially became the northeast's eighth state.

Thus, through political wheeling and dealing and ethnic gerrymandering, India created its smallest, and economically least viable, administrative units. The four states forged out of colonial Assam, plus the former kingdoms of Manipur, Tripura, and Sikkim, are (along with tiny Goa) the least populous of India's twenty-nine states. The granting of statehood may have satisfied ethnic aspirations, but the region remains economically marginalized and performs poorly on indicators for health and education.

After administratively carving up northeast India, the politicians faced an image and marketing challenge: How could they create a sense of togetherness and interdependence for the region? Calling it northeast India seemed too prosaic. They were rescued by Jyoti Prasad Saikia, a journalist in Tripura. During a radio talk show, he coined the term "Seven Sister States," and later he developed his thesis on their shared characteristics and heritage in a book, *The Land of Seven Sisters*. The name quickly caught on and is widely used as a slogan by state and private tourism operators.

The "Seven Sisters" label may lure tourists, but as political rhetoric it has limited appeal. In 2014 at a rally in Imphal, the capital of Manipur, Modi, running as the BJP's candidate for prime minister, optimistically rebranded the seven plus Sikkim as the Ashta Lakshmi States. In Hindi, Ashta means eight and Lakshmi is the Hindu goddess of wealth and prosperity, so literally they were the "eight wealthy and prosperous states of India." The description spectacularly defies the data, because most are as poor as any states in mainland India, but Modi's language was meant to be aspirational, not descriptive. Criticizing the Congress Party for sixty years of neglect in the region, he said that India will prosper only if the northeast gains, and that it was "time to offer lotus (BJP) to this Ashta Lakshmi."

Other BJP politicians picked up on the theme. In his address to parliament in 2017, President Pranab Mukherjee boasted of his government's investments in infrastructure: "My government sees the NE states as the Ashta Lakshmi that can take India to new heights. The northeast is the gateway to Southeast Asia. We are opening up road and rail routes to our neighboring countries to boost economic development of the region."[3] Mukherjee's reference to "neighboring countries" is significant, reflecting what has been called the "Look East" policy. It recognizes the geographical reality that more than 90 percent of the northeast's borders are with neighboring countries—Bangladesh, China, Myanmar, Bhutan, and Nepal. For the region to develop economically, trade with mainland India is less important than trade with and via its neighbors. India is working to conclude trade and tariff agreements and improve road, rail, and river transportation in the region. In an ideal scenario, the northeast will be economically integrated with East and Southeast Asia while politically integrated with India.

Many in the northeast and elsewhere in India would agree that government neglect has left the region lagging behind the rest of the country on most development indicators. Adding poverty to the demands of ethnic and indigenous groups for political power creates a volatile mix. For half a century, the Seven Sisters have been engaged in spats with each other as well as with their absent parents in Delhi.

An Alphabet Soup of Insurgency

Bhrigu is studying how the Assamese media portrayed the United Liberation Front of Assam (ULFA), formed in 1979 to wage an armed struggle for independence. With the arrest of its leaders, ULFA morphed from militant action—blowing up bridges and murdering local officials—to a political movement, working within the system to improve living conditions, education, and health for Assamese. At least three other insurgent movements are active in the state, demanding self-rule, land rights, native-language instruction, and other rights for ethnic and tribal groups.

For more than half a century, security forces in the northeast have had authority under a special powers act to arrest people or search properties without a warrant, and to use deadly force if they have "reasonable suspicion" that a person is acting against the state. Even Indian citizens who travel to Arunachal Pradesh, Mizoram, and Nagaland need to obtain a special permit.

As with all insurgent movements, these groups have tended to merge, splinter into factions, and merge again, creating an alphabet soup of insurgency. At one time or another, the demands of one hill tribe, the Karbi, were represented by the United People's Democratic Solidarity (UPDS), its political wing, the Karbi Longri North Cachar Hills Liberation Front (KLNLF), and its armed wing, the Karbi Longri North Cachar Hills Resistance Movement (KNPR), in addition to two separate groups, the Karbi National Volunteers (KNV) and the Karbi

People's Front (KPF). Fortunately for everyone concerned, but especially for acronym-weary newspaper readers, these groups disbanded in 2014 following the surrender of their cadres and leaders.

The proliferation of armed groups, most based on ethnic or tribal identities, indicates the level of discontent in the region, always simmering and occasionally boiling over. For five years, from 1979, Assam was wracked by strikes, protests, and mass picketing in front of polling places. The student-led Assam Movement brought to a head long-standing grievances over the growing economic power and political clout of Bengali Muslims who had migrated to the state, both before and after the Bangladesh Liberation War of 1971. The Assamese claimed they were becoming a minority in their own homeland and faced the loss of their language and culture. In 1983, during the so-called Nellie massacre in fourteen villages in the Nagaon district, indigenous Assamese killed more than two thousand suspected illegal immigrants, including women and children. In August 1985, after lengthy negotiations, the central government and the Assam groups signed the Assam Accord, under which immigrants who entered illegally after January 1966 were to be deported.

Easier said than done. There was little motivation for the Congress Party, which had long ruled the state and takes a secular approach to politics, to boot out the Muslims who supported it in elections. Tensions continued, as new arrivals from Bangladesh competed with indigenous groups for low-wage jobs as construction workers, domestics, rickshaw pullers, and vegetable sellers. In 2012, at least seventy-seven died and four hundred thousand fled their homes following violence in western Assam between indigenous Bodos and Bengali Muslims. However, it was not until 2016, when the BJP deployed it as an election issue, that deportation returned to the top of the political agenda. With a majority in the state assembly, the BJP made it a priority to update India's National Register of Citizens (NRC). Currently, about four million Assam residents, most of them Muslim, are not listed. Both the Assam and central governments say there will be an appeal process to prove residency, but fears are mounting that some will be deported. Densely populated Bangladesh, already struggling to deal with Rohingya refugees from Myanmar, is ill prepared to handle another influx from the north.

In August 2015, India's government signed what Modi called a "historic" agreement with the main Naga insurgent group, the National

Socialist Council of Nagaland (NSCN), technically ending six decades of lingering conflict. Most of the fighting had ended in 1997 when, as the *Economist* put it, "guitar-strumming rebels agreed to a ceasefire and quit guerrilla life in the forests for comforts in town, where many are lauded like rock stars."[4] However, previous peace deals have failed after breakaway factions took to the hills. There are more than twenty Naga tribal groups in Nagaland and Manipur, and some have formed alliances with Naga living across the border in Myanmar; in June 2015, one ambushed an Indian Army convoy near the border, killing eighteen soldiers. The government of Myanmar, which has its own agenda, has quietly supported militant groups in the northeast and hosted a 2015 meeting at which nine formed the United Liberation Front of Western Southeast Asia. Journalists covering the meeting were grateful that they abbreviated the acronym to UNLFW, rather than UNLFWESEA.

The China Syndrome

As if the Indian Army did not have its hands full with insurgents, there's on-and-off tension along the mountainous northern border in Arunachal Pradesh with the old enemy, China. In October 1962, Chinese artillery shelled Indian positions, and the People's Liberation Army (PLA) advanced south; by mid-November, it had taken the town of Bomdila, about one hundred miles from Tezpur, the headquarters of India's IV Corps and the major army base in the region. Although a ceasefire was declared, Tezpur residents, already overwhelmed by refugees fleeing the PLA, feared their town would be the next target. They recall the roads choked with cars, bullock carts, and families with suitcases; at the Brahmaputra *ghat* (terminal), there was chaos as people fought for places on the ferries. Government officials fled the town, but a group of students volunteered to stay to guard the power station and other installations. At the state bank, according to historian Neville Maxwell, officials burned half a million dollars in bills. They also "tried to get rid of the coins by throwing them in a lake but gave up the idea when people began diving for them."[5]

The Chinese never reached Tezpur, but the construction of the bridge across the Brahmaputra makes its location even more strategic than it was in 1962. It's estimated that China, which in its belligerent moments describes Arunachal Pradesh as "South Tibet," has 180,000 troops, including motorized divisions, stationed along the border. Tezpur is still the base for the IV Corps, and two tank brigades have been deployed to the region. The air force has taken over the local airport, restricting commercial flights. While I was teaching in Tezpur, there was a minor scuffle between the PLA and Indian troops. The *Assam Tribune* reported that it was resolved when the Chinese commander presented his Indian counterpart with two boxes of chocolate. Peace at any price . . .

Boarding on the Brahmaputra

The Assam Tourism representative in Jorhat looked puzzled. "Hotel?" he asked. "Yes, a hotel," I repeated. "Can you recommend a hotel?" Remembering that in northeast India, the term "hotel" can also refer to a roadside café, I tilted my head to the right to rest on the palm of my hand.

"Ah, hotel! You can stay here," he said triumphantly.

Stephanie and I were at the front desk of the Assam Tourism Lodge at this midsized city on the south bank of the Brahmaputra. Like most government establishments, it had seen better days. Indeed, we had been warned to stay away from government lodges. Except for a few well-maintained lodges at the national parks, most had fallen into disrepair after years of underfunding. In the lobby, paint was peeling from the walls. The place had a musty smell. Out in the parking lot, weeds sprouted from cracks in the concrete. A few guests were sitting in the lobby looking bored. There was a soap opera on the TV but either the volume wasn't working or no one had bothered to turn it up. It was swelteringly hot, the single fan simply moving around the humid air.

The representative gestured toward the room tariff on the wall. A standard room (communal bathroom) was a backpacker's bargain at $8. From there, the rate ascended through different options to the "deluxe, executive" at 1,200 rupees (under $20).

Stephanie and I don't like paying over the odds for accommodation, but we have some basic criteria—AC if possible (if not, at least a fan), a bathroom, and a bug-free bed. Our chances of getting that for under $20 were remote.

"Would you like to see a room?" asked the representative.

"Thanks, but I think we want a hotel closer to the city center," I replied tactfully. In truth, I had no idea where the center was, but it seemed the best way to extricate ourselves without causing loss of face.

"There is the MD," said the representative. We had already heard about the MD from the loquacious, I-know-everyone-in-Jorhat-and-because-you-are-my-friends-they-will-give-you-a-special-price taxi driver who had cornered us at the airport and driven us into town. He boasted of taking oil executives and other business travelers to the MD, and surely that would suit us too.

As a transport hub in the Brahmaputra valley and the gateway to eastern Assam, with its oil fields and tea estates, Jorhat needs at least one business hotel, a place with anonymous architecture where the Wi-Fi works, and the room service includes Western fare. I use business hotels when I travel, but Stephanie and I were on vacation, so we wanted something comfortable, but less bland.

"We know about the MD. Are there other hotels?" The question seemed to fluster the representative. He reached behind the desk and pulled out a tattered notebook containing names, addresses, and phone numbers. "You don't have a list of hotels?" I asked, almost rhetorically. After all, this was the *tourism* office. He shook his head.

"Well, do you have a city map?" I was subconsciously trying to support my nearer-the-city-center thesis. More head shaking. He handed us a regional map of Assam. Stephanie said we already had a better one.

"But there is the Nikita Hotel," he added, his face brightening.

We decided to check out the MD. It was Sunday afternoon, with little traffic on the streets, so we were stuck with our taxi driver. Along the road, billboards advertised quick-fix schools for high school students preparing for entrance exams at medical and engineering institutes—Brilliance Academy, Radiant Academy, and Transcend Coaching Centre. And, for that quick, exam-cram snack, "US Pizza. The Taste of America. New at Jorhat. *Conditions apply." Conditions apply? I suppose they want you to pay for the pizza.

The MD was one floor up from street level. Behind the desk in the dimly lit lobby sat three uniformed receptionists, waiting for oil executives and tea tycoons. We were not dressed for business, but at least we were Westerners and presumably had credit cards. The cheapest room with AC would run us almost $75 but we were tired and decided to look at it anyway. "Fourth floor," said the receptionist. "We are sorry the lift is not working today." Not a good omen. We trekked up the flights of stairs and then wandered down long dark corridors to a clean, but awkwardly designed room. We decided it wasn't worth the price—or the long walk.

So on to the Nikita. "The manager, he is my friend," our taxi driver informed us, although by now we assumed that anyone in Jorhat who would take our money was in his social circle. At least the lift was working. The room was sparse, and a little dirty, but the AC worked. We decided we had exhausted Jorhat's limited hotel options and checked in.

A couple of hours later, I was fighting the temptation to climb onto the reception desk and enhance the "May I help you?" sign with the words, "I wish you would."

We ignored the unemptied ashtray and the grease marks on the floor. It took an hour and three phone calls for the staff to produce two extra pillows and one more threadbare towel. The small refrigerator wasn't working. A staff member came to the room, plugged and unplugged it and confirmed the diagnosis. He disappeared, without proposing a solution. Eventually, after more calls, we suggested an option: bring in a working refrigerator from another room. It arrived, but not soon enough to keep our Kingfisher beers cool.

We called room service to order a pot of tea and curd (a yoghurt drink, usually slightly salted). "We have no teapots," answered the staff member. And curd? No curd. It was reminiscent of my experiences (described in *Postcards from Stanland*) of staying in Soviet-era hotels in Central Asia where surly staff ignore hotel guests and most of the items on menus are not available.

We decided to take our chances downstairs at the room with a restaurant sign on the door. It reminded me again of Central Asian hotel restaurants—high ceilings, bare fluorescent lights, torn window shades, two wall clocks stopped at different times, a few electrical wires hanging out of the walls, tables with chipped Formica tops. The chairs were those steel-framed things that are standard issue in conference rooms and allow you to gently rock back and forth. I reminded myself to ask for the name of the Nikita's interior designer.

It was too late for the "Morning Glory" breakfast, and the "Nil Grey Soup" did not sound appetizing, so we ordered vegetable pakoras and fried cashew nuts, which both turned out to be tasty. At 5:30 p.m., we were the only souls in the place. A few staff loitered near the kitchen, carefully avoiding any eye contact that might have required them to check if we needed anything. Outside in the lobby, other staff were pinning balloons to the stairs, presumably for a birthday party. A manager walked in and out, locking and unlocking doors and occasionally remonstrating with staff. We asked for the bill. The server asked for our room number. No, we want to pay now, I insisted. After more fruitless exchanges, she referred the problem to the front desk.

The next morning, the restaurant tables had been moved out and a banner hung across the windows. The Nikita was gearing up for real business—a four-day workshop, sponsored by the Ministry of Agriculture and Farmers Welfare, on "Development Cooperatives as Rural Growth Centres." As we checked out, I asked the question I'd wanted to ask all along, "Why is the hotel called Nikita?" I was hoping for a reference to Nikita Khrushchev, or Soviet influence in the Brahmaputra Valley, but I also remembered that Nikita was the name of an Elton John song and a short-lived American TV series with improbable plots about a secret agent with long and shapely legs. I got the answer I deserved. "It is named for the owner's daughter."

Boating on the Brahmaputra

At 8:20 a.m., ten minutes before its scheduled departure, the ferry from Neemati, on the south bank of the Brahmaputra near Jorhat, was already packed. The open deck area was filled with motorcycles and cars, and the shaded cabin area with passengers. We found a place for our bags, and passengers shifted to give Stephanie a seat on a bench. I moved to the rear deck, which offered a view of the river and overlooked the engine room. The engineer connected cables to two large batteries, weighed them down with bricks to prevent them from shifting, and kicked on the diesel engine. He lowered a bucket into the water and topped up the tank that cooled the engine. And then we were off downstream with the current.

The ferry was a catamaran with a wooden platform straddling two wooden cargo craft with high prows. These are the all-purpose vessels that carry building materials, gasoline, food, and other supplies up and down the Brahmaputra. Because of the river's width and the long distances between bridges, most communities depend on ferries and cargo boats. Our ferry looked seriously overcrowded, and I doubted there were enough life jackets for all the passengers. Maybe if they charged more than 20 rupees (30¢) for the trip they could buy a few more. We were thankful the water was calm; in stormy weather, it would have been a dicey crossing.

FIGURE 7.1 With few bridges over the Brahmaputra, most people travel by ferry

FIGURE 7.2 A river cargo boat moored at the *ghat* (terminal) on Majuli Island, Assam

We were on our way to Majuli Island, which at one time claimed to be the largest river island in the world. The island was formed at the point where a tributary of the Brahmaputra enters, creating a new channel; sixty miles downstream, the channels rejoin. At one time, Majuli had a total area of almost five hundred square miles, but as the river has shifted, eroding banks, it has shrunk and today is about one-third of its original size.

The Brahmaputra is sacred to Hindus, and the main attraction on Majuli are the *satras,* the monasteries where traditional Assamese arts have been practiced since the fifteenth century. With a willing driver who knew the narrow island roads, we visited the Shamaguri *satra,* famous for its mask making, and the large Dakhinpat *satra,* where more than 350 monks live and worship, the site for major Hindu festivals. Majuli's indigenous group, the Mising, are fishing people, living in bamboo houses with thatched or metal roofs raised on stilts above the marshlands. Majuli is also a nesting and feeding ground for thousands of water birds—snowy egrets, storks, kingfishers.

By late afternoon we were exhausted. It had been hot in Jorhat, but on the island the heat and humidity were almost unbearable. And we had no AC refuge. The first guest house we visited, the Bamboo Cottage, lived up to its name—six bamboo huts on stilts, reached by a precarious bamboo bridge and rickety steps. We checked out a *satra* guesthouse, a bare room with rough beds and no fan; it was probably better appointed than the rooms where the monks lived, but we were not ready for a dose of Hindu asceticism. We ended up at a small guest house in the village of Kalambari. The room was basic but clean; however, even with the ceiling fan, it was swelteringly hot. We decided to cut the trip short and left the next morning. As someone remarked to us later, "Majuli—interesting place, no facilities."

We planned to take the 8:00 a.m. ferry to Neemati, but when we arrived at the *ghat,* we were disappointed. "Assam is closed today," another passenger solemnly informed us. This seemed like a rather broad statement. On further inquiry, it emerged that the state's trade unions had called a one-day general strike or *bandh* to protest the central government's plans to auction oil leases to private companies. No commercial trucks were moving, and most public transport was off the road. We faced the prospect of another hot day on the island. We retreated to the shade of one of the food stalls that lined the dirt road to the *ghat* and had breakfast. I wandered along the litter-strewn shore where cargo boats were tied up and pigs grazed on food scraps. Our hopes were briefly raised at 10:30 when a ferry from Neemati docked. We got on board but were told to get off because there were not enough passengers to justify the trip. Eventually, the first ferry of the day left at 12:30; upstream against the current, the return journey took more than two hours, twice as long as the outbound trip.

Empire of the Ahoms

About 250 miles upstream from Saraighat, where the Ahom army threw back the Mughal invaders in 1671, lies the capital of the Ahom Empire, Sibsagar. The kingdom was established in 1228 when the first ruler, Chao Lung Siu-Ka-Pha, crossed the Paktai mountain range from what today is China's Yunnan Province with his court and an army of nine thousand. Making alliances with local ethnic groups, the Ahoms expanded their empire along the Brahmaputra valley and into the hill country, establishing a system of local administration and tax collection and introducing wet rice cultivation to the economy. The Ahom dynasty ruled Assam for almost six hundred years, despite internal rebellions and Mughal attempts to conquer the region.

The dynasty reached its zenith in the early eighteenth century when its kings displayed their power and wealth by building fortresses, palaces, and public works in Sibsagar. In the middle of town is the Sibsagar Tank, an artificial lake created in 1734 to supply water to inhabitants. A few miles outside town, the massive fortress of Talatal Ghar, built of bricks and surrounded by a moat, had two secret tunnels and three floors below ground level, later used as exit routes during wars with the Burmese. The two-storied Rang Ghar, with its roof shaped like an inverted Ahom longboat with a decorative pair of carved stone crocodiles, served as a royal sports pavilion. The king and nobles sat in the shade under its arches, looking down on an amphitheater. Sports included wrestling and cockfights, and major spectacles where water buffalo locked horns and elephants fought to the death.

By the end of the eighteenth century, the empire had been weakened by internal rebellions and rivalry among the nobility. In 1817, the Burmese invaded, and the Ahom army surrendered. The Ahom king bought a temporary peace by paying off the Burmese army and sending a prince's daughter to the king of Burma with fifty elephants and a dowry. Two more invasions followed, with most of Assam finally coming under Burmese rule in 1822. With the end of the Ahom dynasty, two expansionist empires—the Burmese and the British East India Company—faced off in the Brahmaputra valley and other areas of the northeast. The British, seeking to expand north and east of Bengal, wanted to open new trade routes and combat French influence at the Burmese court. The first Anglo-Burmese War (1824–26) ended in a decisive victory for the British, giving them control of the northeast, including Assam, and some areas of Burma.

Today, Sibsagar is a pleasant laid-back town with a lively central market. Most of its tourists come from mainland India, and the rare sight of two Westerners exploring the fortress of Talatal Ghar encouraged some to ask to have their pictures taken with us. We found an excellent hotel, the Shiva Palace. Its restaurant, the Skychef, sounded like a franchise of an airport fast food chain, but our guide book assured us that it had the best Indian and Chinese food in town. Indeed, it did. We saw no reason to eat anywhere else, although I did wonder what was on the menu at the Kremlin Hotel a few doors down. Perhaps I was still thinking about Nikita.

Scotland of the East

"Welcome to the Scotland of the East." The battered road sign on a hairpin curve on NH40 looked incongruous amid the stands of bamboo and subtropical vegetation. For a moment, I wondered if I was hallucinating. The scenery didn't look any different from that Stephanie and I had seen for the past hour as our shared taxi labored up the twisting highway into the Khasi Hills, passing villages that looked much like other villages in northeast India. No medieval castles shrouded in mist. No sweeping views of lochs and glens. No sheep (only the usual cattle and goats on the road). Not a single sprig of heather. And definitely no kilts. But I wasn't dreaming. The sign contained the imprimatur of the Meghalaya Tourism Board, so at least someone thought we were in Scotland.

We were on our way to Shillong, the capital of Meghalaya, the small, hilly state sandwiched between western Assam to the north and Bangladesh to the south. The end of the first Anglo-Burmese War in 1826 left the East India Company in control of Assam and the northeast. The company depended on the river system for transportation, with steamers from Kolkata and other ports carrying troops, supplies, merchants, and missionaries up the Brahmaputra. The company's regional administrator, David Scott, devised a plan to build a road from the plains of Bengal through the hills to the Brahmaputra to provide an alternative route that would not be affected by annual flooding. After a four-year war with the Khasi, the British took control of the hill country south of the Brahmaputra and posted a political agent to the settlement of Cherrapunjee. In 1864, the administration established a hill station at Shillong. A decade later, it became the capital of the province of Assam, and it retained its status until 1972 when it became capital of the newly created state of Meghalaya.

The "Scotland" story goes something like this (there is no official version, so I am taking literary license). Reaching the crest of a hill, the East India Company agents, weary from their journey from the sweltering lowlands, looked out through the drizzle on a landscape of grassy, treeless hills, mountain streams, and clear lakes. "Reminds me of Ben Lomond," said one. "Nay, Speyside," replied another. Either way, it looked like Scotland, or as close to Scotland as homesick, tired, and dehydrated East India Company agents could imagine. History—or at least the Meghalaya Tourist Board road sign—would have been different if those first agents had come from the Lake District, Yorkshire, Northumberland, or North Wales.

Whatever the origin of the Scotland label, it stuck. At an elevation of almost five thousand feet, the hill station of Shillong had a mild climate—cool and rainy in summer, cool and dry in winter—offering welcome relief from the searing temperatures of the lowlands. The British planted pine trees and built Victorian bungalows, churches, a polo ground, and a golf course called Gleneagles. For half a century, Shillong resembled a transplanted British country town. Then India crowded in. Today, with a population of 150,000, Shillong is (by Indian standards) a large town; its suburbs, sprawling across the hills, add another 200,000 to the metropolitan area. Khasis make up most of the population, with other northeastern tribes represented, as well as Assamese, Bengalis, and migrants from mainland India.

The Christian Hills

"Smile—Jesus Loves You." The sign with a cross hung over a metal fabrication shop in Jorabat, the crossroads town where NH40 to Shillong branches off from NH37, which follows the south bank of the Brahmaputra from Guwahati toward Tezpur, Jorhat, and eastern Assam. The sign was the first indication that we had reached a predominantly Christian region of the northeast. We had arrived on an early morning bus from Tezpur and planned to pick up a shared taxi to Shillong. We squeezed into the backseat of a high-riding Mahindra Maxx with another passenger, our suitcases strapped to the roof. In the middle row sat four young men. There were three in the front seat until a backup driver joined them, sitting across the driver's lap. We stopped to pick up another passenger. He would have had to join us on the backseat. One passenger in the front turned around. "The driver wants to know if you'll pay for three seats. It's not expensive." He was polite enough not to comment on the size of our butts. We agreed. For $3 more, it was worth upgrading to Economy Comfort for the two-and-a-half-hour trip.

"I'm an evangelical and I work for a faith-based NGO," the front-seat passenger Mango (he said his full name was too long for us to pronounce) told us. Over lunch in Shillong, where he helped us fend off the taxi touts and carried one of our suitcases, he explained that his work had become more difficult since the Hindu nationalist party (the BJP) had come to power. There was no outright religious discrimination, of course. Just more bureaucratic regulations on NGOs, questions about their foreign funding sources, new registration requirements, permit delays. Niggling problems that made it more difficult to offer the social services that the central and state governments were not providing.

I'd met a Christian from Meghalaya three weeks earlier at Delhi's domestic terminal as we waited for the flight to Guwahati. He was a young engineer going home to Shillong to visit his parents. "I'm a Presbyterian," he told me. "Most people in Shillong are. Well, I suppose we do have a few Anglicans too." He did not mention Catholics.

Protestant and French Catholic missionaries had followed the colonial administrators into the hill country and found willing converts among the tribes—the Khasi, the Jaintia, and the Garo—many of whom mixed Christianity with traditional beliefs. About half the population of Meghalaya, and two-thirds of Shillong, listed themselves as Christian on the 2011 census. Not surprisingly for the "Scotland of the East," Presbyterians form the largest denomination; they built sturdy stone and timber churches in Shillong and other towns. Immigrants from Assam and mainland India have recently led to a resurgence of Hinduism, with about one in four in Shillong listing it as their religion.

The Presbyterians win in the numbers game, but it's the Catholics who win the architectural prize for the Cathedral of Mary Help of Christians, situated on a hill a mile south of the center of Shillong. It is the principal place of worship for the Shillong Archdiocese, which has thirty-three parishes and an estimated three hundred thousand adherents. The cathedral stands out not only because of its art deco style but because of its color—a striking shade of blue, which also brands the schools, social service centers, and shrine around the cathedral—and its foundation. Or rather, lack of foundation. Because the Shillong region is prone to earthquakes, the church was built on trenches filled with sand and has no direct connection with the rock. Theoretically, during an earthquake, the building can shift safely on the shock-absorbing sand.

We visited the cathedral with Ratul Baruah, the news editor of the English-language *Meghalaya Guardian,* whom I had met on the flight from Delhi to Guwahati. With its high arches and long stained-glass windows, the cathedral has been described as modern Gothic. By Catholic standards, its interior seemed uncluttered, with just a few large paintings and banners. The banners, explained Ratul, were in the Khasi language, indicating how the missionaries had adapted their religion to local sensibilities.

After the visit, Ratul took us for lunch at a restaurant owned by his friend, Raphael, an artist and local TV station owner. We talked about the vibrant local media scene; in addition to Ratul's newspaper, three other English-language weeklies and newspapers in indigenous languages—Khasi, Jaintia, and Garo—circulate in Meghalaya. I told Raphael I was curious about his name. "Well, I have a Khasi name," he told me, "but my family is Catholic, so my mother had to give me a Christian name. Don't you think Raphael is a pretty good name for an artist?"

The Wettest Place in the World

"Anything we need to bring on the trip?" The agent at the Meghalaya Tourist Board office in Shillong looked up from her ledger and smiled. It must have been a familiar question. "I'd recommend umbrellas," she said matter-of-factly.

We had booked a day trip to the must-see destination of Cherrapunjee, an area of scenic waterfalls and caves about a two-hour drive south from Shillong near the border with Bangladesh. At 400 rupees ($6 each) it was a bargain. We could have paid more and hired a car, but we prefer traveling with other people. It was raining hard when we left the hotel. I was thinking that the "Scotland of the East" label had as much to do with the weather as with the scenery. Technically, Shillong has a subtropical highland climate; in practice, that means that during the monsoon season, it rains most days. And some days it rains most of the day. Not the persistent drizzle I remember from hikes in the Lake District, Pennines, and Yorkshire Moors, but a steady downpour.

We were the first to board the thirty-seat bus and did not notice that our tickets had seat numbers. Other tourists—mostly from Delhi and Kolkata—got on and chose their places. As the bus filled, new arrivals started demanding their assigned seats. The young tour guide who had shown up late was not having much success mediating the seat disputes. People jammed into the narrow aisle or climbed over seats as everyone moved to their assigned places. Eventually, everyone was seated, if not happily. The seating disputes delayed our departure by almost half an hour, and the guide warned us we would have less time at the still-undisclosed number of stops. I wiped the condensation off the window and peered out into the driving rain, wondering if all the seating fuss was worth it because no one could see much anyway. As we left the outskirts of Shillong, the mist thickened, further obscuring visibility. The road wound through low, grassy hills, with rice paddies in the valleys and terraced rows of tea plants on the hillsides; in places the hills were gouged open for sand, gravel, and rock quarries. We passed small churches, with cemeteries on hilltops.

Our first stop was at a waterfall. "Just ten minutes, please," the guide said. Stephanie and I surveyed the mist-filled valley and the treacherous, slippery steps descending to the viewing platform and decided to have a cup of tea instead. We crossed the road to the small "hotel" and claimed a wooden bench. The guide had ordered his breakfast of eggs and Maggi noodles. The other tourists wandered in later, many of them ordering food. The ten-minute stop lasted almost an hour.

At our next stop—an ecological park where one waterfall begins its deep plunge—the rain had, if anything, intensified. We almost waded out to the viewing terrace and looked down to see not mist but clouds, with the occasional glimpse of the green valley below. Back on the bus, tension was rising. The guide was describing the sights in English, angering two passengers who insisted he speak in Bengali. "It is the official policy to speak in English," said the guide, who made no attempt to disguise his contempt for the request. Fortunately for him, passengers came to his defense, pointing out that they were Hindi speakers and did not understand Bengali.

We passed through the small town of Cherrapunjee, where the East India political agent had first set up shop, a straggle of houses and commercial buildings clinging to the slopes. In the Khasi language, the settlement was called Sohra; the British called it "Churra," which may have been how it sounded to them, and eventually it became Cherrapunjee. Today, its main claim to fame is that it is the wettest place in the world, holding the record for the most rainfall in one month (370 inches in July 1861) and in a year (1,042 inches between August 1, 1860, and July 31, 1861). That proved to be too much for even the rain-resistant British administrators, which is why they decamped to the balmier climes of Shillong a couple of years later. Cherrapunjee's claims are hotly disputed by a nearby Khasi village, Mawsynram, which receives an average of 467 inches a year and got 1,000 inches dumped on it in 1985. "It used to rain every day," a fellow passenger told me. "Now there are some dry days in December and January. Climate change, I suppose." Despite all the rain, both places face an acute water shortage and the inhabitants often trek long distances to obtain potable water.

Our next stop, near the rainy village of Mawsynram, was the Mawsmai cave, known for its impressive stalagmites and stalactites. I made it about as far as most of the tourists—the first chamber. The passage ahead was narrow and under several inches of water. My feet were already wet. I figured I'd buy a postcard instead and went back to the bus.

At the final stop the rain had eased and we looked out toward Nohkalikai Falls, at 1,115 feet (340 meters) the highest plunge waterfall in India, and reportedly the sixth highest in the world. The name in the Khasi language means "jump of Ka Likai." According to legend, a poor woman named Ka Likai struggled to take care of her infant daughter after her husband's death. She was forced to remarry, and her jealous new husband killed and cooked up the daughter. Returning from work as a porter, Ka Likai unknowingly ate the meat and then discovered a severed finger. Distraught, she flung herself over the cliff to her death.

As usual, mist and clouds blocked the view. Then a breeze moved through the valley, breaking the clouds. And suddenly there it was, the majestic Nohkalikai, plunging into a green pool below. Cameras clicked before the clouds moved in again.

The sun came out in midafternoon as the bus topped a ridge. There below us lay the plains of northern Bangladesh. Or rather the sea of northern Bangladesh. Rivers flowing south from the hills of Meghalaya and the state of Manipur, combined with the Barak of South Assam, converge in the Surma River. A few weeks into monsoon season, it was already out of its banks, flooding farmland and washing out bridges.

A Linguistic Hodgepodge

On our last day in Shillong, we visited the Museum for Indigenous Cultures named for Don Bosco, the Catholic priest and educator whose Salesian Order accepted the pope's request to take over the church's Assam mission in the 1920s. The museum houses eight floors of well-displayed and interpreted exhibits on every aspect of culture and society in northeast India—agriculture, fishing, domestic industry, indigenous technology, warfare, and religion (a predictable emphasis on Catholicism, with the Presbyterians as a footnote).

I lingered in the linguistics gallery where the language families of Asia, India, and the northeast were meticulously charted. What was the origin of the local language, Khasi? Well, it's in the second branch of Austro-Asiatic languages in the Mon Khmer group, which includes Khmer, Vietnamese, Malaya, and Nicobarese. It's several steps from Mon Khmer to Khasi, which itself has five dialects—War, Bhoi, Pnar, Khyrian, and Lyngngam. Are you following this? Let's move on to the lineage of the Garo language, spoken in western Meghalaya, which is from the Sino-Tibetan group. Here's the family tree: Tibeto-Myanmar > Jingpho > Konyak > Bodo > Konyak-Bodo-Garo > Garo. Both are different from the widely spoken Assamese and Bengali, which are, like Hindi, Indo-Aryan languages.

I counted thirty-nine languages on the chart for the northeast. Many are struggling to survive. Two of my Tezpur workshop participants from Manipur had given me a collection of short stories translated into English from Manipuri, an Indo-Aryan language. Driven from their homelands by Burmese invasions and political unrest, Manipuri speakers scattered across the region and struggled to retain their ethnic identity and language. Virtually extinct at the end of the nineteenth century, Manipuri has made a comeback and is now spoken by perhaps half a million people. I started reading the book as we waited in our hotel room in Shillong for the rain to stop. The title of the first story, "Seducing the Rain God," seemed ironically appropriate. In the Scotland of the East, no seduction is needed.

eight

Joy Bangla (Victory to Bengal)

"I lost my father. I lost my sister. How do you expect me to forget? Is it even possible for me to forget? For me, it's still real."

Museum guide Mitua Momataj paused while my colleague Suruchi Sood translated. For a moment, Suruchi wondered if she had misunderstood the Bangla (Bengali). How could this woman, born at least a decade after Bangladesh's Liberation War of 1971, have lost her father?

Then it became clear. "She's not talking about herself," said Suruchi. "She's talking about the sentiment that's still in people's hearts. For them, the war isn't something that happened almost half a century ago. It's yesterday."

Standing in a gallery of Bangladesh's new Liberation War Museum, surrounded by photos and testimonies of victims and *mukti bahini* (freedom fighters), it's easy to understand why the violent and bitter struggle for independence from Pakistan is still widely discussed and memorialized today.

Depending on which source you accept, as many as three million Bangladeshis lost their lives in the nine-month conflict. Ten million fled to refugee camps in India. Pakistan's army, backed by hardline clerics who declared that it was fighting a righteous war to defend Islam, used religion to justify rape, torture, and murder. It ruthlessly targeted the minority Hindu population, particularly in Dhaka. To destroy the leadership of the independence movement, it singled out professionals—politicians, academics, journalists, writers, artists, and musicians—for imprisonment, torture, and summary execution. The war left the country's economy in shambles.

The museum in the sprawling district of Agargaon in northwest Dhaka was opened by the prime minister, Sheikh Hasina, daughter of the charismatic leader of the independence movement, Sheikh Mujibur Rahman, in April 2017. The former museum, located in an old but graceful nineteenth-century house in Old Dhaka, had ambience, but not enough exhibit space and no parking. The new concrete colossus has large, well-lit, air-conditioned galleries and research facilities for scholars. Most days of the week, it is crowded with schoolchildren, bussed in from the suburbs.

Momataj, a postgraduate history student who has worked as an archivist and guide for the museum for more than a decade, believes children need to understand the conflict that created and defines their country. "I would not be able to love my country if I did not know where I came from, I could not be a good citizen," she said.

I asked her how she felt about Pakistan. "We get a few Pakistani visitors and this all comes as a huge shock to them," she said. "They have no idea that their country or their countrymen were involved in something like this."

Most Pakistanis, I reminded her, took no part in the war because, like her, they were born after it.

"I don't have strongly negative feelings, but I'm also not neutral," she said. She related the story of how Pakistani soldiers, searching for a *mukti bahini,* bayoneted his four-month-old child and threw the body into the road. "When you know they have done things like that you can't forgive them. The stories of what people experienced have been passed on through their children so it's not history to them, it's current."

You cannot begin to understand Bangladesh, its politics, society, or culture, without recognizing how the struggle for independence figures into collective memory. Beside every poster of the prime minister Sheikh Hasina, striking her stock pose of maternal benevolence, is an image of her father, Sheikh Mujibur Rahman, popularly known as *Bangabandhu* (friend of Bengal), looking cerebral and statesmanlike with his slicked-back hair and thick glasses. He became the independent country's first president but was assassinated, along with members of his family, in a 1975 coup led by army officers.

In public speeches, Sheikh Hasina, her ministers, and members of the ruling Awami League frequently refer to the liberation struggle. Memorials to the martyrs of 1971 and the earlier language movement that stirred nationalist feelings are under construction in schools and public places all over the country. Advocates for social and economic reforms reference the struggle in arguments that go something like this: "What would those who fought and died for our independence have said about Dhaka's traffic congestion? About factory waste polluting our streams? About election-rigging? About Hindi and English words corrupting the Bangla language?" Academics and social commentators publish lengthy opinion pieces on the legacy of the conflict in newspapers and magazines. Some include the war cry of the *mukti bahini*, "Joy Bangla" (Victory to Bengal), or the year 1971 in their e-mail signature line.

Not all Bangladeshis supported independence. Some joined paramilitary groups, the *razakars*, that fought alongside the Pakistani military. In Arabic and Urdu, *razakar* means "volunteer." In Bangladesh, it has become a pejorative term meaning "traitor." Others, members of the innocuous-sounding Peace Committees, collaborated, providing the military with support and supplies and spying on neighbors with suspected pro-independence tendencies.

For almost forty years, the authorities left *razakars* and collaborators pretty much alone, to the chagrin of those who knew what they had done. Finally, in 2009, the government of Sheikh Hasina established the International Crimes Tribunal (ICT) to try some of the sixteen hundred suspects identified by a fact-finding committee. Some, including members of the opposition, the Bangladesh Nationalist Party (BNP), and its ally, Jamaat-e-Islami, the largest Islamist party, have been executed. Every week, the press reports the roundup of more suspects, most of them now in their seventies and eighties. Campaigners want the government and international community to classify the 1971 war as a genocide. As Dhaka University history professor and war crimes trial campaigner Muntassir Mamoon put it, "It is disgraceful that the country observes a day for handwashing, while it is yet to dedicate a day for the genocide victims."[1]

In official circles, any favorable comment on Pakistan is viewed as subversive. In August 2017, the chief justice, Surendra Kumar Sinha, a

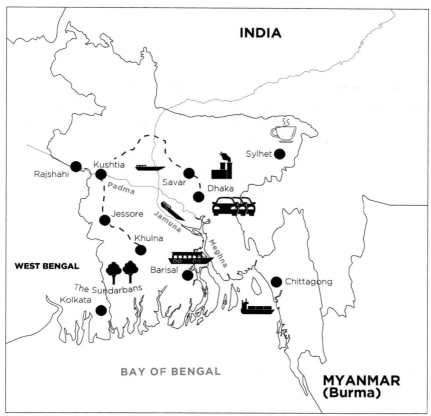

MAP 8.1 Bangladesh (map by Belén Marco Crespo)

Hindu, pointedly criticized political interference in the judicial system by congratulating his counterparts in Pakistan's supreme court for quickly removing from office Prime Minister Nawaz Sharif, who faced corruption charges. The response was immediate and virulent. "We can tolerate a lot of things, but not comparisons to Pakistan," Sheikh Hasina told a rally. Awami League leaders called for the chief justice's resignation. "If you have love and sympathy for Pakistan, you should go to Pakistan," said one.[2]

The Failure of Religious Partition

With historical hindsight, the decision to carve up British India into two countries along religious lines seems fatally flawed. The Muslims of what became East Pakistan shared language, ethnicity, and culture with the Hindus of what became the Indian state of West Bengal. Over time, the ties that bound proved to be stronger than religion.

For almost two centuries, since Colonel Robert Clive's East India Company army retook Calcutta from the Nawab of Bengal, Siraj-uh-Daulah, and then defeated his army at the 1757 Battle of Plassey, Britain had drained Bengal's wealth. Landowners and tenant farmers paid heavy taxes. British-made goods, supported by subsidies and low customs duties, flooded the market. Dhaka, once the center of the Mughal textile industry, faded in importance.

Agitation for Bengali independence grew in the second half of the nineteenth century, particularly among the Hindu intellectual class in Calcutta, the political and commercial capital of British India. The Bengal Renaissance, with its ideas of liberalism, democracy, science, and education, produced writers, musicians, and artists who challenged colonial political and economic power. Most of the economy was controlled from Calcutta by Hindu factory owners, merchants, and *zamindars* (landlord tax collectors); the Muslim-majority east was poorer and less developed, a source of food and raw materials for the west.

In 1905, the viceroy, Lord Curzon, announced that Bengal was to be divided into two provinces along religious lines. The official reason was that the region, which included Assam and parts of Bihar and Orissa, was too large to govern effectively, but the real motive was political—to suppress the nascent independence movement in the west. Muslims in the east resented Hindu economic dominance and hoped that creating a separate province would lead to spending on roads and railways, industrial development, and improved education. The policy of divide-and-rule gave new impetus to India's Swadeshi movement that encouraged domestic production and the boycott of foreign, especially British, goods as a first step toward political independence. The partition decision was reversed six years later. The British left in a huff, moving their capital to Delhi. Bengal became a backwater of empire.

The 1905 partition may have failed, but it set the stage for the eventual division of British India along religious lines. After World War II, Bengali nationalists called for the creation of an independent, united Bengal. "Let us pause for a moment to consider what Bengal can be if it remains united," wrote Shaheed Suhrawardy, the last prime minister of Bengal under the British, in April 1947. "It will be a great country, indeed the richest and the most prosperous in India capable of giving to its people a high standard of living. . . . It will be rich in agriculture, rich in industry and commerce and in course of time it will be one of the powerful and progressive states of the world. If Bengal remains united this will be no dream, no fantasy."[3]

The forces for division proved stronger than the dreams of unity. In the year leading up to partition, Bengal saw some of the worst communal violence anywhere in the country. In October 1946, gangs went on an anti-Hindu rampage in the southeast; at least five thousand Hindus were killed, hundreds of women raped, and thousands forcibly converted to Islam. Hindus fled to relief camps while some who remained had to obtain permits from Muslim leaders to travel outside their villages. Gandhi spent several months walking barefoot from village to village, trying to restore communal harmony, but his mission failed, and most survivors migrated to India. Partition by religion seemed inevitable. On August 15, 1947, East Pakistan was created, with borders similar to those drawn in 1905.

From the beginning, the bifurcated country of Pakistan was difficult to govern. The challenge was not only that its two parts were separated by more than one thousand miles of India. From the early 1950s, power began shifting from the elected National Assembly and prime minister to the president, and then to two military dictators who ruled from 1958 to 1971. East Pakistan politicians whose parties gained enough seats in the assembly to form a government were quickly deposed. Despite having a slightly larger population than West Pakistan, East Pakistan regularly received only 40 percent of the government budget. Bengalis were underrepresented in the military, with few in command positions. The balance of power was firmly tilted in favor of West Pakistan; however, the breaking point came over language.

Bangla is the sixth most widely spoken language in the world, with an estimated 250 million native speakers. Although derived from Sanskrit, and with close links to Hindi, modern Bangla has been influenced by many other languages, including Arabic and English—the result of centuries of trade and cultural contacts. The nineteenth-century Bengal Renaissance gave Bangla a rich literary tradition. Language and identity were closely related.

In 1948, Pakistan's leader, Muhammad Ali Jinnah, declared that "Urdu, and only Urdu" would be the language of Pakistan. Because Pakistan was an Islamic state and most religious literature was in Urdu, he argued that making it the official language would preserve Islamic culture. Opponents pointed out that no language had a special status in Islam, and there was no bar against Bangla becoming the official language of an Islamic state. Jinnah's decree stood, and the Bengali script was removed from currency and stamps. Protests erupted in East Pakistan, and on February 21, 1952, police fired on Dhaka University students, killing twelve. The victims are commemorated in *Shahid Minars* (Martyr monuments) throughout the country and in the annual *Amar Ekushey* (Our twenty-first) tributes. The killings stirred nationalist sentiments. In 1956, the government relented, declaring Bangla a second national language, but the policy reversal only emboldened East Pakistan nationalist politicians.

Every House a Fortress

In 1970, East Pakistan's leading political party, the Awami League, led by Sheikh Mujibur Rahman, won a majority in the National Assembly, giving it the constitutional right to form a government with Rahman as prime minister. The political establishment reacted by dissolving the assembly's first session. In early March 1971, President Yahya Khan, Zulfikar Ali Bhutto, leader of the Pakistan People's Party, and other West Pakistan political leaders met Rahman and Awami League leaders in Dhaka, ostensibly to discuss power sharing and to grant more autonomy to East Pakistan. Meanwhile, Pakistan's military secretly prepared for action.

On March 7, Rahman addressed a crowd estimated at two million people at Dhaka's Ramna horse racecourse. He called for an end to martial law and for troops to return to their barracks. In the tradition of Gandhi, he proposed a campaign of civil disobedience, calling for "every house to turn into a fortress." He asked people to stay away from work, schools, and universities, to refuse to pay taxes, and to take their protests to the streets.

Black-and-white film footage of the twenty-minute speech runs on a loop in the Liberation War Museum. The display includes a transcript, a 45-rpm disc recording of the speech, and press reports. Rahman concluded with a de facto declaration of independence: "Our struggle, this time, is a struggle for our freedom. Our struggle, this time, is a struggle for our independence. Joy Bangla! [Victory to Bengal]"

Rahman's call for passive resistance was heeded throughout the country. Government offices were closed. Dockworkers in Chittagong refused to unload a Pakistan navy ship carrying military supplies. A unit of the East Pakistan Rifles refused to fire on demonstrators. Rahman still hoped a settlement could be reached, but on the night of March 25, the Pakistan Army struck.

Operation Searchlight

At the Liberation War Museum, you step from the well-lit display of Rahman's March 7 racecourse speech to a dimly lit area illuminated only by the headlights of an army jeep. A tree branch blocks a passageway. The soundtrack—muffled voices, gunshots—is ominous.

On the night of March 25, units from the Pakistan Army launched Operation Searchlight—coordinated attacks to crush military and political resistance and take control of major cities. Politicians, journalists, writers, artists, and other members of the intelligentsia were rounded up and executed or imprisoned. Bengali soldiers were disarmed, and some killed. Police stations were attacked, and newspaper offices burned to the ground. The central *Shahid Minar*, symbol of the language movement, was blown up. Hindu neighborhoods in Dhaka were shelled and temples destroyed. At Dhaka University, the army targeted the residence halls. The display features a chilling radio exchange between army headquarters and the field unit:

> HQ: Highest control wants to know as to what type of opposition has been faced in areas of Jagannath, Iqbal, and Niakhut [university residence halls], over.

> UNIT: Initially a lot of fire was received from Jagannath and Iqbal Halls, roger, over.

> HQ: What do you think would be the approximate number of casualties at the university? Just give me an approximate number in your view. What would be the number killed or wounded or captured? Just give me a rough figure, over.

> Unit: Wait. Approximately three hundred, over.

> HQ: Well done. Three hundred killed? Or anybody wounded, captured, over.

UNIT: I believe only in one thing. Three hundred killed, over.

HQ: Yes, once again I would like to give you *shabash* [well done] to all the boys for wonderful job done in this area. I am very pleased, over.

Film secretly taken by an engineering professor who lived opposite the residence halls documented the slaughter. At dawn, eyewitnesses found the halls and courtyards littered with corpses. Jagannath, the only Hindu residence hall, was destroyed and six hundred to seven hundred of its students killed.

Estimates of the number killed that night vary widely, but most historians put the death toll in Dhaka at five thousand to seven thousand. By systematically targeting the intelligentsia, the Pakistan military hoped to remove the leadership of the resistance movement. Bhutto, who had taken part in the talks with Rahman, returned to Karachi to tell the media, "Thank God, Pakistan has been saved." Shortly before he was arrested and flown to West Pakistan to await trial, Rahman declared independence on government radio:

> This may be my last message, from today Bangladesh is independent. I call upon the people of Bangladesh wherever you might be and with whatever you have, to resist the army of occupation to the last. Your fight must go on until the last soldier of the Pakistan occupation army is expelled from the soil of Bangladesh and final victory is achieved.[4]

The broadcast had limited reach and few people heard the announcement. The next day, a telegram with the text of the announcement was received by students in Chittagong. Translated into Bangla, it was read over the air by army major Ziaur Rahman, whose forces had taken over a radio transmitter. The broadcast was picked up by a Japanese ship in the Bay of Bengal and later retransmitted by Radio Australia and the BBC.

More than two hundred foreign journalists were in Dhaka, covering the talks and the resistance movement. Hours before Operation Searchlight was launched, they were herded into the Intercontinental Hotel. They could see flames rising from Dhaka University, a mile and a half away, but they were not allowed to leave the hotel. The next day, they were taken to the airport and flown out.

Three managed to evade their minders. Simon Dring of the *Daily Telegraph* hid in the hotel's laundry, kitchen, and rooftop for thirty-two hours until the curfew was lifted on March 27. He visited the university, government buildings, and Hindu neighborhoods. His report, filed from Bangkok, gained worldwide attention:

> In the name of "God and a united Pakistan," Dacca is today a crushed and frightened city. After 24 hours of ruthless, cold-blooded shelling by the Pakistan Army, as many as 7,000 people are dead, large areas have been levelled and East Pakistan's fight for independence has been put to an end. Despite claims by President Yahya Khan, head of the country's military government, that the situation is now calm, tens of thousands of people are fleeing to the countryside, the city streets are almost deserted, and the killings are still going on in other parts of the province. . . . Only the horror of the military action can be properly gauged—the students dead in their beds, the butchers in the markets killed behind their stalls, the women and children roasted alive in their houses, the Pakistanis of Hindu religion taken out and shot en masse, the bazaars and shopping areas razed by fire.[5]

Pakistan's leaders expected Operation Searchlight, the arrest of Rahman and other political leaders, the banning of the Awami League, and the disarming and killing of Bengali military personnel to crush the revolution. "Kill three million of them and the rest will eat out of our hands," President Yahya Khan is reported to have told his military top brass.[6] He was wrong. On April 4, senior army officers met in Sylhet in the northeast to divide the country into military zones, with General Muhammad Ataul Ghani Osmani as commander-in-chief. Bengali soldiers defected to the new Bangladesh army, taking their arms with them. On April 17, political leaders who had escaped Operation Searchlight set up camp in Meherpur, a remote village near the western border with India, declared a provisional government, and began radio broadcasts. They later moved, as a government-in-exile, to Calcutta. As millions of refugees, Hindu and Muslim, poured across the border—to West Bengal, Assam in the north, and Tripura in the east—India faced a massive refugee crisis. Bands of *mukti bahini* guerrillas, at first acting independently but later under military command, attacked army units and bases, power plants, bridges, and railroads. Many received arms and training across the border, as India secretly aided the independence struggle.

Until recently, the story of India's support of clandestine operations in East Pakistan went largely untold. All records of the training and arms supply of the *mukti bahini* were classified, and military officers who supervised it were prohibited by India's Official Secrets Act from talking about their experiences. With most records now declassified, historians are now able to trace how India's secret support sustained the resistance movement.

On my third trip to Bangladesh in August 2017, my UNICEF colleague Neha Kapil invited me to her apartment in Dhaka for dinner. "My dad's just arrived from Delhi. Retired from the navy. I think you'd like to meet him. He's here on a research trip to interview Operation Jackpot veterans for an upcoming book."

Operation Jackpot

In March 1971, as the political crisis intensified in East Pakistan, India's Western Naval Command headquarters in Bombay buzzed with speculation. Since partition, India and Pakistan had fought two wars—the most recent in 1965—over the disputed territories of Jammu and Kashmir. Tensions were high. Would the Pakistan navy launch a preemptive strike to prevent India from helping the Bangladeshis? How could the navy prepare to defend Bombay's naval dockyard and commercial harbor? Naval lieutenant Vijai Kapil, the twenty-nine-year-old commander of the fleet diving team, had a lot on his mind.[7]

More than four thousand miles away, another group of seamen was anxiously following events. Pakistan's French-built Daphné-class submarine, the *Mangro*, was being readied for sea duty at the Mediterranean port of Toulon. When they heard of Sheikh Mujibur Rahman's declaration of independence, eight Bangladeshi submariners came up with a risky escape plan. They knew that if they were caught, they would be flown to Pakistan, tried as deserters, and likely executed.

Radio operator A.W. Chowdury, who had the code for the combination lock of the captain's safe, quietly removed the group's passports. The eight slipped ashore, crossed the Spanish border, and reached Madrid, where they asked the Indian embassy for political asylum. The embassy informed the Indian Research and Analysis Wing (RAW),[8]

FIGURE 8.1 Vijai Kapil (*back row, second from left*) on a Royal Navy training course at Portsmouth (UK) in 1969. The group includes three Indian Navy colleagues and three from Pakistan.

which arranged for them to fly via Geneva to Delhi for debriefing by Indian naval intelligence. Kapil's naval classmate and fellow diving officer, Lieutenant Samir Das, was flown in from the naval base at Cochin in southern India. As a Bengali, he could not only interpret but build trust with the submariners.

The eight brought special skills in underwater warfare. Naval intelligence wondered if they could be trained as specialized divers to attack Pakistani shipping. From Delhi, they were flown to Eastern Command's naval base at Kolkata.

Kapil received orders to join Das. He knew the mission must be important because at that time the Indian Navy had an acute shortage of diving officers.

"All clandestine operations were under heavy wraps," he told me after dinner at Neha's. "India was not yet at war with Pakistan, and if it leaked out that we were helping the *mukti bahini* it would have caused a major international incident. This was all done by naval intelligence. Even the navy did not know what was happening."

Kapil and Das realized they did not have enough time to train the submariners in underwater sabotage. "It's highly specialized," said Kapil. "You need dedicated equipment and a lot of training, and there's the danger of underwater sickness. Unless a diver is fully trained, it's very risky." Instead, they recommended that the eight lead groups of naval commandos in surface sabotage against Pakistani merchant shipping.

From early April, the Indian army set up secret training bases for *mukti bahini* across its long border with Bangladesh. For naval commando training, Kapil and Das had to find a secluded riverside location with water conditions similar to those the commandos would encounter on inland shipping channels.

"Secrecy was of the utmost importance, so we needed the camp to be out of sight," said Kapil. "Not even our families knew where we were." Together, they explored the Indian portion of the Sundarbans, the vast mangrove forest delta region on the Bay of Bengal shared by India and Bangladesh.

"One day we came to a place on the Bhagirathi, a channel of the Ganges," said Kapil. "I looked at Das and he looked at me. We said, 'This is it.' Here, the channel was broad, with moderate to strong currents—the right training conditions."

It was here, on marshland about ninety miles north of Kolkata, that the fate of Bengal had been sealed more than two hundred years earlier. The camp was on the site of the 1757 Battle of Plassey, where Clive had routed the forces of the Nawab of Bengal, securing Britain's control of the region. Was Plassey again going to change the course of history?

An abandoned sugar mill provided a secluded storage area for the camp's transport and equipment. Kapil, who had joined the navy just one week before Das, was rewarded for his marginal seniority by being made the temporary commandant of Camp C2P, the "P" for Plassey. Together, they devised a training plan. "We knew scuba diving would not work, because it leaves a trail of bubbles," said Kapil. "We settled on camouflaged swimming. The commando floats downstream under vegetation or debris, breathing through a bamboo or papaya reed. We needed to train the boys to be good swimmers, to build up their endurance. And how to handle explosives, including making improvised devices."

While Kapil and Das set up the camp, the Indian Army, working with the *mukti bahini*, scouted potential recruits from refugee camps. Kapil and Das needed an ethnic mix, recruits from all over the country who spoke local dialects. "Guerrillas have to melt into the crowd, they have to escape after the attack," said Kapil. "We needed men from the region, with local knowledge and contacts. We looked at their motivation level, their physical strength, and their educational background. When you're handling explosives, you need a certain level of comprehension."

Most of those selected were fifteen to twenty years old. Some were college students—a group the Pakistani army had targeted in Operation Searchlight. "They were really fired up," said Kapil. "They had faced atrocities. They had seen their mothers and sisters being ill-treated and raped. They were young, dedicated to the cause." By the end of April, about one hundred were being trained, with new recruits arriving each week. By late September, when training began to wind down, more than five hundred commandos had been prepared.

Obtaining equipment was a challenge. India depended on the British Royal Navy for swimming gear. Placing an order for several hundred sets of fins and goggles would have raised suspicions. Kapil and Das looked up a retired navy diving officer who had opened a small factory in Calcutta. "We said we need the gear now, price no problem," said Kapil. "It has to be good quality so don't cut corners on rubbers and molds."

Munitions—the limpet mines to attach to ships—proved a greater obstacle. Again, Kapil and Das could not go through naval supply and procurement channels and issue a public tender on the world market, not only because questions would be asked, but because India lacked foreign exchange. Naval armaments experts managed to develop a rudimentary limpet mine, but it lacked a key component—the clockwork mechanism that sets a time delay for detonation.

"Then someone had a bright idea," Kapil recalled. "Why not put in soluble plugs, the kind used in depth charges to attack submarines?" That presented a new timing problem. The plug begins to dissolve on contact with water. How could the commando swim downstream for at least one hour to reach his target without the mine exploding and killing him?

"We needed a sheath for the plug—one that could be removed after arming the mine and attaching it to the hull of the ship," said Kapil. The solution was simple, cheap and readily available—a condom. No one would ask a young, healthy man who walked into a village pharmacy to buy a pack of condoms how he was going to use them. The low-tech limpet mine, fitted with a plug that dissolved in thirty to forty minutes and a removable condom sheath, went into production.

At the camp, training began at 6:00 a.m. and often ended at 10:00 p.m. The training team led by Kapil and Das consisted of seven Indian Navy divers, with the eight *Mangro* submariners and the best recruits serving as assistant trainers. General Osmani and his Indian liaison made secret visits to the camp to talk about the independence struggle and motivate the men. They were given meat and eggs in addition to the normal diet of fish and rice. In this isolated location, living in tents through the monsoon, eating the same food and fighting off the same mosquitoes, customary distinctions between officers and men began to melt away. The recruits, said Kapil, felt free to talk with their trainers about their experiences. "The boys had seen horrible things, and were emotional," said Kapil, "so we had to instill discipline and the camaraderie that is so important in guerrilla training."

By the end of July, the commandos were ready for operations. Indian army and navy commands, working with Bangladesh's regular army, *mukti bahini* commanders, and the Bangladesh government-in-exile, selected the night of August 15–16 to deal a psychological blow to the Pakistani forces. Symbolically, it came on India's independence day, and one day after Pakistan celebrated its independence. It was called Operation Jackpot.[9]

The targets were the ports on which the Pakistan Army depended for supplies of oil, military hardware, and food: Chittagong, on the Bay of Bengal, and ports on the inland waterway system—Chalna in the southwest, Naryanganj near Dhaka, and Chandpur and Barisal in the south. "The element of surprise was crucial," said Kapil. "The operation had to be coordinated precisely so that the attacks took place at about the same time, because once the Pakistanis were alerted, the chances of success were lessened."

Groups of commandos, some led by *Mangro* submariners, were deployed to different regions and told to wait for the signal to travel to their targets. Each man, dressed in a traditional *lungi* (loin cloth), was equipped with fins, goggles, a limpet mine, a knife, a grenade, Pakistani cash, and a fake certificate of residence for a village in the region; around his waist, he strapped plastic explosives. Each group had one submachine gun and a transistor radio.

The radio was essential. The groups could not use bulky radio transmitters and receivers, and walkie-talkies were restricted to line of sight. Instead, the time-tested radio broadcast—the kind that alerted French resistance fighters to operations and parachute drops in World War

II—was used. At an appointed time, All India Radio (AIR) in Calcutta, which reached western and central Bangladesh, played Bengali songs in a specific sequence; the broadcast was relayed by AIR in Guwahati (Assam) to northern, eastern, and southern parts of the country, including Chittagong. This was the signal to travel toward the target.

The journey—always at night, on foot, and by boat—took four to five days, with local guides and a network of safe havens where the commandos rested during the daytime. After a second sequence of songs on AIR, the groups moved into position. At the port, the group commander surveyed the shipping and selected targets.

A limpet mine typically weighs about 2.5 kilograms and contains 2 kilograms of explosive. "To pack a bigger punch, ours had more explosive and weighed up to four kilograms," said Kapil. The added weight reduced buoyancy, so styrofoam pads were attached, which reduced the weight in water to under half a kilogram, making it easier for a commando to swim with a mine tied to his waist. Working in pairs, the commandos floated downstream under vegetation and debris to attach the limpets to ships' hulls.

Although several large cargo ships at the port of Chittagong were sunk, most of the targets were smaller freighters and barges—from eight hundred to twenty-five hundred metric tons—that operated on the inland waterways system. "We did not go for high-value targets because they were heavily guarded, and the commandos were more likely to get caught," said Kapil. "The aim was to cause as much damage as possible. On that night, we sank ships carrying rations, munitions, troops, and export goods—forty-five thousand tons in all."

The attack came at a crucial time in the conflict. By early August, the Pakistan military controlled most of the country, *mukti bahini* units had been driven across the border into India, and morale was wavering. "The commando attacks were a devastating blow to the Pakistanis because up to that time they had been saying that everything in the war was going hunky-dory," said Kapil. "The psychological impact was more important than what was destroyed."

Media coverage of Operation Jackpot exposed the vulnerability of the Pakistan military. Lloyds of London raised insurance rates on ships entering Bangladeshi waters, and foreign merchant ships refused to enter the inland waterway system, cutting off supplies and choking the export trade.

Later attacks on shipping, with local *mukti bahini* commanders deciding on timing and targets, lacked coordination. However, the threat forced the Pakistani army to increase troop strength at ports. When the Indian Army invaded in December, the Pakistanis were unable to mount a concerted defense because *mukti bahini* operations had forced the army to spread its troops across the country to guard railroads, bridges, power plants, river ports, and other strategic assets.

It is estimated that fewer than fifteen commandos died in attacks on ships. By the end of operations, they had sunk more than one hundred thousand tons of shipping. "Their achievements were phenomenal compared to our inputs," said Kapil.

In 2016, Kapil, who later saw action in a gunboat raid in Bangladesh, returned to the country for the first time in forty-five years. He was recognized by Prime Minister Sheikh Hasina and had an emotional reunion with some of the commandos he trained. I asked him how it felt to be back in a country in whose liberation he had played a part. "Pretty good," he answered modestly.

The *Mukti Bahini*

As guerrilla forces go, the *mukti bahini* defied the stereotype of ill-trained, trigger-happy irregulars, led by self-appointed warlords and contemptuous of military and political authority. Their coordination with regular military units and the military and political leadership was key to the campaign. They moved back and forth between training camps in India and their villages, concealing themselves and their arms in the holds of high-prow *nouka*, the all-purpose river boat used to carry sacks of rice, vegetables, and passengers. "The boatman would tell the river patrol he was transporting people who needed medical care," said museum guide Momataj. "Sometimes, pregnant women would sit on deck and pretend to be in labor."

The *mukti bahini* conducted most operations at night, targeting power stations, fuel and storage depots, bridges, ferry terminals, railroad lines, and communications networks. By day, they melted into the rural landscape. The mock-up guerrilla camp in the museum "looks just like a normal village," said Momataj. "Pots and pans, laundry hanging on lines, houses and people." By November, the *mukti bahini* controlled a large area of rural Bangladesh, and most Pakistani units were confined to their barracks at night.

I had expected fighters who needed to avoid detection to have kept few records, lest they were betrayed by collaborators. Instead, the museum displays long, handwritten lists of *mukti bahini* members, with their ages, fathers' names, their home districts and villages, and other personal information, maps of their bases, and detailed accounts of training and other activities. Momataj pointed to a framed certificate of training from the Indian Army. "There's a list of fifty thousand fighters with certificates, and they all receive stipends from the government," she said. The documentation shows that Osmani and his zone commanders were in regular contact with *mukti bahini* units and strategically deployed them alongside regular forces. To do so, they needed to know the units' strength and capacity. In the midst of a chaotic struggle, the bureaucrats—the *babus*—still maintained their records. The *mukti bahini* are remarkably well documented.

For months, the conflict ebbed and flowed, but growing attacks from regular and *mukti bahini* forces forced Pakistan to fly in more troops. As the refugee crisis intensified, Indian prime minister Indira Gandhi and her cabinet discussed direct armed intervention. War broke out in early December 1971, after Pakistan's air force launched a preemptive strike on Indian Air Force bases, intending to destroy planes on the ground. India quickly retaliated, flying sorties over Bangladesh to attack airfields, military bases, shipping, and infrastructure.

Lights Out in Calcutta

It usually happened in the middle of the family dinner. "The sirens would start blasting throughout the city," said Suruchi. "It was total panic. My parents would insist that all the lights were turned off, so we were in total darkness, and then we would be asked to hide under the bed."

For Suruchi, seven years old and living with her family and her uncle's family in a small apartment in southern Kolkata, the blackout "seemed like an adventure." There were five children in the home—Suruchi, her older sister, and three cousins. "We made it into this hide-and-seek game. My grandmother got really agitated with us, but we said we might as well enjoy the pitch darkness." She admits that the blackout sometimes scared her. There was always the chance that a stray bomb or missile would land on the city.

For several months before the conflict began, Suruchi had sensed that something was up. "Another uncle was an intelligence officer with

RAW and he was assigned to Bangladesh. He would often fly in from Delhi and spend an evening or a weekend with us before traveling to Dhaka. At that age we were like, 'Oooh, clandestine operations.' It was all very cloak-and-dagger because he couldn't tell us what he did. He was a lot of fun and we always looked forward to his visits. We had an idea that something was coming, but I think we were still too young to understand until it affected us personally."

The sirens and blackouts lasted only two weeks. Three Indian corps, with air support and reinforced by Bangladesh regulars and *mukti bahini,* advanced rapidly. The Pakistan Army, which had deployed units around the country to defend towns, ports, and infrastructure, was unable to resist the advance. In a final atrocity on December 14, the army rounded up 250 intellectuals, professionals, and journalists, shot them, and dumped their bodies in a killing field outside Dhaka. On December 16, at the Ramna racecourse where Rahman had made his historic March 7 speech, the Pakistan commander signed the instrument of surrender. More than ninety-three thousand troops surrendered to Indian and Bangladeshi forces, the largest surrender since World War II. "We celebrated when we read about the surrender in the newspapers," Suruchi recalls. "We knew how heavily the Indian army had been involved."

Victims of War

> A schoolboy of Jamalpur narrated the experience of his father who was a schoolboy at the time. While crossing the street with a can of milk he was called by the sentry to come in the camp. There the soldier took the milk from him and paid with a two *anna* coin. Inside the room the boy saw three naked women with marks of torture all over their bodies. The boy could never forget the scene and he did not spend the coin. [Plaque at Liberation War Museum]

Who are the victims of war? In Bangladesh, the count must go beyond those killed and wounded, those imprisoned, those whose homes, crops, and businesses were destroyed, the refugees who fled to India. It must include the sexual victims of war.

Outside a darkened gallery section, a letter from a Pakistani military commander to the Peace Committee of a southern district is displayed.

The commander asks, in a matter-of-fact tone, for the collaborators to supply his men with "beautiful women," and he lists the physical features of what he calls a "good product." There is no evidence that the collaborators delivered the goods, but throughout the country young women were taken from their homes, schools, and workplaces and pressed into sexual slavery. Religion was used to justify rape, torture, and murder. Pakistan had declared that it was fighting a holy war to defend Islam, and some clerics issued fatwas in support of raping women, especially Hindu women. Many were held in army barracks or prisons and some tortured; one wall in the gallery reproduces sexual graffiti from a prison wall. Some committed suicide, using their saris to hang themselves.

Those who survived, and the babies born of the sexual violence, were often treated as social outcasts. Some children were adopted by families outside Bangladesh. As prime minister, Rahman established halfway houses to try to reintegrate the victims, providing them with education and handicrafts skills. Momataj pointed to a letter written by a father to Rahman, describing how his only daughter, a college student, was taken away by Pakistani soldiers. What made it worse, he wrote, was that the soldiers "came with the *razakars* [traitors]." He described the conditions in which his daughter was imprisoned, and how she appeared when she was freed. "I cannot take her back," he wrote, asking Rahman to find a place for her.

The room includes a few photos and stories of survivors. Museum staff know of more such women, said Momataj, but because of the stigma they have not agreed to share their testimonies. For them, as for many other Bangladeshis, the war isn't something that happened almost half a century ago. It's still going on for them.

nine

Swimming to Bangladesh

Midway through the first afternoon of the August 2017 workshop for university faculty on communication for development, one participant rubbed his head and glanced toward the ceiling. Sure enough, a steady drip of water was coming through the acoustic tile. He shifted his chair. Soon, drips appeared in other places. People started moving tables and chairs, and a janitor placed a bucket below the leakiest spot. Then someone noticed water dripping onto the lectern and rescued the laptop. I looked up at the acoustic tiles, many of which were stained brown and black. This was evidently not the first time rain had come through the roof of the University Grants Commission building in Dhaka. No one complained or even commented. In monsoon season, you expect to get wet.

There is flooding in Bangladesh every year, but the floods of 2017 were the worst in a decade. The first rains came in April, fully three months ahead of the normal monsoon season, inundating paddies before farmers could harvest the first of the three annual rice crops. After several weeks of rain in July and August, rivers and streams in the north burst their banks, inundating thousands of acres of farmland and washing away homes, schools, shops, vehicles, and livestock. According to the government's Meteorological Department, on a single day, August 11, almost a week's worth of average monsoon rainfall was dumped across parts of the country in the space of a few hours. By the time the rains eased, and the floodwaters began to recede, almost 150 people had

Figure 9.1 Rickshaws and vans push through the water in Chittagong after six hours of heavy rain in April 2017 left many areas of the port city flooded. Courtesy *Daily Star* (Anurup Kanti Das)

Figure 9.2 Three days of monsoon rains in July 2017 left many roads in Dhaka under water. Courtesy *Daily Star* (Amran Hossain)

lost their lives, seven hundred thousand homes had been damaged or destroyed, and up to a third of agricultural land submerged. The waters destroyed rice crops and washed out the fish ponds that provide the main source of protein for the rural population. More than eight million people sought shelter on higher ground or on narrow levees, erecting flimsy shelters of bamboo poles and tarpaulins, without food, clothes, clean water, or sanitation facilities.

"People are used to seasonal flooding but nothing to this degree," Corinne Ambler of the International Federation of Red Cross and Red Crescent Societies (IFRC) told CNN. "This is a different level—for miles around all you can see is water, the flooding has transformed the countryside. People were fearful they would soon begin to starve." By the third week in August, most vegetable prices had shot up by at least 50 percent, with the price of onions and chili—essential ingredients in many dishes—doubling. The flooding was the most serious since 2007 when more than half the country was affected and more than one thousand people, most of them children, died. In August 2017, across India, Nepal, and Bangladesh, more than twelve hundred people died from flooding and landslides, and forty million were affected.[1]

For the Bangladesh government, NGOs, and international relief organizations, providing clean water and sanitation were the major priorities. Floodwaters provide breeding grounds for waterborne diseases such as diarrhea, malaria, dengue, and Japanese encephalitis. Reaching stranded communities was challenging because the floods washed away roads, bridges, and railroads. A newspaper front page photo showed a woman walking along the buckled tracks of a railroad in a badly hit region of the northwest. The force of the waters had washed away the track bed and submerged the tracks for three days, leaving them looking "like those of a roller-coaster."[2]

Dhaka escaped the worst of the flooding, although rising water in streams and lakes washed away banks and inundated the rough shacks and market stalls where poor families, many of them migrants from rural areas, eke out a living as bicycle rickshaw drivers and roadside vendors. Roads in low-lying areas were under knee-to-waist-high water. Urban planners blamed the waterlogging on inadequate drainage and pumping systems and accused government officials and contractors of corruption, shoddy construction, and poor maintenance. Over the years, private developers have filled in sections of the canals and rivers

FIGURE 9.3   Roller-coaster railroad—the Dhaka-Dinajpur line at Kauguan in August 2017 after flood waters washed away the track bed. Courtesy *Daily Star* (Kongkon Karmaker)

that serve as the city's main drainage channels. Culverts that feed into the waterways are often clogged with garbage and building materials.

It seems strange to say so, but it could have been worse. In 2002, in a move that could well be emulated by other less flood-prone cities, the authorities banned the use of plastic shopping bags that clog drains and waterways. When you shop in a supermarket or a smaller "super-store" in Dhaka, the clerk puts your purchases into a paper sack or bag made from thin cotton or muslin. The city's action was followed by a national law that imposed fines and prison terms for the import, distribution, and sale of plastic bags. Enforcement has been sporadic, partly because of corruption, but environmental groups have praised Bangladesh as a world leader in banning plastic bags. There is still plastic around—for example, in water bottles—but plastic bags are no longer a major cause of flooding.

The morning after the laptop rescue the rains came again, heavier than the day before. In the lobby of the Ascott Palace Hotel, my colleagues and I waited for the hotel van, wondering how we would reach it without being soaked to the skin. For the staff, it was a familiar challenge. At the entrance, a canopy extended several feet into the street. The van drew up and a guard held up a brightly colored umbrella, almost four feet in diameter, to cover the three steps from the canopy to the door, while still remembering to give us the customary salute. Most travelers were not so lucky. Bicycle and bicycle rickshaw drivers pedaled unsteadily through the torrent, one hand on the handlebars and the other clutching an umbrella. Cars sped by, their tires splashing them; one poor cyclist got a double whammy when cars passed him simultaneously on both sides. Auto rickshaws—the so-called CNGs, powered by compressed natural gas—stalled out, forcing their drivers to push them to the roadside. At junctions where the traffic was stopped, a colorful stream of umbrellas crossed the road. Street cleaners and construction workers, carrying bricks in baskets on their heads, had no protection from the downpour.

Most workshop participants showed up late that morning. One said it had taken him two and a half hours to make a five-mile trip across the city, but he was nonplussed; he was from Chittagong, where flooding is usually much worse than in Dhaka. On my previous visit in April, my UNICEF colleague Yasmin Khan had translated a newspaper cartoon. It depicted the portly, bespectacled mayor of Chittagong, happily floating on an inner tube, while his constituents struggled through the floodwaters. The caption read: "Mayors come and go but citizens continue to suffer."

The Traffic Jam That Never Ends

Even when it's not raining, Dhaka, like Delhi or Jakarta, is notorious for traffic snarls that can make even the shortest (in distance) journeys frustratingly long. The traffic flow is also unpredictable; if you leave ten minutes later than planned, what would normally be a twenty-minute trip can turn into a two-hour marathon. Although the city has morning and evening rush hours, you are just as likely to be stuck in traffic at 2:00 p.m. or 11:00 p.m. On three visits to Dhaka over a year, I was almost always at least half an hour late—but occasionally half an hour early—for appointments.

According to a World Bank analysis, over the course of a decade average traffic speed dropped from 21 km (13 miles) to 7 km (less than 5 miles) per hour, slightly above the average walking speed. Another study estimates that if vehicle growth continues at its present rate without improvements in public transport, the average speed will be down to 4.7 km (less than 3 miles) per hour by 2035. At that point, sensible city

FIGURE 9.4 Dhaka, the traffic jam that never ends. Courtesy *Daily Star* (Palash Khan)

dwellers would leave their cars at home and use their two feet, although that scenario seems unlikely.

The World Bank estimates that traffic gridlock eats up 3.2 million work hours per day, a significant impact in an urban area that contributes more than one-third of the country's GDP and more than 40 percent of total employment.[3] "Like other cities of the developing world," writes Jay Rosen in the *New York Times,* "Dhaka is both a boomtown and a necropolis, with a thriving real-estate market, a growing middle class and a lively cultural and intellectual life that is offset by rampant misery, poverty, pollution, disease and terror attacks. But it is traffic that has sealed Dhaka's reputation among academics and development specialists as the great symbol of twenty-first century dysfunction, the world's most broken city."[4]

The roads are filled with cars, buses, trucks, auto rickshaws, and tricycle rickshaws carrying passengers and cargo. The fastest-growing species is the motorcycle, with an average of more than one thousand new machines being registered every day. Official estimates in July 2018 put the number of motorcycles on the roads of Bangladesh at 2.27 million, but all transport experts agree that's a gross underestimate because many owners don't register their machines. Less than half the drivers of registered machines hold a valid license, so at least one in three should technically not be on the roads at all. Accidents are common, as riders drive on the wrong side of the highway or on sidewalks, or carry more than one passenger. Transport Minister Obaidul Quader described motorcycles as "terror incarnate." In one ten-day clampdown in August 2018, more than half of the eighty-three thousand traffic citations handed out by police went to motorcycle riders. In Dhaka, the number of motorcycles doubled to almost half a million in eight years, with a big bump in 2017 when Uber and other ride-sharing services were introduced. As in other crowded south and southeast Asian cities, motorcycles significantly reduce commuting time.[5]

There would be fewer motorcycles if Dhaka's public transport system was more reliable. Its challenges are symbolized by the aging maroon-colored Ashok Leyland double-decker buses, operated by the government public transport agency, the Bangladesh Road Transport Corporation (BRTC). It is the Indian version of the Leyland Titan, developed in the UK and a common sight on British city roads until the 1970s. The last was manufactured in 1968; one year earlier, the first Titan rolled off the Ashok Leyland production line, and for many years it was a big seller in the subcontinent. Keeping the fleet on the road is a challenge; old buses go into assisted living and eventually expire in a massive yard outside Dhaka where BRTC mechanics painstakingly salvage their organs for transplant.

Many of BRTC's single-decker buses are also showing their age. Like the buses operated by private companies, they look as if they have run the traffic gauntlet, with their panels scraped and dented, their windows missing or shattered, headlamps broken, their exhausts belching smoke. To offset their appearance, many sport upbeat slogans: God Bless You with his Love, Have a Nice Tour, Super, Hi-tech Travel, Dream Line, All Way First Class, Exclusive Journey, Heppy [sic] New Year. The government estimates that about forty-five hundred private buses, owned by almost two thousand small companies, are on the road in Dhaka, competing on a maze of 165 routes, stopping wherever they can pick up passengers. Competition is fierce, with some drivers pulling fourteen-hour shifts in packed, stiflingly hot vehicles. Some admit to taking drugs, including the stimulant yaba, a mix of caffeine and methamphetamine (crystal meth), to stay awake, but road fatigue and accidents are frequent. Efforts by the city authorities to regulate the private bus industry, including issuing tenders for routes, designating where buses are allowed to stop, and setting an eight-hour limit on driving time, have so far come to nothing. However, the authorities have clamped down on the smaller, privately owned *lagunas*, minivans with bench seats, that often carry a dozen passengers, some hanging on the back of the vehicle. In September 2018, the 5,000-plus registered *lagunas*, some operated by underage drivers, were banned from major roads in the city. It did little to relieve congestion; for most residents, it meant longer waits for crowded buses and more business for auto rickshaw drivers.

Many of the auto rickshaws, the CNGs, are also casualties of the daily jousts and standoffs on city roads. Because they are smaller than buses and cars, their operators, who sometimes stretch their leg muscles by propping their feet on the handlebars while driving, believe they can squeeze into the smallest gap between larger vehicles. Passengers on the narrow bench seat—it can accommodate three or four Bangladeshis or one or two reasonably well-fed Westerners—are not protected from accidents, but at least they do not have to clutch their bags tightly while stopped in traffic; a heavy metal grille door, locked from the inside, insulates them from beggars and purse snatchers. Lane discipline is not part of driving culture; vehicles dodge, weave, and cut across oncoming traffic, with collisions missed by important inches. Traffic signals and stop signs are often merely roadside ornaments. "These traffic lights were a bad investment for Bangladesh," Yasmin told me.

The government has ambitious plans to relieve the city's traffic crisis and thus deny foreign journalists literary license in describing Dhaka's urban dysfunctionality. It plans to build five metropolitan rail lines to carry sixty thousand passengers an hour. It is also planning two dedicated BRTC bus routes to carry twenty thousand passengers an hour and has promised to build 750 miles of new roads, three new ring roads, and six new interchanges by 2035. Passengers will be able to use smart cards on metro rail, BRTC, and water taxi routes. A digital system will allow traffic police to remotely control stop lights to improve traffic flow.

From a writer's perspective, one benefit of getting stuck in traffic is having the time to read and record entertaining commercial signs. Tippera Iron and Tin Factory, manufacturer of water bucks, cooking pans, and all kinds of domestic hardware. Choiceful Granite & Slate, Decent Sanitaryware, Bengal Foam (a clothing store), Aluminium World, Dominous Pizza, Right Aid Pharmacy, Heartiest Welcome—Bangladesh

Railway. In the upscale Gulshan-2 area, where many expatriates live, real estate developers compete for pretentiousness: Navana Real Estate, Different, Dependable, Definitive. Definitive? Dhaka has several large military bases, their entrance gates graced with an assortment of military hardware—fighter planes, naval patrol boats, tanks and armored personnel carriers—and banners exhorting young people to join up. Some sport slogans: the army engineering base welcomes visitors to "Sapper's Dell—Disciplined, Efficient, Loyal, Laborious." Laborious? I think they mean hardworking.

The UNICEF faculty workshop was held at the University Grants Commission on Statistics Road, prosaically named for the Central Bureau of Statistics a few doors down. As we jogged along the wide, dirt road in an Uber, feeling every bump, my colleague Amy Chadwick said she thought it was aptly named. In statistical research, she dryly noted, you need to wade through potholes and garbage to get to the other side.

In the Zone

The Ascott Palace Hotel is in Baridhara, or, to give it its full name, the Baridhara Diplomatic Zone. It's a large, gated community, separated from the commercial district of Gulshan-2 by a lake and from the traffic-clogged Jamuna Future Park Road by a long wall. It has only two entrances, both with security checkpoints and concrete roadblocks. Each morning, street cleaners, construction workers, and service staff line up at the guard posts to show their entry permits. All vehicles, including taxis, require a special permit to enter. Traffic within the zone is light. That's mainly because there are no commercial businesses—only apartment blocks, hotels, and embassies.

The US embassy (or Fortress America, as I call it), an ugly red-brick collection of buildings, is technically outside the zone, across the road from one checkpoint. It has high walls topped with metal spikes and security cameras; at night, the sidewalk is closed to pedestrians. Inside the zone, every embassy and apartment block has armed guards; police in camouflage fatigues and semiautomatic weapons are deployed at key locations.

Because of its high security, the zone is favored by expatriates, government officials, and business people who rent or own apartments. Baridhara's real estate is booming. Streets are lined with stacks of bricks and stones, piles of sand and cement, and long strands of rebar; sidewalks, roadways, and drainage channels are under construction. Work starts early in the morning and often goes on late into the evening, but after 10:00 p.m. the zone is almost eerily quiet, with only the occasional car or truck and few pedestrians on the streets. The embassy and apartment building guards sit in their wooden sentry posts, reading or watching TV, and stray dogs sleep or root around in the garbage. *Fajar*, the first call to prayer, comes just before dawn. By 6:30, the zone has woken up. Workers on foot and on bicycles are on their way to construction sites, street cleaners in yellow jackets are brushing away trash, leaves, and tree branches after the previous evening's storm, drivers are picking up children to take them to school. It's also time for the changing of the guard. Trucks carrying police armed with semiautomatic rifles pull up; the day shift disembarks and the night shift, yawning and stretching, gets on board. Life in the zone has its daily rhythms.

Fortunately, it's only a ten-minute walk from Baridhara to the commercial district of Gulshan-2, which centers on a large, traffic-clogged, roundabout. On my first visit to Dhaka, I strolled there from the hotel on my first night. The next morning, my UNICEF colleague Neha Kapil pointed it out to me from the car. "Oh, I was here last night," I said offhandedly.

"What? You walked here? On your own?" Clearly, Neha was uncomfortable with my wanderings. She had reason to be concerned. On the evening of July 1, 2016, five gunmen burst into a popular Western-style café in Gulshan-2, the Holey Artisan Bakery, shouting "Allahu Akbar," and started firing indiscriminately. They turned off the lights and held the customers at gunpoint. They separated Muslims from non-Muslims by asking them to recite verses from the Koran. Twenty hostages, seventeen of them foreigners, were killed—shot or stabbed with machetes. As police closed in, the gunmen opened fire and hurled grenades, killing two officers. Commandos stormed the restaurant twelve hours later; the five terrorists and a chef died during the operation, and another staff member died later in the hospital.

The brazen attack—the country's worst-ever hostage crisis—shocked the government and the international community. Law enforcement agencies launched a nationwide crackdown on suspected Islamic militants. Security measures in Gulshan-2 and Baridhara were stepped up, with extra army and police patrols and checkpoints. Embassies, development organizations, and international NGOs reviewed security measures at hotels, restaurants, stores, and commercial establishments and declared some off limits.

In between the boutiques, Italian restaurants, European bakeries, and coffee shops of Gulshan-2, you can glimpse the real Bangladesh. On the roadside or under tarpaulins, people squat, selling fruits and vegetables. Tailors sit behind their sewing machines, ready to make running repairs. There are hole-in-the-wall pharmacies, copy and lamination shops, fabric shops, grocery "super-stores," and tea stalls. At the roadside, under palm trees, drivers nap on the beds of their bicycle vans or play board games with pebbles.

Because it's now rare in the United States to find anyone who can repair shoes, I had packed my Birkenstock sandals, hoping to get them resoled. Down an alley, I found a cobbler, squatting under a tarpaulin. He pulled out a length of rubber and indicated where he would cut and replace the soles. An hour later, the work was done. "How much?" I asked. He shrugged. I offered 200 taka. He looked a little disappointed, so I added 100 more. That's about $3.50. He smiled and shook my hand.

Old Dhaka

Wandering around a modern commercial district is one thing. Even with a good map and a guidebook, I was not prepared to single-handedly tackle the old city of Dhaka with its winding, unnamed streets and back alleys. I pulled out my travel guide and called Taimur Islam, director of the Urban Study Group, an NGO that offers walking tours of Old Dhaka. Was there a tour I could join? He said the morning tour had already left, but that he would call one of his volunteers and see if I could join the group. He called back a few minutes later. I passed the phone to my CNG driver, and Taimur gave him directions. We set off on a harrowing and bumpy ride through the narrow streets.

I met Ana, one of the volunteer guides, at a nineteenth-century merchant's home, built in brick with colonnades and balconies. Like most of the historic structures in Old Dhaka, it is in serious need of restoration. Years of baking heat and monsoon rains have taken their toll. The stucco had peeled off the walls and columns, exposing the brick, and the wooden balconies sagged, but at least it was still standing and, with investment, could be restored to some of its former splendor.

Old Dhaka, the area between the central part of the city and the River Buriganga, began its life as a small river port with bazaars. From the seventeenth century, under the Mughal emperors, it became a major commercial center, based largely on the production of muslin, a high-quality woven cotton exported to Europe. The city thrived until the nineteenth century, when British merchants took advantage of favorable tariffs to flood the market with imported cotton goods, sending the local industry into decline.

Several Mughal-era buildings—the Lalbagh Fort and Choto Katra, a large merchant's house—survive. From the late seventeenth century, Armenian merchants became prominent in the muslin export trade. They built large houses and became rich landlords; in 1771, they built an Armenian church and gave their name to the Armanitola neighborhood. The city also attracted Hindu artisans, who established workshops and small shops. The names of the two bazaars, Tanti (weaver) and Shakhari (craftsman), mark their importance in the commercial life of the city; today, many Hindus still live in Old Dhaka, and the side streets have small Hindu temples.

In 2004, an old building in Shakhari Bazaar collapsed. The government, supported by developers who saw an opportunity to grab prime real estate, proposed that many historic buildings, some from the British colonial era, be demolished for safety reasons. Historians and conservationists were outraged, arguing the city's cultural heritage would be destroyed. The controversy was the impetus for the founding of the Urban Study Group (USG) by Taimur, a trained architect. The USG campaigned to have several streets and buildings designated as historically significant, and so protected from demolition. Some building owners opposed the designation, saying they did not have the money to maintain or restore their properties. The debate over preserving Old Dhaka echoes conflicts in other cities, with government agencies, developers, property owners, and preservationists taking their disputes to the courts and the media.

The USG may have met its original goal of saving the buildings from demolition but restoring them will be a longer struggle. Some are being used as homes by dozens of families. Only the most philanthropic of landlords will throw out the tenants, lose the rental income, and invest in restoration. In Western countries, a government agency might buy the buildings and restore them, but in Bangladesh the government has other budget priorities. It's difficult to argue for the allocation of public funds when schools and health clinics are understaffed, roads need to be repaired, and flood levees built.

One example is the so-called Water Palace on the bank of the Buriganga River. "These are residences for families of the Army Corps of Engineers," said Ana. We were standing in the stone central courtyard, looking up at washing draped over the balconies as children played hide-and-seek among the pillars and narrow passageways. Many government agencies provide free or low-cost housing for their staff, partly to compensate for low salaries. It's doubtful the Army Corps of Engineers will support preservation efforts. Part of the palace has been taken over by Old Dhaka's spice bazaar. Outside, trucks were unloading sacks of garlic. We wandered through the bazaar—a feast of colors and aromas—and emerged at the waterfront.

FIGURE 9.5 History under threat—the Water Palace in Old Dhaka. It's used to provide low-cost housing for military families.

Figure 9.6   Selling garlic at Old Dhaka's spice bazaar

The river was busy—large passenger boats (called launches) embarking for destinations in southern Bangladesh, small freighters unloading cargo, and motor-powered *nouka* loaded with vegetables for the city's markets. The nearest was piled high with cauliflowers. "They have come from Barisal," said Sunny, another volunteer who had joined us, naming a port city in the southern delta. Porters piled the cauliflowers into broad baskets and formed a human chain, carrying them on their heads and passing them on to the next link. On the dirt bank, pumpkins, gourds, and other vegetables were stacked high. Below us, a group of boatmen waited for passengers to ferry to the other side of the river. Sunny asked if I would like a boat trip. I looked at the wobbling craft and the dirty water and decided that walking was safer.

Our next stop was Dhaka's main Shi'a mosque, Hossaini Dalan. Most Bangladeshis are Sunni Moslems, but a small Shi'a community exists in the old city. The women in our group had only two headscarves between them, so it took fifteen minutes or so for the whole group to visit the mosque. From there, we walked to the merchant houses of the so-called French Quarter, or Farashganj (the name is a corruption

FIGURE 9.7 The Buriganga River waterfront in Old Dhaka—*nouka* loaded with vegetables for the city markets, passenger boats bound for delta ports

of *Frenchganj*, meaning French market-town). The French East India Company began operations in Dhaka in 1740, trading in spices such as turmeric, ginger, garlic, and chili, as well as other goods. The French got into sporadic disputes with the British East India Company over trading privileges, forcing the Nawab of Bengal to mediate. The French were eventually kicked out after the Nawab, with French support, was defeated by Clive at Plassey in 1756, but they left behind stylish mansions with balconies and wrought-iron balustrades.

The tour group kept getting larger as more volunteers—all of them students—joined us; at one time, I counted at least a dozen volunteers. All were enthusiastic about their work and proud to show us the city's heritage. "We learned from the preservation movements in the West," Sunny told me. "They inspired us."

FIGURE 9.8 Two porters in Old Dhaka. They carry bricks or produce sacks in baskets on their heads.

We arrived at a large, colonial-era house, with emblems for Bangladesh's professional cricket clubs painted on the walls. It is now a student residence hall, and some volunteers lived there. Each room housed four male students in basic conditions—hard wood beds, a couple of chairs, and a small balcony. We shared samosa and bananas in one room and took a group picture outside. In the dirt yard, some students were tending a large iron cooking pot over an open fire. They said they were fortunate to have the cheapest accommodation in Dhaka—3,000 taka (about $35) for the year.

Our final visit was to Shakhari Bazaar, where most shopkeepers and workshop owners are Hindus. The bazaar was one of the neighborhoods targeted by the Pakistani army in Operation Searchlight in 1971. On the street, we were stopped by two men who wanted to show us their Hindu temple. The temple president explained that developers were trying to take the land to build a high-rise and were buying off politicians to make the deal go through. The temple was not particularly old so could not be designated as a historic structure, but it was where the president and his neighbors had worshipped all their lives. At his request, we took a group picture, hoping that the image of the temple president and a group of concerned *bideshi* (foreigners) would end up on social media and perhaps help in the campaign.

Bangladesh's Friendly Skies

Fly Your Own Airline. That's the slogan of United Airways (not to be confused with the larger US-based carrier, United Airlines), one of Bangladesh's four private airlines. It's emblazoned across the aircraft and at the check-in counter at the domestic terminal of Dhaka's Hazrat Shahjalal Airport. I'd like to think it means the crew will invite you to take over the controls once the plane has reached a safe cruising altitude and take a selfie in the cockpit against a background of flashing instrument lights, but it's probably just the product of a brainstorming session with a marketing team to make passengers feel part of the airline family.

I haven't had the opportunity to test the slogan because I haven't flown with United, but I've taken flights on the three other private airlines—Regent Airlines, Novo Air, and US Bangla. All connect to domestic destinations and offer a few international flights, mostly to India and Southeast Asia. After the government airline, Biman Bangladesh (Air Bangladesh), lost its monopoly of the skies in 1996, the airline industry literally took off, and competition is cutthroat. My total bill for three round-trip domestic flights came to under $250, and all airlines offer special discounted fares. If you plan ahead, you can fly almost anywhere in the country for under $60 round trip.

Bangladesh is a small country, so the flights are short. My first flight to Jessore in the west on Novo Air took just thirty minutes; it was forty-five minutes to Chittagong on Regent and a seemingly interminable fifty minutes to Sylhet in the north on US Bangla. With short flight times, everything in the cabin happens at breakneck speed. The attendants race through the routine announcements and safety demonstration (in both Bangla and English) in a couple of minutes, including the requisite quotation from the Koran, roughly translated as "God (Allah) is almighty, without him we would not be safe." Immediately after the seat belt sign is turned off, and almost before you have time to lower your tray table, the cabin attendants are running up and down the aisle, doling out boxes with sandwiches, cookies, or cake and a bottle of water. There's more glitz to the packaging than the food inside the box. "Celebrate Spring with the bite of true delight," promises US Bangla on its bright yellow boxes with a floral design. "True delight" consists of a soggy bun wrapped around processed chicken, a slice of sponge cake, and a mint wrapped in teeth-challenging plastic. But there's no time to debate truth in advertising because it's a mad rush to collect the trash before the seat belt sign goes on again and the plane begins its descent. The standard request to "sit back, relax, and enjoy your flight" seems irrelevant because it's nonstop action most of the way.

For those of us accustomed to long lines at check-in, surly gate agents, and tiresome security checks, taking a domestic flight in Bangladesh is remarkably hassle-free, the security measures relaxed and the staff helpful and friendly. At the terminal entrance, your luggage goes through a scanner while you walk through the security gate. No one tells you to remove your belt or empty your pockets, so you invariably set off the alarm. The security agent points a scanner in your general direction, then waves you through. No ID is required at check-in. There's one more scanner for carry-on, but you don't have to remove your laptop, or take off your jacket, belt, or shoes. There's a list of prohibited carry-on items—the usual ones (handguns, knives, and other sharp objects) and a few oddball items such as tape measures, tennis rackets, cricket bats, pool cues, and catapults. Your one-liter water bottle? Carry it on board. The value-sized shampoo bottle? No problem.

I got to know the departure lounge at Dhaka's domestic terminal pretty well. I usually headed for a corner area where there's a sofa and two easy chairs—a standard living room suite that would not look out of place in a low-rent apartment. The fake leather is showing its age, but it's the most comfortable place in the lounge. The thrift store ambience is enhanced by a couple of other upholstered bench chairs across the room. There's a small tea and coffee stall and a place to buy sweets and pastries. It all feels rather homey.

You have no problem finding your gate because there's only one. Although the domestic terminal handles between fifty and sixty flights a day, the system works well. There are a couple of monitors for departures, but the standard announcement to board is made by airline agents strolling around barking, "Regent—Chittagong" or "US Bangla—Sylhet." If you're dozing, they'll wake you up to check where you're going. The slightly surreal atmosphere continues on the bus, where the soothing preflight Muzak track is distinctively but confusingly Celtic—soft acoustic melodies on piano, flute, and harp.

Or perhaps you will travel by car. For no clear reason, every airline provides a couple of cars to shuttle passengers to the plane. I assumed this service was for VIPs, government officials, and disabled passengers who found it difficult to board a bus. But it seemed entirely random. For the first flight to Jessore, Yasmin and I had chauffeur service to the plane, with the driver stashing our carry-on in the trunk.

After a short flight and fast onboard service, you expect your checked baggage to arrive promptly and intact. Unfortunately, although Biman Bangladesh surrendered its monopoly of domestic routes, it still handles—or rather mishandles—baggage at every airport. Delays are longest for international flights because of lack of equipment and baggage-handling staff. It's a forty-five-minute flight from Kolkata to Dhaka, but one passenger told the *Dhaka Tribune* that it took five hours for the luggage to reach the carousel. According to a report by the airport authority, an average of more than one hundred passengers a day file claims at the lost and found office; either their luggage went missing or items were stolen. According to the *Tribune,* "ground handlers routinely pick out suitcases from flights they know are bound to be filled with valuable goods, such as flights from the Middle East or India." Closed-circuit TV has failed to stop the pilfering by Biman Bangladesh staff. Private airlines and consumer advocates are pressing for an open tender to allow a private company to take over baggage handling.[6]

Bangladesh has a long list of items subject to customs duties, with electronic goods as the main targets. There's a sliding scale of duties for plasma, LCD, and LED TVs, based on screen size; home theater systems, digital cameras, and satellite dishes are also on the list. So are home appliances such as dishwashers, refrigerators, and freezers. Carpets are taxed by the square meter, chandeliers by the point.

The baggage declaration form provides a snapshot of Bangladesh's consumer economy. In a country where most basic items—foodstuffs, clothes, and household goods—are grown or manufactured domestically, imports are expensive. Just scan the shelves of a supermarket where there are separate racks for domestic and imported products; the Doreo cookies are half the price of the Oreos, the domestically bottled Coke and Sprite cheaper than the imports.

According to the 2011 census, nine out of ten Bangladeshis are Muslims, for whom alcohol is forbidden. Certainly, a few of them drink, but the penalties for possession of alcohol, except with a doctor's prescription, are severe. The same strictures do not apply to ethnic and religious minorities. Among Hindus, who make up about 8 percent of the population, and smaller numbers of Buddhists and Christians, attitudes and practice vary. Indigenous groups in the Chittagong Hill Tracts distill their own high-octane brews from rice, while the Christian Garo people near the border with Meghalaya make a rice wine. For foreign visitors, alcohol is available in a few hotels and bars in Dhaka, and in international clubs patronized by expatriates and wealthy Bangladeshis. It's hard to imagine establishments such as the Aussie Club, the Dutch Club, the German Club, and the Nordic Club *without* alcohol. Foreign residents purchase alcohol at a government warehouse, using a customs passport in which their purchases are recorded. An individual is allowed a set number of points a month, with each bottle or can adding to the total. If this sounds like an effort to control alcohol use, it does not work very well. "Unless I'm throwing a big party, there's no way I can spend my 250 points in a month," one friend confided. "And the alcohol is cheap." Most foreigners keep their alcohol use discreet so as not to offend Muslim sensibilities. At a hotel restaurant, I observed the Chinese family at the next table enjoying a bottle of *merlot*, but the bottle was never left on the table; after glasses were refilled it was stashed under an empty chair.

Dhaka's Dominance

Although most of Bangladesh's people still live in the countryside and depend directly or indirectly on the agricultural economy, migration to urban areas—as in Madagascar, India, and Indonesia—has been steadily increasing. Although some is seasonal, with farmers working construction or pulling rickshaws in the months between seedtime and harvest, an increasing number of rural migrants decide to stay because the opportunities are better. Although all urban areas draw in migrants, the greatest influx is to Dhaka for jobs in the formal and informal economies. The population of Dhaka itself is estimated at about 8.5 million, that of the metropolitan area at more than 18 million (as of 2016). It is one of the most densely populated areas in the world.

Dhaka's demographics are staggering, but it still accounts for less than 10 percent of Bangladesh's population of 163 million. For its population, the city punches above its weight in the economy. The World Bank estimates that the Dhaka area contributes more than one-third of the country's GDP and more than 40 percent of total employment. It is the seat of government and the judiciary, and the headquarters of international organizations, multinational corporations, financial institutions, major media groups, and NGOs. Dhaka has the most advanced hospitals and medical facilities. Dhaka University is the largest and oldest academic institution in the country and is only one of several public universities in the capital; the number of private universities, many specializing in business or technology, has been growing steadily. All major conferences and trade exhibitions are held in Dhaka. If you can live with the traffic, pollution, and seasonal flooding, it's the place to be.

Urban historian Adnan Morshed captures the paradox. "The city feels infernal," he writes, "an urban tornado sucking everything into a dizzying vortex of traffic congestion, wild land speculation, economic disparities, and environmental challenges. Yet, neither despair nor hope can account for the city's exhilarating urbanity."[7] Dhaka can be infernal and exciting, often at the same time. But it is not a microcosm of the country. I knew I needed to leave the city to see the Bangladesh where most people live.

ten

On the Road and on the Water

Get Your Kicks on Route 6

"It's my tribute to Route 66!" Sujoy Vai struck a pose under the sign of his roadside eatery in Rajshahi. He gestured toward the midday melee of auto rickshaws, carts, and battered buses. "We're on Bangladesh Route 6."

With his shoulder-length graying hair, sun-beaten face, faded salmon-pink T-shirt, jeans, and sandals, Sujoy could have passed for an extra from the cult classic *Easy Rider*, or a member of a rock band that had never abandoned its studiously scruffy dress code. I guessed he was in his early fifties. The Rolling Stones' rendition of the rhythm and blues standard, released on their 1964 debut album, had inspired the restaurant name.

"Route 66" is a story by itself. Composed in 1946 by songwriter Bobby Troup after a ten-day cross-country trip with his wife in their 1941 Buick, two versions—an upbeat, jazzy one by Nat King Cole and a softer, swing-style rendering by Bing Crosby with the Andrews Sisters—hit the *Billboard* charts that year. Other artists—from Chuck Berry to Van Morrison to Perry Como—went on to record it. For Sujoy, it was the Stones' version that conjured up his American dream of the open road, where he could "go take that California trip."

FIGURE 10.1 Getting his kicks on Route 6—Rajshahi restauranteur and Rolling Stones fan Sujoy Vai

National Route 6 in Bangladesh does not evoke the same feelings. It winds a mere ninety miles southeast from Rajshahi in western Bangladesh along the Padma (Ganges) valley before dead-ending at the river port of Kashinathpur on the Jamuna (Brahmaputra). The only kicks you're likely to get are from goats straying onto the road.

At the Route 6 De Lounge (to give it its full name), Sujoy looked a little out of place among a young, mostly male, clean-cut clientele, with neatly pressed shirts and pants and short haircuts. Sujoy, who may have renounced capitalism at one time in his life, is now a successful entrepreneur—the restaurant cum coffeehouse cum smoothie bar just outside the main gate of the University of Rajshahi is a popular hangout for students and faculty. Sujoy's customers buy into the American popular culture motif with Facebook endorsements. "Oh man, it is simply awesome," wrote one. "I am just loving it, dude." This is probably untranslatable into Bangla.

The original US Route 66 signs had black lettering on a white background, not the red, white, and blue logo of the interstate highway Sujoy chose for his Route 6 sign. I decided not to quibble about accuracy in signage, but to bring him a black-and-white version if I ever visit Rajshahi again. Of course, most of the original signs along the US highway were stolen by collectors and Stones' fans years ago; today, the online trade is in embossed aluminum reproductions, touched up with lithographed rust stains and bullet holes to look like the real thing. At least Sujoy is more creative than the owner of the Outback Fast Food & Coffee House down the road, which shamelessly reproduces the restaurant chain's logo. And the Route 6 food is good, if not exactly what you'd find winding from Chicago to LA—the standard Bangladesh mixed menu of Bangla, Indian, Chinese, Thai, and Continental dishes, along with the signature Route 6 burger.

I was on the second of two trips to Bangladesh in early 2017 to visit universities and talk with faculty from several disciplines, including anthropology, sociology, journalism, and mass communication, about introducing classes in communication for development to the curriculum. There were only three flights a week from Dhaka to Rajshahi, but none worked with my schedule, so Yasmin and I made the trip by road. In most parts of the United States, I'd allow three hours for a 150-mile highway trip, more if it includes some city driving. In Bangladesh, the standard driving time from Dhaka to Rajshahi is twice that—six hours.

Garment District

Leaving Dhaka at 6:30 to avoid the early rush hour traffic, we drove northwest through an industrial region. We passed dozens of garment factories; at one factory gate, a large concrete blue and white sewing machine welcomed workers to another long, hot day of sewing, dyeing, and finishing. It was time for the morning shift; on both sides of the road, women were getting off company buses or walking to the factories. Bangladesh is the world's second-leading clothing exporter after China, supplying global chains such as Walmart. The garment industry is a major driver of the economy, providing employment and a measure of financial independence for thousands of women, who were once mostly confined to domestic or part-time work. Low production costs give the industry a competitive advantage, but market share comes at a price in terms of working conditions, safety, and pollution. Factory owners pay low wages, spend little on workplace safety, and routinely evade environmental regulations. The authorities periodically crack down on violators but have too few fire and building inspectors; officials are easily bribed to overlook violations. The industry is powerful, with links to politicians, and has forced the resignation or transfer of overzealous regulators. The mayor of the industrial suburb of Savar, Mohammed Abdul Kader, told the *New York Times* that he was powerless to resist political pressure. "You should understand the reality in Bangladesh," he said. "These people who are setting up industries and factories here are much more powerful than me. When a government minister calls me and tells me to give permission to someone to set up a factory in Savar, I can't refuse."[1]

Kader became mayor after his predecessor was suspended following what the Bangladesh media call "the world's worst workplace disaster." On April 24, 2013, the nine-story Rana Plaza building, which housed several garment factories, collapsed, leaving more than eleven hundred dead and hundreds injured. My second visit coincided with the fourth anniversary of the tragedy. More than five hundred mourners gathered at a monument to lay wreathes and hear speeches from workers and trade union leaders criticizing lax regulation. Although several criminal cases have been brought, none had yet gone to trial. The judicial system moves slowly, and activists fear factory owners will bribe lawyers and judges to delay or dismiss cases.

Beyond the garment factories, the landscape turned dark and desolate—mile on mile of smoking brick kilns and power plants, grime-covered buildings, and loading yards lined with rows of trucks, their brightly painted and decorated bodies spattered with mud. We took the bridge over a canal that crosses the industrial region, where trucks were off-loading building supplies from *nouka*. Under overcast skies, the water looked dark and stagnant, devoid of life. Although tanneries and pharmaceutical plants add to the pollution, most untreated wastewater comes from textile and dyeing factories. It fills canals and inundates wetlands. "Sometimes it is red," a teacher in Savar told the *New York Times*. "Or gray. Sometimes it is blue. It depends on the colors they are using in the factories." He said the fumes made his children choke or become dizzy.

Dhaka's canal system was designed to supply the city with water and serve as a natural drainage system, disposing of rainwater during monsoon season and preventing stagnation, but the waterways are dying. "Look, it's not only in Savar," said Kader. "The whole country is suffering from pollution. In Savar, we have lots of coconut trees, but they don't produce coconuts anymore. Industrial pollution is damaging our fish stocks, our fruit produce, our vegetables." Environmentalists hope polluted waterways can be brought back to life, and they point to successful cleanup efforts in other countries, including the United States. Could Dhaka follow the example of Cleveland? The reference is to the stinking waters of the Cuyahoga River, which famously caught on fire in June 1969, capturing headlines across the world. The catastrophe contributed to the passage of the 1972 Clean Water Act. Today the Cuyahoga, if not exactly pristine, is no longer a smelly sewer and runs through a vibrant waterfront area, lined with bars, restaurants, and shops.

With economic pressures from the garment industry and corruption, it's difficult to imagine how Dhaka can do a Cleveland and save its canals. It's not a question of legislation because tough antipollution laws are on the books. The issue is whether they are enforced, and for years factory owners have managed to lobby, schmooze, and bribe their way out of trouble. The occasional fines they pay are a trifle compared with the costs of installing wastewater treatment equipment and utility costs.

River Grabbers

Along both banks of the Turag River in Savar, wooden cargo boats are moored, bobbing gently in the slow current, their once brightly painted colors faded from the tropical sun. Unlike most cargo boats, they're not going anywhere, or at least not far. Metal tubing—about the diameter of a furnace pipe—extends from each boat's hold, then loops down into the water. A diesel-powered motor sucks sand from the river bottom. The water line around the boat rises slowly as it fills with wet sand; when the crew reckon it can hold no more without sinking, it limps a short distance downstream to a makeshift dock where the sand is off-loaded onto trucks.

What looks like a dredging operation to improve river navigation is in fact part of a money-making scheme by land developers. Most of the gritty, greyish sand mined from the Turag and Dhaka's other rivers—the Buriganga, Balu, Shitalakkhaya, and Shaleshwari—does not travel far. Trucks dump huge piles along the river banks to form the shaky foundation on which homes, apartments, and factories will be built. Hand-lettered "Land for sale" signs promise future profits. Yasmin translated: "You buy the land now, and you can build in five years."

It's all about population pressures. The Dhaka area is experiencing a residential and commercial construction boom, and land is at a premium. For years, so-called river-grabbers have been filling up the foreshore—the area between the high- and low-water marks—erecting retaining walls, planting trees, and building homes, factories, and commercial establishments. A landmark 2009 High Court judgment was supposed to rescue Dhaka's rivers by delineating their boundaries. According to the *Daily Star*, the decision became "the death warrant" for the rivers. Demarcation pillars were set up along the banks during the dry season when the water level was low. It's estimated that twenty-five hundred acres of foreshore and wetlands were left outside the official boundaries—an open invitation to developers to move in and start filling in the banks.

In 2016, the *Daily Star* used photos of the Turag over a five-year span to document its slow decline into what one local farmer called "a drainage ditch." In mixed industrial-residential areas such as Savar, most development goes unregulated; a government inspector may levy (and then pocket) a fine, but business interests, allied with government officials, act with impunity. The "river-gobblers," writes the *Daily Star*, are "powerful, rich and ruthless" and "have no difficulty maneuvering the legal system and the land administration." Reclaimed land is now occupied by sand and concrete companies, private universities, and mosques. As one local official complained: "The river encroachers come back immediately after being evicted and we don't have adequate manpower to constantly guard against that."[2] It's rare that building projects are shut down. Even those on shifting sands.

The industrial wasteland of Savar finally gave way to an agricultural landscape of rice paddies, interspersed with fields of corn and mango plantations. The region also produces jute, used to make rope and fabrics. Along the roadside, farmers were selling seasonal vegetables and fruits—eggplants, watermelons, cantaloupes, bananas, and pineapple.

As we moved beyond the industrial suburbs, the truck traffic became lighter. In rural areas, almost everything—farm produce, cattle, firewood, plastic water containers, and people—is transported by "van."

Van *Chalaks* and Bus Bosses

Somewhere in the linguistic transfer between English and Bangla, the imported word "van" lost its original reference to a sturdy vehicle of transportation with a cab and enclosed cargo area, powered by an internal combustion engine. It also lost a lot of RPM. The Bangladesh "van" is a tricycle with a seat for the driver and a short flatbed. It's the low-cost

Figure 10.2 Traffic hazard—a slow-moving motorized van defies a High Court ban to transport bamboo on the Dhaka–Sylhet highway. Courtesy *Daily Star* (Anisur Rahman)

and low-emission utility transport found everywhere from country roads to crowded urban highways. You can carry almost anything on it—cattle fodder and sugarcane, sacks of rice and vegetables, a basket full of live chickens or a couple of goats, household furniture, metal pipes, bamboo scaffolding poles, or your family of six. The van has no gears (and perhaps no brakes), making for tough pedaling with a heavy load on the back. Fortunately, most of Bangladesh is as flat as a pancake, so the main challenges are the potholes, speed bumps, and trucks and buses that careen wildly across the road, forcing the van *chalaks* (drivers) onto the dirt berms. There's an upscale motorized version of the three-wheeler van with a longer bed. Most are homemade, with a tiller engine—the kind used for irrigation pumps—adapted to provide power. These are used for transporting bricks, lumber, and building materials. You can fit two cows, a stack of tires and mattresses, or a couple of beds and tables on the motor-van. Or a couple of families.

Any road trip in Bangladesh is a study in the social hierarchy of transportation. Next up from the motor-van is the three-wheeled auto rickshaw, often referred to by its fuel source as a CNG (compressed natural gas). It doesn't move much faster than a motor-van, especially when it's carrying five or six passengers, a couple of them hanging precariously out of the sides of the cab. Then there are Chinese-made pickup trucks with narrow beds and cabs so tiny that you'd think there was a height and weight limit for drivers. The passenger cars are mostly made in India: models of Tata, Maruti Suzuki, and Mahindra SUVs, and foreign brands, manufactured under license—Isuzu, Mazda, Mitsubishi, Opel, Renault, and others. The Indian industry also dominates the commercial vehicle market—Tata and Ashok Leyland trucks and Mahindra tractors. And finally, there's the king—or rather tyrant—of the road, the bus. They come in many forms—from sleek, air-conditioned luxury vehicles to stifling, exhaust-belching claptraps with broken windshields, torn seats and panels, and long scrape marks that would challenge the best body shop to knock into shape. The roughest-looking vehicles are often the ones with the fanciest names—the "International Super Express" and the "All the Way First Class Bus." They all go too fast.

I can't decide whether it's more terrifying to watch a bus speed along, swerving wildly to avoid other vehicles, or to be a passenger in the bus itself, taking your life in your hands. I'll assume that passengers are either inured to danger, resigned to their fate, reciting prayers, or heavily sedated. The buses, some with passengers sitting on the roofs, relentlessly charge ahead, their horns blaring, with the driver's assistant, usually a skinny teenager, hanging out of the door, waving at slower and smaller vehicles to move aside. I don't think bus drivers are culturally more inclined to reckless maneuvers than other drivers. The problem, according to Yasmin, is that bus companies operate on low profit margins and insist their drivers make so many trips per day; knowing they will get stuck in traffic at some point, they hit the gas when traffic is moving, and other vehicles had better move aside. The brightly painted trucks join in the discordant chorus of horns—some monotone, some playing annoyingly repetitive short melodies. With almost every vehicle using its horn, it's difficult to figure out who's getting in the way of whom. I started to wonder if the bus and truck drivers use a jumper wire to bypass the horn on the steering wheel so that the blast is constant. If you're dodging and weaving and riding the bumps, you don't want to add the tiresome task of having to push the horn.

The government has embarked on an ambitious road-building program, widening two-lane roads into divided highways, but high population density and rapid economic growth place severe strains on the network. Several studies have shown that the road system is totally inadequate for the traffic it carries, but shortage of funds and corruption have left many major highways, especially in rural regions, in disrepair. In monsoon season, roads and bridges are washed away, and traffic faces long detours. One night in early 2017, on the two-lane highway northwest from Dhaka to Tangail on which we were traveling, a combination of accidents, broken-down vehicles, and road construction caused a twenty-five-mile tailback, delaying traffic for up to eleven hours; even after the vehicles were cleared, the traffic did not move because truck drivers had fallen asleep in their cabs. The highways also take a heavy pounding from overloaded vehicles. Trucks are piled high with bricks, building materials, and agricultural produce, lashed down with ropes; often the tailgate is left open, so that the load hangs a foot or so off the back of the bed. When a truck is loaded high, the center of gravity shifts upward, making the vehicle liable to tip over if the driver turns sharply to avoid oncoming traffic. We saw a couple of trucks lying on their sides on the road bank and another jacked up with its cargo precariously leaning to the left.

The statistics are terrifying. On average, road accidents claim the lives of twelve thousand people a year, or about thirty-three per day, with another thirty-five thousand—almost one hundred per day—injured. No one knows exactly how many vehicles are on the roads because some vehicles—perhaps as many as 1.5 million, according to the Bangladesh Passenger Welfare Association—are not registered. In 2017, according to the Bangladesh Road Transport Authority (BRTA), about 3.42 million vehicles were registered. The same agency reported only 1.7 million driver license holders—in other words, one for every two registered vehicles. Except among government ministers and the business elite, multivehicle households are rare. Adding in the number of unregistered vehicles means that almost two-thirds, or more than three million, could be driven by unqualified drivers. The *Dhaka Tribune* reports that the country has only 142 BRTA-approved driving instructors and fewer than one hundred training centers, with long waits for training and licenses. Most people learn to drive from family members, friends, or coworkers.[3]

In 2011, there was a public outcry when a bus overtaking a vehicle on a curve hit a minibus head-on, killing five of the occupants, among them a well-known filmmaker and a media personality. The unlicensed driver had been driving the poorly maintained bus all night in the rain. Activists accused the government of ignoring "road terrorism" and demanded the resignation of the communications minister for his inaction. In a rare verdict almost six years later, the driver was sentenced to life imprisonment for "reckless driving and negligence."[4]

Transportation experts identify several reasons for accidents. Although some drivers may be naturally reckless (and some drive without training or licenses), congestion can make even a good driver take unnecessary risks. Some vehicles are poorly maintained: nontechnical translation—no brakes. And then there's that distinctively Asian and African practice of setting up a market or food stall on the highway itself. Economically, it's a smart move because the stall is in the right place to, so to speak, catch the passing traffic. Narrowing the roadway without warning, however, increases the risk of accidents. Sometimes the passing traffic catches the stall, or another vehicle.

The combination of fast-moving buses, trucks, and cars, slow-moving bicycle and motor-vans and auto rickshaws, and animals—goats and cattle—on two-lane roads is a recipe for accidents. Twice, the Bangladesh High Court has banned bicycle and motor-vans from national highways, while allowing them to operate on local roads. The ban has gone largely unenforced. The government has ordered local authorities to shut down the small factories that turn out the motorized three-wheelers, but has been stymied by political and business interests. "The implementation rate is zero . . . sometimes I feel helpless," admitted Transport minister Obaidul Quader.[5] Van drivers will not take local roads if the shortest distance between two points is on the national highway. How best to accommodate fast- and slow-moving vehicles? We saw one solution on the road to Rajshahi—the equivalent of a broad cycle path, a strip of blacktop parallel to the highway reserved for vans, bicycles, animals, and people. Much safer.

Rice Bowl

Bangladeshis like to tell you they are blessed with six seasons. The Bangla year begins on April 14 with the summer *grismo* season, running to mid-June. It is followed by *borsha,* the monsoon season to mid-August, then the fall season *sharat* to mid-October, and *hemonto* (late fall) to mid-December. *Sheet* (winter) lasts from December to mid-February, and the year ends with *bashonto,* the spring season to mid-April. I haven't spent long enough in the country to enjoy all the seasonal nuances, but at least they made me rethink my simplistic classification of the weather in tropical countries as either hot and wet (monsoon) or hot and dry. Of course, seasonal terms are relative. In the Bangladesh "winter," daytime temperatures are often in the 15–25 degrees Celsius (60–77 degrees Fahrenheit) range, dipping down to a teeth-chattering 4 degrees Celsius (40 degrees Fahrenheit) at night, with fog lingering into the morning. For those from northern climes, such winter weather feels almost balmy; Bangladeshis wrap up with sweaters, scarves, and hats.

The warm climate, monsoon rains, rivers, and rich alluvial soil make Bangladesh one of the most productive agricultural countries in Asia. Traveling northwest from Dhaka, the countryside around us was lush green. This land produces three rice harvests a year—the *Boro* (April to May), the *Aus* (July to August), and the *Aman* (November to December)—with different varieties planted to suit soil and weather conditions. Between the rice seasons, farmers plant crops such as mustard, chili, sesame, linseed, and coriander leaf that require little water, fertilizer, or pesticide, and can be harvested thirty to sixty days after planting. With four or five annual crops, the land is productive year-round.

Rice is a staple in the diet, especially for rural families. In most years, the seasons are predictable enough to allow farmers to know when to plant and harvest, but in 2017 the weather turned ugly with heavy storms in late March and early April—three months ahead of the usual start of the monsoon season. The intense rainfall caused flash flooding and created conditions for fungi to attack the rice plants while the grain was in its formative stage. In some regions, the *Boro* crop was ruined; in others, farmers harvested early, salvaging what they could. With stocks in public granaries low and a 25 percent import tariff on cheap rice from India, prices reached a three-year high.

The *haor* (wetland) areas in the northeast near the border with the Indian state of Meghalaya were particularly hard hit, as poorly built embankments collapsed; there were accusations of shoddy construction, poor oversight of contractors, and corruption. Flash floods in these areas ruined at least 80 percent of the *Boro* crop and submerged pastures, resulting in a shortage of fodder; some farmers had to sell their cattle because they could no longer feed them. "Nature turns her back on the *haor* people," ran the headline in the *Daily Star*. It was the first of a triple blow to farmers in one of the poorest regions of the country. As the floods receded, thousands of dead fish were found floating in the *haors*, forcing the authorities to temporarily ban fishing. Then ducks, the other major source of income, started dying, apparently from the same contamination. No one was sure what caused the pollution—the rotting of rice paddy under the water, or, perhaps more ominously, toxic waste from uranium mines across the border in India. The region was devastated, with farmers unable to pay loans taken out to plant the *Boro* rice crop. Some sold their livestock and abandoned their fields to seek work in the cities on construction sites and as rickshaw pullers. Although seasonal migration to urban areas happens every year, it usually occurs after the harvest. "Many farmers," noted one *Daily Star* writer, "are forced to become climate refugees, constantly on the move in search of a shelter and an opportunity to earn a livelihood."[6]

Along the road northwest from Dhaka, the rice fields were a patchwork—large areas of dark green, broken by squares of a lighter green where the rice had been cut. The harvested bundles are fed into machines that separate the rice from the stalks. Small trucks and vans loaded with rice and corn stalks wobbled along the road. Outside almost every house, the stalks were piled high. When the fields flood, cattle will not be able to forage, and the stalks will be the only fodder available. The people have adapted to the climate, building levees lined with banana trees that lead from their homes to the main road; when the rains come, these pathways—just wide enough for a motor-van—will be the only safe way to travel. The levees also protect fish ponds—a vital source of protein for the population.

Mango and jackfruit trees provide lumber for the small sawmills and furniture workshops in almost every village. Sections of tree trunks, golden-brown in color, are stacked along the roadside, ready to be cut into planks, then fashioned into beds, chairs, tables, chests, and trunks. Most furniture making is done by hand. Bare-chested craftsmen, wearing the traditional, checkered-pattern *lungi* (loin cloth), cut, plane, shape, and sand arms, legs, and headboards to standard dimensions and patterns. Most furniture is not stained or painted and has a rough, unfinished look, but it is sturdier than the mass-produced furniture from factories and more easily repaired. It's a low-cost, efficient manufacturing process with little waste; the wood scraps—and the odd miscast table or chair leg—are stacked in piles to be sold as firewood for cooking stoves. Shipment is by bicycle or motor-van, a whole bedroom or living room suite secured to the bed with ropes. On the roadside, the piles of uncut logs alternated with what looked to me like stacks of huge clay pots, enough to cook up *dahl* for a small village. I asked Yasmin if I was correct. She smiled. "They're pit toilets, and sold in sections," she said.

Land of Rivers

For a small country, close in size to its near neighbor, Nepal, or about the size of Illinois or Iowa, Bangladesh has an exceptionally large number of rivers, around seven hundred according to most estimates. Roughly 10 percent of its land area is water, a high proportion considering that it has no large lakes. In other words, most of that water is moving, at least in the monsoon season. And when Bangladesh floods, as much as one-third of its land area may be under water. The rivers are constantly shifting course, creating new channels or distributaries, making accurate mapping a frustrating exercise.

Three major river systems combine and empty into the Bay of Bengal. After flowing 450 miles southwest across Assam, the Brahmaputra turns south around the Garo Hills to enter Bangladesh, where it is called the Jamuna. South of the border, it is joined by a major tributary, the Tista, which rises in the Himalayas in Sikkim. The Jamuna then splits into two distributaries. For centuries, it flowed through central Bangladesh to join the second major river system, the Meghna, which brings together the Surma and Kushiyara, also flowing out of India's northeast. In the mid-eighteenth century, a major flood caused the Jamuna to change course over a thirty-year period. The larger, western channel now flows south 150 miles to join the third major river system, the Padma, the name given to the Ganges in Bangladesh. The smaller eastern channel, the old or lower Brahmaputra, flows southeast to join the Meghna.

The combined waters of the Padma and western Jamuna join the Meghna south of Dhaka to form the Lower Meghna. At its widest point, the Lower Meghna is almost eight miles across, land, river, and ocean merging into one hazy landscape. A maze of channels and distributaries combine into the great Gangetic Delta. At twenty-three thousand square miles, it's the largest delta in the world—the size of Lake Huron or almost as large as the state of West Virginia. The delta is ground zero for climate change, with floods and cyclones blowing up from the Bay of Bengal to submerge low-lying islands and push brackish salt water inland.

For Bangladesh's rural population, the river is interwoven with every aspect of their lives. It sustains agriculture—rice paddies, fields of corn, mango orchards, fish and shrimp farms, herds of cattle, and flocks of ducks. It is the main highway for commerce, with *nouka* carrying fruit, vegetables, livestock, and building materials. In many places, you need to travel by river to reach the school, the health clinic, or the government office.

The river, its seasons and rhythms, are common themes in Bangla literature. They figure prominently in the novels, short stories, plays, poems, and songs of Rabindranath Tagore (1861–1941), a leading figure in the Bengal Renaissance and the first non-European to win the Nobel Prize for Literature in 1913. An upper-class Brahmin from Calcutta, Tagore was raised in a literary family and attended public school in Sussex, England. From 1890, he began managing his family's estates on the Padma River in Kushtia district. As a *zamindar*—a hereditary landlord with the right to collect taxes from farmers—he and his entourage cruised the Padma and its tributaries on the well-appointed family houseboat. He witnessed the grinding poverty of rural Bengal

FIGURE 10.3 A *nouka* leaving the port at Barisal to carry passengers across the Kirtankhola River

and studied its folk traditions and songs. Several works from this period focus on the river, both literally and metaphorically, as in his famous poem, "The Golden Boat" (1894):

> Clouds rumbling in the sky; teeming rain.
> I sit on the river bank, sad and alone.
> The sheaves lie gathered, harvest has ended,
> The river is swollen and fierce in its flow.
> As we cut the paddy it started to rain.
>
> Who is this, steering close to the shore
> Singing? I feel that she is someone I know.
> The sails are filled wide, she gazes ahead,
> Waves break helplessly against the boat each side.
> I watch and feel I have seen her face before.
>
> Oh, to what foreign land do you sail?
> Come to the bank and moor your boat for a while.

Go where you want to, give where you care to,
But come to the bank a moment, show your smile
Take away my golden paddy when you sail.

For Tagore, the river was more than a setting for tales of love won and lost, or a place to marvel at the beauty and power of nature. From the 1920s, he became increasingly involved in social and political causes. He supported Indian independence while denouncing the elitism of its educated, urban leaders who, he felt, put political goals ahead of relieving poverty and suffering. In his later works, the river becomes a metaphor for class and social justice. In the poem "Kopai," he compares a small river "intimate with the villages" where "the land and water exist in no hostility" to the majestic Padma, which, like the Brahmaputra of Bhupen Hazarika's "Bisitirno Paarore" (On your wide banks), is indifferent to humanity:

She's different. She flows by the localities,
She tolerates them but does not acknowledge;
Pure is her aristocratic rhythm.

Across the Wide Jamuna

For centuries, the Jamuna, like Tagore's Padma, had its own "aristocratic rhythm," dividing the country vertically into two nearly equal halves. It was both a highway and a barrier to travel and trade. The only east–west links were by ferries carrying vehicles, rail cars, freight, and passengers. Ferry traffic depended on navigability; in rough weather or in the dry season, east–west commerce was practically halted.

Soon after partition in 1947, political parties and businesses began campaigning for a bridge across the Jamuna. Consultants were hired, feasibility studies commissioned, and committees appointed. The project was abandoned more than once. By 1982, the estimated cost had climbed from $175 to $420 million. The clincher was to make it a multipurpose bridge, carrying a two-lane roadway, a dual-gauge railroad line, a natural gas pipeline, and power and telecommunications lines. It was named the Bangabandhu Bridge, in honor of the hero of the independence movement, Sheikh Mujibur Rahman, known popularly as Bangabandhu (Friend of Bengal). By the time his daughter and then-president Sheikh Hasina opened it in 1998, the cost had risen to almost $700 million.

Building the bridge meant taming the river. Records showed that at flood stage, the Jamuna could stretch almost nine miles across. A nine-mile bridge was not in anyone's cost calculations, so engineers built a channel to confine the Jamuna, keeping the bridge length down to three and a half miles. Construction required anchoring forty-nine spans in the river bed and building east and west viaducts, each with twelve spans. When opened, it was the eleventh longest bridge in the world. As we crossed, we looked down on fishing boats; the Silk City Express, one of three weekly trains on the Rajshahi route, passed on its way to Dhaka, a six-and-a-half-hour trip.

For most people traveling between Dhaka and Rajshahi, the town of Sirajganj, west of the Bangabandhu Bridge, is a convenient place to break the journey. Bus companies and their drivers take commissions to disgorge passengers at roadside restaurants, some of which have expanded to become small shopping centers. As we arrived, the Michi No Eki Food Village Plus was doing a booming business, with six buses in the dirt parking lot. In the cutthroat world of roadside eateries, it's useful to have a distinctive, fashionable foreign name. The owners of the Michi No Eki had done their research, using the Japanese name for a government-designated highway rest area with shops and restaurants. Good street food, but no sushi.

After a hair-raising three hours on a bus, I'd expect the passengers to stumble out and kiss the earth, thanking Allah that they are still breathing, but instead they amble into the restaurant to order lunch and buy desserts to sustain them for the road ahead. We stopped across the road at the Aristocrat restaurant. Yasmin told me it was the first, upscale roadside eatery established after the bridge was opened. The staff take the Aristocrat name seriously. As we pulled up, uniformed security guards moved forward to open our car doors and saluted; more staff opened doors and saluted as we entered the restaurant. I felt a little guilty that we had just stopped for tea. Yet this is how one is greeted and treated at most restaurants and hotels that have staff (usually more than one) stationed at every point where a customer might need something. We departed to more saluting and door opening. One security guard walked into the road, held up his hand to halt traffic and shooed away a goat. He snapped to attention and saluted again. And we were on our way.

Rajshahi, an agricultural processing center famous for its silk industry, sits on the north bank of the Padma. On a hazy morning, the south bank—the Indian state of West Bengal—was a distant blur. In the river, low-lying islands formed by silt deposits are submerged during monsoon season; when the waters subside, some islands have shifted, changed shape, or disappeared altogether as the river keeps redefining the land. My companions and I walked from the levee to the shoreline across a floodplain of sand, mud, and long grasses. Ice cream vendors were setting up their stalls, and a boy was wiping tables at a restaurant. When the weather is nice, this is a popular spot for paddling and picnics. In monsoon season, the river laps at the edge of the levee and sometimes covers the road. This morning all was calm. A few fishing boats were pulled up on the shore, others were out catching *hilsha*, a popular fish served fried, grilled, and in curries.

I pointed to a line of boats with radio aerials. "That's the border patrol," said Rama Saha, the local UNICEF officer. "They're trying to stop smuggling from India." I asked her what was smuggled. "Cattle are the major contraband," she said. "The Hindus can't eat beef, so there's money to be made bringing cattle across the river." I asked her what else was smuggled. It was a diverse list—saris, matches, medicines, and fentanyl, the notorious heroin additive. Much is sold on Rajshahi's central bazaar, where Indian-made goods (legally and illegally imported) dominate.

After the chaos of Dhaka, Rajshahi was a relaxed place, relatively free of pollution and traffic jams, with parks, gardens, and some stylish British colonial buildings, including the Rajshahi College, built in 1873. A week after crowds had turned out to celebrate the Bengali New Year on April 14, the surfaces of several streets were still covered with colorful, intricate traditional designs called *alpona*, derived from the Sanskrit *alimpana*, which means "to plaster." The art form, also common in several regions of India, uses rice powder mixed with water to form a liquid paste, with leaves added to provide coloration and glue to help it stick, at least through a few rain showers. The artwork, mainly done by women, marks the changing of the seasons.

Our hotel booking was at the "Seiz Razzak." This puzzled Yasmin. "The word makes no sense in Bangla," she said. I checked online. "Oh, it's Chez Razzak," I said. "It means 'at the home of' in French." The desk clerk confirmed that Razzak, the owner, often traveled to France and had decided to give his establishment a French name.

That evening, Rajshahi was lashed by what Yasmin called an "evil storm." At Chez Razzak, the power went off, then on again, then off; puddles formed on the floors of the stairways as rain seeped through the roof. Not wanting to risk the elevator, Yasmin and I took the stairs to the seventh-floor restaurant. I was hoping that the French name extended to the menu and was looking forward to some haute cuisine à la Bangladeshi. Perhaps the local *pâté* de foie gras as a starter? I had seen lots of ducks along the road. Unfortunately, at Chez Razzak, you must order meals in advance. There's no menu and certainly no haute cuisine. All the staff could manage was tea and a packet of cookies. Bon appétit.

Literary Kushtia

For ninety miles, the Padma forms the western boundary with India. South of Rajshahi, the river turns west before dividing into two channels near the city of Kushtia. The main channel flows southeast to join the Jamuna. The smaller channel meanders south through the districts of Jessore and Khulna to the vast mangrove forest of the Sundarbans—home to the Bengal tiger and other endangered species—and to the Bay of Bengal.

It was on the south bank of the Padma, at Shilaidaha Kuthibari, the country house built by his father in the mid-nineteenth century, that Tagore lived for more than ten years after returning from England in 1880. In between his duties as a *zamindar*, traveling up and down the Padma and tributaries, Tagore wrote some of his most famous poems, short stories, and songs. Some were influenced by the folk songs of the philosopher, mystic, songwriter, and social reformer Lalon Shah, who lived on the Tagore estates and often visited the family. Lalon came from a group of nineteenth-century hippies called the Bauls, engagingly described in one travel guide as "singing, marijuana-smoking bards who espouse a love of the land while shunning the mainstream." The Bauls were a mixed group of moderate Hindus and Sufi Muslims, known for their colorful clothes, musical instruments, and back-to-the-land lifestyles. In his folk songs, Lalon called for religious tolerance and the rejection of class and creed. By the time he died in 1890, reportedly at the age of 116, he is said to have composed more than eight hundred songs and to have influenced many poets and thinkers—from Tagore to Allen Ginsberg. Tagore published and popularized some of his songs.

Tagore returned to Shilaidaha Kuthibari in 1912 to translate the *Gitanjali*, a collection of more than one hundred of his poems, into English—the work that earned him the 1913 Nobel Prize for Literature. The open terraces of the three-story mansion, built from brick, tile, and timber with a corrugated metal roof, look out on landscaped gardens and orchards of mango, jackfruit, and other evergreen trees, a flower garden, and two ponds. The house is now a museum, with annual festivals honoring Tagore. For many Bangladeshis, particularly those who value the tolerant philosophies of Lalon Shah and Tagore, the city of Kushtia is the capital of Bengali culture. Twice a year, in March and October, thousands make the pilgrimage for two folk music festivals held on the grounds of Lalon Shah's *mazar* (gravesite).

The city of Kushtia, with a population of more than one hundred thousand, is an educational center with public and private universities and government colleges, and a commercial and transportation hub with textile and sugar mills. And it was in Meherpur, a remote village in Kushtia district near the Indian border, that in 1971 the country's political leaders, fleeing from the Pakistani army, set up their government.

On Jessore Road

Millions of babies watching the skies
Bellies swollen, with big round eyes
On Jessore Road—long bamboo huts
No place to shit but sand channel ruts

. . . .

Millions of souls nineteen seventy-one
Homeless on Jessore under grey sun
A million are dead, the millions who can
Walk toward Calcutta from East Pakistan

Historians estimate that ten million refugees, most of them Hindus but at least one in five Muslims, fled to India during the nine-month Liberation War. Allen Ginsberg's 152-line poem "September on Jessore Road" vividly depicts their suffering on the main road west from the city of Jessore to the border. They left farms and towns, traveling by van, rickshaw, and on foot, carrying what belongings they could. Along the road, they faced attacks by the Pakistani army and the *razakars,* the pro-Pakistani militia. Many died of exhaustion and hunger in the mud of the late monsoon rains, their bodies abandoned by their families. Ginsberg, who had been traveling in India, was in Kolkata during the war and visited refugee camps in West Bengal. Although many world leaders supported the liberation struggle, the United States, embroiled in Vietnam and afraid of jeopardizing its new relationship with Pakistan's ally, China, did not. Ginsberg, along with other poets, writers, journalists, and musicians, was sharply critical of the Nixon administration:

> Where are the helicopters of U.S. AID?
> Smuggling dope in Bangkok's green shade.
> Where is America's Air Force of Light?
> Bombing North Laos all day and all night?

Ginsberg's friend Bob Dylan arranged and played guitar on a song version of the poem and performed it at two concerts for refugee relief at Madison Square Garden organized by George Harrison and sitar maestro Ravi Shankar. "September on Jessore Road" remains a moving testament to the victims of the conflict.

The strategic location of Jessore, where the north–south highway from Kushtia and Rajshahi to Khulna meets the east–west route from Dhaka and central Bangladesh to India, gave it a key role in the Liberation War. On March 29, a few days after the Pakistan Army launched Operation Searchlight, a contingent of Bengali soldiers in Jessore mutinied against their Pakistani commanders. The city became a center of resistance activity. On December 7, the advancing Indian Army captured it after a fierce twenty-four-hour battle. Its Pakistani defenders—estimated before the battle at about five thousand men—fled south. The capture of Jessore virtually assured the Indian Army of control of the western half of the country. A week later, the war was over.

The Industrial West

Jessore, an old city with fine colonial-era buildings, twisting alleys, and a lively bazaar, retains its strategic importance as a center in cross-border commerce. The border crossing at Benapole, an untidy cluster of hotels, restaurants, warehouses, and transport facilities, is less than thirty miles west, and the Jessore road is the main overland commercial route between the two countries. Trucks rumble west, carrying textiles, jute products such as rope and sacks, scrap metal, and agricultural produce. Bangladesh imports coal, petroleum, chemicals, rice, and manufactured goods, including cars and trucks. On the road south from Jessore to Khulna, we passed rail junctions where laborers off-loaded coal from trucks into rail cars, part of a supply chain that begins in the mines of Bihar and West Bengal and ends at the power stations that supply Dhaka's garment factories and residents.

In contrast to the northern section of the road from Kushtia to Jessore, which is bordered by rice paddies, corn fields, and mango plantations, the southern section is more industrial. The region has deposits of mica and bauxite and produces building materials; we passed the tall chimneys of brick kilns, cement plants, and factories with rows of bicycles parked outside. The dull grey concrete buildings were interrupted by unexpected splashes of color—apartment blocks and commercial buildings painted from basement to roof in bright red or green, advertising cement, chips, tea, and mobile phone services. Perhaps only in South Asia can you buy not only a roadside billboard but a whole building to push your product. On some, an uplifting slogan was added to the product name and logo, a small dash of corporate social responsibility to atone for dunking yet another block in company colors. It was nice to know that the company that sold you chips also believed that "The Learned are Judicious."

Beyond the kilns and plants, the rice paddies stretched far into the distance, irrigated by diesel-powered pumps drawing water from the aquifer. Along the road, lined with eucalyptus trees, peanuts were laid out on tarpaulins to dry. The most important cash crop is shrimp, raised in fresh and saltwater ponds; we saw blue nets stretched across the ponds and small fields of red—harvested shrimp drying in the sun. Logs were piled on the roadside, ready to be fashioned into furniture. South of Jessore, the logs came in more varieties—not only golden-brown mango and the lighter jackfruit, but darker woods. South of Khulna is the Sundarbans, the delta area with the largest continuous mangrove forest in the world. It is home to deer, wild boar, otter, saltwater crocodiles, river dolphins, and the last surviving Bengal tigers. Officially, it's a protected area, but its vastness and lack of roads make it difficult to police. Illegal logging has become a lucrative industry.

Khulna, where we stayed overnight after a visit to the university, is an old river port on a distributary of the Padma. It used to be a center

of the jute industry, but today shrimp is its major export. With a population of just over one million, it's the third-largest city in Bangladesh, but
a distant third; Dhaka has a population of 8.5 million and Chittagong,
the major port on the Bay of Bengal, 4.5 million. It's still a bustling place,
crowded with trucks, buses, auto rickshaws, and cars. We stayed at the
City Inn, a three-star establishment with a temperamental elevator that
promoted itself as the "symbol of elegance."

From UNICEF's perspective, there's a lot to do in western Bangladesh.
Poverty rates are high, and many children suffer from poor nutrition. Over-
all, the country has improved its maternal and childhood mortality rates,
but some western districts are lagging. Many children work in agriculture
and small industry, so child labor is an issue. On the other hand, why would
parents send their children to school when the quality of primary education is low, and poorly paid teachers sometimes don't show up for class?
The government's failure to provide education, health, and social services
has created needs that are partly filled by development agencies and by
the mosques that operate madrassas. As in other Muslim-majority regions,
girls are often married off in their teens. It's a social norm that's hard to
break, but it's also driven by poverty; marrying your daughters early re-
duces dowry amounts and the number of mouths to feed.

I was told there were Islamic State-affiliated training camps in this
region where young Muslim men are radicalized and then sent to Iraq
or Syria. At the Islamic University of Kushtia, which has a large department of religious studies, I trod carefully in my discussions with faculty
members. I need not have worried because they were typical academics,
contemptuous of all authority. I would have likely faced more hostility
from the motorcycle gang we passed on the road near Jessore, waving
red flags. The region, like its Indian neighbor West Bengal, is a strong-
hold of the Communist Party. I thought the bikers all looked rather
revolutionary chic—sooooo Che Guevara with their red bandanas embossed with the hammer and sickle. But I was not about to stop and
commend them on their sense of fashion.

Bangladesh's East End

"Don't take the piss, luv. I'm bleedin' knackered." I caught the last part
of the mobile phone conversation in the lobby of the Valley Garden
Hotel in Sylhet, a bustling city in northeastern Bangladesh. By his dress

and skin color, the speaker—a man in his thirties—looked Bangladeshi, but the accent and word choice were purely London. The man picked up his bag and went to the elevator. He looked as if he'd just arrived after a long flight.

Which he probably had. There are flights from Heathrow via Dhaka to Sylhet on Biman Bangladesh, and other connections via Dubai and Delhi. They serve a community of Bangladeshis—or Sylhetis as they prefer to be called—who have settled in East London since the nineteenth century. They first came as merchant seamen, hired on in Chittagong by British trading ships. When World War I broke out and young British men were conscripted, demand for seamen increased and more Sylhetis took to the seas. Leaving their families was difficult, but they earned more money than they could in the tea plantations. Between voyages, they lived in cramped quarters in London's docklands. Some left the ships to take factory jobs and sent the money home.

As Muslims, they maintained their culinary practices. In the 1920s, a Sylheti opened a curry shop that became the foundation for a thriving Bengali restaurant industry, centered on Brick Lane in Tower Hamlets. Of course, the Brick Lane entrepreneurs adapted to British taste and climate, cutting down on the heat and spices. They have been remarkably successful. Today, the Bangladeshi restaurant industry in Britain is estimated to be worth $6 billion a year.

Some of that money comes home to Sylhet to support family members. It goes toward medical and educational expenses, and daily living needs. British Bangladeshis have built mansions outside the city to use when they visit. Most of the time, a colleague told me, they stand empty, with a guard, a maid, and a gardener on staff. In a society where, despite its Muslim principles, material possessions are valued, the mansion represents a family's social standing—a status symbol in a region where many people remain desperately poor.

According to economic statistics, Sylhet Division is the wealthiest region of Bangladesh outside Dhaka, but the wealth is unevenly distributed, and the division lags behind others on indicators for health, nutrition, and education. On the tea plantations, many workers are from the Indian states of Orissa and Bihar. They are descendants of workers brought in by the British in the colonial era; they have struggled to preserve their Hindu religion and native languages and have never fully integrated into Sylheti society. In the months before partition in 1947, the Muslim League encouraged Bengali Muslims to move north to Assam, hoping a Muslim majority in its southern districts would expand East Pakistan's frontiers; ultimately, only the Sylhet district became part of Pakistan. Bordered on the north by the Indian state of Meghalaya and on the east by Manipur, the district is among the most ethnically diverse in the country, with villages of Manipuri, Khasis, and Tripura people in the hills, practicing Hinduism, Buddhism, and Christianity. It has its own language, Sylhoti, with ties to both Bangla and Assamese.

The tea plantations—or tea gardens, as they are somewhat romantically termed—stretch across the low hills along the road from the airport to the city. Compared with the rest of the country, the region's climate is cool and wet, making it (like Assam) ideal for growing tea, most of it for export. The day Yasmin and I arrived, there was a *hartal*—a strike by transport workers protesting an increase in the price of CNG, which fuels all the auto rickshaws and many buses, trucks, and cars. UNICEF's security people had warned us to be careful because some roads had been blocked by strikers, but the main road was clear and mercifully free of traffic, so we reached the hotel in what our driver assured us was record time.

By early evening, the strike was over, and Sylhet returned to its normal traffic congestion. The city is a major shopping destination, with some of the best discount clothing outlets in the country. Many British Bangladeshis (perhaps including the man in the hotel) come here on shopping trips; after paying for the flight and excess baggage, they'll still come out ahead compared with shopping in the UK.

Every hotel I've stayed at outside Dhaka has its idiosyncrasies, and the Hotel Valley Garden was no exception. The main challenge was figuring out which button to push in the elevator. Our rooms were on the sixth floor, but if you pressed "6" you ended up on the seventh floor. The restaurant was on the fourth floor, but accessible only by pressing "3." The hotel staff were used to it and reflexively deducted one from the desired destination, but we made a few detours before figuring it out. Unfortunately, the card in the room with instructions on how to stay safe during an earthquake did not include "Do not use the elevator, or if you do, remember to deduct one." Maybe it was installed by the same company responsible for a restaurant menu that offered "milk sheik," "corn flacks," and "poltry."

"Your passport, please sir. Why are you coming to Barisal? What is your organization? Where are you staying? The mobile phone number of your host, please." The questions came thick and fast from the young security service agent at Barisal Airport. He was polite, if a little officious. I fumbled in my briefcase for papers and scrolled through the contacts on my phone while he took notes. I hadn't expected a security check after a domestic flight and was feeling concerned. Was I required to inform the security service of my travels within the country? If so, no one in Dhaka had warned me. Or perhaps the agent was just hassling me and hoping for a bribe. I couldn't be sure. At that point, the driver from the local UNICEF office appeared. The agent asked for his name and mobile number, then told us to wait in the car.

As we walked out of the terminal, we passed a pickup truck with half a dozen uniformed men with semiautomatics sitting on benches on the bed. "The RAB," said the driver. "Assigned to guard the airport." The RAB (Rapid Action Battalion) is an elite anticrime and antiterrorism unit drawn from the police, army, navy, and coast guard. With their neatly pressed dark-gray uniforms, jauntily reversed caps, and designer sunglasses, the officers looked not only menacing, but fashionably so. Indeed, the power and swagger of the RAB may be enough to deter some criminals and terrorists. The unit has developed an unsavory reputation for ignoring normal legal procedures and human rights. Warrantless searches. Forced confessions, sometimes extracted by roughing up suspects. Accused terrorists mysteriously disappearing after arrest. Extrajudicial killings. The RAB does not mess around.

It was swelteringly hot, and I was happy for the air-conditioning of the Toyota Land Cruiser. A Mahindra auto rickshaw pulled up in front of us. Its driver sported a bright yellow T-shirt with the word "Broken" in black letters across the front—another one of those puzzling (or perhaps completely meaningless) English words that crop up on cheap clothing throughout South Asia. At least his passengers—three young policemen armed with rifles—were appropriately dressed. One signaled for us to follow and at last I realized that I was not going to pay the price for some bureaucratic oversight and spend the night in a filthy jail cell but was being escorted into the city. Behind us, two SUVs, both carrying foreigners who had arrived on the same flight from Dhaka, followed. A half hour later, near the city center, the convoy halted, and the police informed us it was now safe to drive without an escort.

For almost a year, the security services in southwestern Bangladesh had been on high alert. In June 2016, a Hindu college teacher was seriously wounded when three machete-wielding men attacked him at his home north of Barisal. Two Hindus were among four people killed in separate machete attacks across the country that week. The machete attacks, usually carried out by young men on motorcycles, followed other violence, with religious minorities, activists, foreigners, and secular bloggers the main targets. The next month saw the attack on the Holey Artisan Bakery in Gulshan-2 in which twenty hostages, including seventeen foreigners, were killed. The attack, the country's worst-ever hostage crisis, sent a shock wave through the expatriate community and led to a crackdown on suspected terrorists by the police and RAB, with thousands rounded up in raids.

Barisal, on the west bank of the Kirtankhola, a distributary of the Lower Meghna, is a river port with a population of 350,000. The commercial gateway to the southwest delta, it's been hyperbolically described as the "Venice of Bengal" or "Venice of the East," although if you're just counting waterways, almost any large town in southwestern Bangladesh is a Venice. Because the region is crisscrossed by rivers and channels, road travel is difficult, so most people and goods move by water. The road from the airport passed through a lush landscape of banana, coconut, and mango trees, separated by wetlands, small channels, and ponds full of lilies, with houses built on stilts. The region is about as disaster-prone as any place in the world; rivers burst their banks from the monsoon rains, and cyclones, with winds sometimes over one hundred miles per hour, blow up from the Bay of Bengal, battering homes and crops and whipping up tidal surges.

Bangladesh's coastal areas are better prepared for natural disasters than they used to be. In 1970, Cyclone Bhola hit East Pakistan, causing an estimated 300,000 to 500,000 deaths. In April 1991, Cyclone Bob, with winds of up to 150 miles per hour and a twenty-foot storm surge, struck the southeastern coast near Chittagong, killing at least 140,000 and leaving more than ten million homeless. Since then, improved forecasting and early warning systems have saved lives. In November 2007, when a cyclone of similar force, Sidr, hit the delta region, property damage was severe, but this time 3,500 lost their lives. Almost every year, one or more cyclones hit coastal areas, but casualty figures for the past decade have been in the hundreds or less, not the thousands. When Cyclone Mora, with winds of seventy miles an hour, made landfall near Chittagong in May 2017, half a million had already moved away from the coast ahead of the storm.

Local authorities have several ways to warn people to move to shelters. Historically, radio was the key electronic medium, but now SMS messages reach many people. In some villages, the most effective warning system is simple and low-tech—a man with a battery-powered loudspeaker on a bicycle, in a van, or on an auto rickshaw. At my hotel, I met a three-person team on its way to Patuakhali, thirty miles south of Barisal, for the formal opening of a "school-cum-cyclone shelter"—one of several hundred built under an Islamic Development Bank project called Fael Khair (Arabic for "philanthropist"). For most of the year, the buildings serve as schools, but when cyclones hit they provide shelter. The team leader, Colin Coyle, a genial civil engineer from Ulster with experience in Afghanistan, Iraq, and Sudan, told me that cyclone-shelter building had run up against the standard if-you-build-it-they-will-come challenge of development work.

"The problem was the farm animals," he said. "The men would come to a shelter, but they would leave the women at home to take care of the animals." Fael Khair's solution? Build ramps so that animals can be herded into the shelters. Men, women, children, cattle, and goats— all safe from the storm.

Since the Mughal period, Barisal's location on a major navigable waterway has made it an important port. In August 1971, it was one of the targets for the naval commandos in Operation Jackpot. The Kirtankhola Channel is not deep enough for the oceangoing cargo ships that steam up the Lower Meghna from the Bay of Bengal, but it can handle smaller freighters that ply between the towns of the delta region, carrying bricks, building materials, and bulk agricultural produce. Motorized *nouka* deliver fruit, vegetables, and fish to villages and ferry passengers, bicycles, and animals across the rivers; the catamaran version—two *nouka* with a wooden platform—is large enough to carry a couple of vehicles. There's a new road bridge across the Kirtankhola at Barisal, but most rivers and channels are not bridged, and ferries are the only way to avoid a long journey on dirt roads.

After meetings at the University of Barisal and the local medical college, my UNICEF host, Sanjit Kumar Das, took me home to his apartment to meet his family. His wife had not only prepared desserts but made up snacks for my return trip to Dhaka. "You'll be on the launch for at least seven hours," said Sanjit. "You can buy food on board, but this will keep you going."

Slow Boat from Barisal

There's something liberating about a long river trip in Bangladesh, and I was happy there were no return flights to Dhaka that day. Sanjit had booked me on the 3:00 p.m. Green Line Waterways launch. In the Bangla transportation vocabulary, the English word "launch," derived from the Spanish *lancha* (barge), is not what you'd expect—one of those sleek party boats that line marinas in Florida, or the kind of patrol boat the coast guard and police use to chase drug runners. The Bangladesh "launch," often four decks high, carries several hundred passengers, and sometimes vehicles and cargo. One type looks like a modern ferry—the kind you'd take across the English Channel, but without the drunken football fans in the bar—while another looks like a Mississippi stern-wheeler, all open decks and verandas but without the stern wheel. From

FIGURE 10.4 The port and ferry terminal at Barisal in the delta region

Dhaka's Sadarghat ferry terminal, launches to southern destinations—Khulna, Barisal, Patuakhali, and islands of the delta—leave in the early evening and offer comfortable cabins with air-conditioning. I haven't done the trip this way, but travelers tell me it's exhilarating to leave behind the noise and pollution of the capital and float off into the sunset.

At the Barisal *ghat* (terminal), Sanjit and his daughter guided me through the stalls selling street food, snacks, fruit, and vegetables. Three launches were moored, and Sanjit wanted to make sure I boarded the right one. I stood on the top deck and waved goodbye. Below me, *nouka* glided in and out of the *ghat*, carrying passengers, bicycles, motorbikes, yellow water barrels, and fruit and vegetables. Small boys jumped into the water, splashed around and climbed back up the wooden pillars supporting the quay. A man emerged from the launch's kitchen and laid a long blue rug on the open deck. Passengers would need to pray during the trip. I wondered if someone with a compass or a smart phone was appointed to adjust the arrow that pointed toward Mecca to the meanders on the river.

After several blasts from the launch's horn, we cast off. For an hour or so, I stood on the open deck enjoying the breeze and watching life on the Kirtankhola—the shoreline of coconut palms, bananas, mango trees, and small settlements, fishermen casting their nets, cattle grazing on low, grassy islands. We passed small freighters heading downstream with loads of gravel, bricks, and sand, and *nouka* crossing the river. After two hours, we joined the Lower Meghna, and the shoreline disappeared into the late afternoon haze. There wasn't much to look at except for larger cargo ships and swooping seagulls, so I retreated to the air-conditioned upper deck. It was a midweek departure, so I had my choice of seats. A steward brought me tea, and I settled down to read a book and make some travel notes.

It was difficult to concentrate because of the constant chatter from the TV monitors, occasionally interrupted by gunshots and car crashes. Green TV was offering a steady stream of Bangla-language movies with routine plots and stock characters. The Dhallywood (Dhaka-based) movie industry is not as large or renowned as its Indian big brother, Bollywood, but it has perfected the mass production process, churning out hundreds of movies a year for domestic audiences and the Bangladeshi diaspora in the Middle East, Malaysia, and the UK. There were shoot-outs on city streets, car chases, and love scenes on beaches and green mountain pastures, the characters' slow-motion passions enhanced by rain, mist, and other artificial weather elements. Most characters appeared to change clothes every couple of minutes, the women dressed in bright colors, the men with slicked black hair usually dressed in smart suits and sporting sunglasses, even during night scenes.

It was night by the time we reached the Buriganga River, the channel of the Padma that flows through Dhaka. We passed overnight launches heading south, their deck lights illuminating them against the dark water. Many passengers were on deck, enjoying the cool night air. We docked at Sadarghat, and I emerged into the maze of Old Dhaka, the streets crowded with auto rickshaws, trucks, buses, and people. I was already missing the river.

eleven

Improbable Indonesia

Noah's Ark

It sits, incongruously, across the roofs of two houses—a one-hundred-foot fishing boat, slightly tilted as if still rocking in an ocean swell. Except that it is nowhere near the sea.

The boat was left high and dry by the 2004 tsunami that struck the province of Aceh in northwest Sumatra, Indonesia's largest island. It's estimated 170,000 people in the province died or disappeared, their bodies swept out to sea or crushed beyond recognition against buildings and trees. In Banda Aceh, the capital, the tsunami swept ashore most of the fishing fleet. Many boats were destroyed, but a dozen or so ended up stuck in buildings.

In the cleanup operations, most boats were removed. This one was left where it landed, a stark memorial to the lives it saved. It's now on the tsunami tourism trail, with street signs pointing to *Kapal di atas rumah* (the boat above the house).

After the earthquake struck early on the morning of December 26, Fauziah Basyariah and her five children found a house that was still standing and reached the second floor. Water started filling the room. "We were floating with our heads touching the ceiling—I thought we would drown," said Basyariah.

FIGURE 11.1   On the tsunami tourism trail in Banda Aceh—Noah's Ark, the "boat above the house." Courtesy Ronnie Muhadi

Then the fishing boat became wedged on the roof. Basyariah's fourteen-year-old son punched a hole in the ceiling, lifted himself through, and pulled the family out, one by one. They climbed aboard the boat and were joined by others. Huddled together, the fifty-nine survivors prayed as the boat, which had taken on water, wobbled on its perch. They were stranded for seven hours until the waters receded. All around them, buildings collapsed, and people, animals, vehicles, and market stalls were swept away. Among the victims was Basyariah's husband, who had taken the family motorbike to go shopping, and her parents. After the disaster, the widow, with five children to support, lived in a temporary shelter and learned new skills. Today, she owns a small business that packages and sells dried tuna. A picture of the boat is on the label. No wonder local people call it Noah's Ark.

Two miles inland, the *Apung I,* a power-generating ship owned by the local electrical company, crashed down on two houses, killing the inhabitants. I joined tourists from Jakarta, pushing past the postcard and souvenir sellers to climb the metal gangplanks, stand on the top deck, and survey the city below. The twenty-six-hundred-ton ship is mostly intact, and some say that there are still bodies beneath it. To many, it testifies to the awesome power of nature. "Who among us could ever move this big ship?" said one tourist. "God can bring it here from the sea, but we just don't have the ability to bring it back."[1]

Standing on the beach that evening with American and Indonesian colleagues, watching the sun set over the Indian Ocean, it was difficult to imagine that this idyllic place had been the scene of such death and destruction. The tsunami was triggered by the world's second-largest recorded earthquake—estimated at 9.1 to 9.3 on the Richter scale—with its epicenter off the west coast of Sumatra. I had watched the TV reports of devastation across the Indian Ocean—from Indonesia to Malaysia, Thailand, India, Sri Lanka, and the Maldives. The news came in, as all news of natural disasters does, in fragments; the death toll kept mounting as the military and emergency services reached communities cut off when the earthquake and tsunami destroyed roads and communications lines.

Some of the video from Aceh was taken by one of my companions on the beach that evening. Dendy Montgomery, a freelance videographer based in Banda Aceh, was out on the streets soon after 8:00 a.m. to shoot the earthquake damage. Then the first wave hit. "I heard my wife yelling, 'Come on—we need to go. The water is coming.'" Dendy kept on filming; he had seen other floods and was not worried. "Then I saw the first water coming from behind the Grand Mosque—it was maybe five to six meters high." A few seconds later came a second, higher wall of water. Dendy started running. "I jumped in my jeep with my wife. Usually, I need at least three times to start the engine, but this time only once and then—vroom!" With other survivors packed inside and hanging on the outside, Dendy sped off. Somehow, he found his mother and younger brother on the street and picked up a blind woman who was begging for money. "Mine was the last car to get out of the area," said Dendy. "The others were swept away."

Members of Dendy's extended family were killed or lost in the tsunami. It was more than a year before he could return to the beach. Ten years later, on the anniversary of the tsunami, he told Britain's Sky News, "I'm still really shaky when I'm at the beach. I'm yelling as loud as I can, 'I'm not scared anymore.'" He will never forget the lives lost. "It was as if all my family was going to Mecca in one big group and never coming back."[2]

Dendy was in a group of eighteen Indonesian TV journalists who took part in a training and exchange program funded by the US Department of State that I managed. The group spent three months in the United States in 2007; the next year I accompanied journalists with whom they had worked on a visit to Indonesia. Dendy and two others were our hosts for a tour of Banda Aceh.

Except for boats on houses, Banda Aceh seemed to show few scars from its near-destruction less than four years earlier. An extensive re-building program, funded by the Indonesian and foreign governments and international aid agencies, had transformed the city, with new apart-ment and office blocks, schools, mosques, hospitals, and government buildings. The roads were wide and well maintained. The markets were busy. A provincial election was coming up, and billboards along the highways featured photos of candidates, all promising a bright future for the province. Banda Aceh looked like a prosperous place.

We visited TV and radio stations and newspapers and the local uni-versity and met with the mayor. Almost everyone talked about how peo-ple had come together to respond to the disaster. The earthquake and waves toppled mobile phone towers and telephone poles and destroyed local radio and TV stations, making communication almost impossible. Aid agencies flew in "suitcase" low-powered FM radio transmitters to broadcast information about shelters and pickup points for food and water, and to air messages from people looking for family members. The daily newspaper *Serambi* (literally "front porch") *Indonesia* lost thir-teen journalists and thirty-seven staff, half its workforce, when its build-ing collapsed. Yet, within a week, *Serambi*, with support from its parent company, the *Kompas* media group, was printing on temporary presses and distributing free copies, helping families reunite by publishing photos of survivors.

Metro TV, Indonesia's first twenty-four-hour news channel, had re-porters and videographers on the ground within hours. With local TV and radio stations off the air, national TV channels played a key role in di-saster recovery and relief. For a time, Metro dropped all advertising spots and ran uninterrupted coverage, while collecting $18 million in contribu-tions from viewers. TV crews brought in food and medical supplies, and many stayed for extended assignments; a year after the tragedy, Metro still had almost one hundred staff in Aceh. The tsunami had psychological effects on journalists, and some needed counseling. "Four days after the tsunami, you could still see hundreds of dead bodies," one told me. "I know I was breaking the rules about showing emotion, but I just cried."

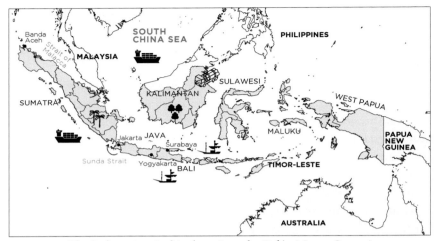

MAP 11.1   The Indonesian Archipelago (map by Belén Marco Crespo)

The Ring of Fire

Unexpected though it was, the 2004 tsunami was simply the latest and largest natural disaster to hit a country that, even for its size, experiences more than its fair share of earthquakes, volcanic eruptions, and tsunamis. Most of Indonesia's islands are strung along the so-called Ring of Fire, a horseshoe-shaped area of the Pacific Ocean basin that stretches from New Zealand to southern Chile. About 90 percent of the world's earthquakes occur along the Ring of Fire, which also contains more than three-quarters of the world's active and dormant volcanoes. The earth movements are caused by plate tectonics, the collision and subduction (overlapping) of sections of the earth's crust, creating mountains, ocean trenches, volcanoes, and earthquakes.

There's more bumping and grinding going on in Sumatra than in most places on earth. The island has almost one hundred volcanoes, fifteen of them still active, and holds the dubious record for the biggest bang ever recorded when, on August 27, 1883, the island volcano of Krakatoa, in the Sunda Strait between Sumatra and Java, blew its top and sides. It spewed a column of ash high into the atmosphere and sent a tsunami more than one hundred feet high crashing over the shores of Sumatra and Java. It's estimated that more than 36,000 people died, and 165 villages were destroyed. The sounds of the explosion were heard thousands of miles away, and measurable wave effects were said to have reached the English Channel. Krakatoa has disappeared, but a smaller and active volcano, known as Anak Krakatau, the "Child of Krakatoa," emerged in its shell. On December 22, 2018, Anak Krakatau erupted and partially collapsed, triggering a tsunami that struck coastal regions of Java and Sumatra, killing at least 426 people and injuring more than 14,000.

Indonesia experiences earthquakes and volcanic eruptions almost every year. Less than two years after the tsunami, Java, the richest and most densely populated of its islands, got a double whammy: in May, an earthquake measuring 6.3 on the Richter scale killed 6,000, left 200,000 homeless, and toppled buildings in the ancient city of Yogyakarta; in July an even heavier undersea earthquake (7.7 on the Richter scale) created a tsunami that washed away coastal villages, killing 550 and leaving close to 50,000 homeless. Despite the devastation and the constant threat of natural disasters, Indonesians always rebuild. Within a year of the 2006 earthquake, most restaurants, hotels, and shops in Yogyakarta had reopened for business; in the countryside, farmers had rebuilt their homes and were planting a new rice crop.

The Tsunami's Peace Bonus

One reason Banda Aceh was booming was that peace had at last come to Aceh. For thirty years, the guerrilla forces of Gerakan Aceh Merdeka (the Free Aceh Movement, usually known by its acronym, GAM) fought the Indonesian Army in the mountains and jungles. Aceh was officially designated as a combat zone, requiring visitors from other parts of Indonesia and foreigners to obtain permits to travel there. Because he worked for international news agencies, Dendy's military press card designated him as a foreign correspondent. "I suppose there's some prestige in that," he told me, "but I've lived in Aceh all my life."

Aceh had once been a rich sultanate, strategically situated at the northern gateway to the Strait of Malacca, on the main route between the Indian Ocean and China, trading in spices, pepper, sandalwood, gold, and ivory. As the saying went, "Whoever is lord of Malacca has his hands on the throat of Venice." By the 1870s, it had become a haven for pirates preying on trading ships and pilgrim vessels bound for Mecca. That gave the region's colonial power, the Dutch, a pretext to declare war. The Acehnese resisted for almost forty years until the last sultan surrendered and Aceh became part of the Dutch East Indies. In 1951, the government of newly independent Indonesia incorporated Aceh, with its Muslim majority, into the religiously mixed province of North Sumatra. Aceh's Islamist party resisted and proclaimed independence; in 1959, Aceh was granted special status, giving it some autonomy in religion, education, and culture.

The special status did not extend to Aceh's wealth. Under Indonesia's constitution, the state owns all natural resources—from oil, gas, and other minerals to forests. The government grants long-term licenses to domestic and foreign companies and state-owned enterprises to exploit resources. Tax revenue goes to the national budget, although some is skimmed off by corrupt officials. Provincial and local governments depend on the largesse of Jakarta for their budgets; even if they are sitting on a wealth of natural resources, they may see little direct revenue from it.

In Aceh, the national government took most of the profits from natural gas exports. It is no coincidence that the declaration of Acehnese independence and GAM's armed struggle came in 1976, just as the massive Exxon-Mobil liquefication plant in the Arun gas field went online. Although the plant created jobs, most local people did not benefit. It's the same story as in Madagascar or northeast India: the profits went to a foreign company and a faraway government that failed to provide health, education, and social services to the province. Exxon-Mobil paid the Indonesian Army to protect the plant. Many of Aceh's 4.5 million people, noted the *Economist*, "clearly resent the government's heavy-handed and arrogant conduct. . . . The word 'Indonesian' is used as a synonym for foreigner, and not in a complimentary sense."[3]

The thirty-year struggle was characterized by atrocities and human rights abuses on both sides. Journalists were restricted in their coverage, but with the expansion of private media in the late 1990s and the loosening of military censorship, Indonesians learned more about the dirty war its army had been fighting. Dendy and several of his colleagues in the group had covered army operations, but also accompanied GAM units on missions, and visited their jungle training camps.

The devastation caused by the tsunami forced the government to open the province to relief organizations and spurred peace talks with GAM. On August 15, 2005, an agreement was signed in Helsinki. GAM guerrillas surrendered their weapons and Indonesian troops withdrew. Aceh is not independent but has a level of autonomy that other regions lack. In Indonesia, all political parties are national, but in Aceh local parties can participate in elections. The religiously conservative province is allowed to enforce sharia law and, importantly, to keep 70 percent of its oil and gas revenues.

Counting Islands

Given its size and diversity, it's not surprising that Indonesia has a history of conflict. Cobbled together for economic gain by a colonial power, it stretches more than three thousand miles east to west and more than one thousand miles north to south. It is the world's largest archipelagic state (although Canada has twice as many islands in its Arctic archipelago). Its islands range in size from Borneo and Sumatra, respectively the third- and sixth-largest islands in the world,[4] to tiny uninhabited islets with only local names.

How many islands? It depends on whom you ask. A 2002 survey by Indonesia's space agency concluded that the archipelago had 18,307 islands; in 2010, Indonesia's mapping agency offered a more conservative estimate of 13,466. The CIA's *World Factbook* uses a 1996 Indonesian government figure of 17,508. Bottom line: no one knows for sure, but the answer has important geopolitical and economic implications.

The problem, of course, is defining an "island." Do you include tidal islands, such as reefs and sand spits that are submerged at high tide? Then there's all that earthquake and volcanic activity that keeps blowing islands apart and creating new ones. Keeping count is like the clichéd Western movie scene where a cowboy stands by the sign, "Dead Man's Gulch, population 200." He hears a gunshot, crosses out 200 and writes 199. I can imagine a similar scene in the control room of the agency that monitors seismic activity. Another eruption? It's time to change the island count.

Despite these challenges, Indonesia has good reason to count all its islands and have the United Nations officially recognize them under the UN Convention on the Law of the Sea. Once an island is recognized, Indonesia can claim an Exclusive Economic Zone (EEZ) for two hundred nautical miles around it, giving it fishing and mineral rights. This brings Indonesia into dispute with neighboring countries that also claim outlying islands. Such territorial spats, often over tiny uninhabited islands, go on throughout the Indian Ocean—from the Îles Éparses (Scattered Islands) off the coast of Madagascar to the Bay of Bengal—but as the world's largest archipelagic state, Indonesia inevitably has more than its fair share of claims and counterclaims. In 2002, the International Court of Justice ruled against Indonesia in a dispute with Malaysia over two islands; the same year, two islands were ceded to East Timor when it became independent. According to Susan Herawati of the Coalition of People for Justice for Fisheries (Kiara), 60 percent of islands "don't have a name or official legal status, so they can easily be taken or claimed by another country." UN status may also protect islands from being grabbed by developers. Herawati says more than one hundred families were expelled without compensation when an island near Lombok was leased to develop a private tourist resort. Although Indonesia officially bans the private ownership of islands, several online real estate companies list islands for sale.

The Ministry of Marine Affairs and Fisheries wants to add at least 1,700 islands to the UN's approved list. The UN defines an island as a naturally formed area of land, surrounded by water, which is still exposed at high tide. That takes tidal islands off the list but leaves a question mark over low-lying islands that may be submerged as sea levels rise. The ministry team must also come up with a name known to local people (even if the island is uninhabited), and a description of the island's history and geography.

With ongoing territorial disputes with China, Vietnam, and the Philippines over the South China Sea, its fishing rights, and mineral resources, Indonesia has strong motives to claim as many islands as it can—not so much for the islands themselves, most of which are not worth inhabiting, but for the maritime real estate all around. "This is about our identity as a nation," Herawati told the BBC. "By clearly listing our islands then our fishermen have legal protection and rights over the islands and our ancestral seas."[5]

Going Dutch

The "ancestral seas" claim seems a stretch because the territorial boundaries of "Indonesia" are not those of some ancient civilization, but of the Dutch East Indies. As in British India, the Dutch colony had its modest origins in a trading post, the port of Batavia in present-day Jakarta. From there, through conquest and alliances, the Dutch came to control the archipelago.

The imperial mission was driven by economic motives, although trade and politics soon became intertwined. From the mid-sixteenth century, the Dutch were duking it out with the Portuguese, Spanish, and English for control of the East Indies trade and sea routes to China. Each established fortified trading posts along the main sea passages; the Portuguese were first to claim the famed spice islands of the Moluccas (Maluku). Realizing the potential of the East Indies trade, the Dutch government merged competing merchant companies into the Vereenigde Osst-Indische Compagnie (VOC), the United East India Company. By 1605, the VOC had driven the Portuguese out of the Moluccas. In 1610, the prince of Jayakarta (Jakarta) granted trading rights to both the VOC and the English. Relations between the two powers were never cordial. In 1619, the English defeated the Dutch in a sea battle and, with the support of the prince's army, besieged the VOC fort. Reinforced by troops from the Moluccas, the Dutch governor Jan Pieterszoon Coen kicked out the English and razed Jayakarta. The VOC named its fortress and trading post Batavia for an ancient Germanic tribe, the Batavi, who lived around the delta of the Rhine.

Batavia became the trading and administrative center of the Dutch East Indies. It was a closed community, with a mixed population of Europeans, Asian laborers, and slaves; Javanese were not allowed inside the walls for fear of an insurrection. The Dutch built canals from the Ciliwung River and lined them with stately mansions. Today, many are abandoned and in poor repair, their roofs leaking and trees sprouting through cracks in the floors. Jakarta's city government wants to revitalize the district, now called Kota

Figure 11.2 Old Amsterdam in the tropics. Some eighteenth-century houses in Kota Tua are being restored, but others are left to decay.

FIGURE 11.3 The *Stadhuis* (City Hall), built in 1710, now the Jakarta History Museum

Tua, but has offered property owners few incentives to restore the buildings. Some Indonesians say good riddance: the country should not be spending money to spiff up relics of its colonial past.

The best example of colonial-era architecture is the palatial *Stadhuis* (City Hall), built in 1710 to serve as the headquarters of the VOC and later the Dutch colonial government. Since 1974, it has housed the Jakarta History Museum. Viewed from Batavia's central cobblestone square, the Taman Fatahillah, it is easy to imagine how Batavia might have looked three hundred years ago when its streets bustled with traders and laborers, hurrying between the harbor, warehouses, and trading offices. One block west of the square is what used to be Batavia's high-rent district. The main canal, the Kali Besar, is lined with stylish three- and four-story eighteenth-century mansions with balconies and arched roofs. The last remaining Dutch drawbridge, dating from the seventeenth century, crosses the north end of the canal. In Batavia, the Dutch created a little corner of Amsterdam, albeit with palm trees and better weather.

From the square, it is a short walk along Kali Besar to the old Dutch port of Sunda Kelapa. It's lined with brightly painted wooden *pinisi*, the traditional two-mast wooden schooners that for centuries have carried cargo and people between islands. The first ships, said to be modeled on

Figure 11.4 *Pinisi* at the port of Sunda Kelapa in Batavia. For centuries, these schooners have carried cargo and people between the islands of the archipelago.

the Dutch pinnace, were built for the spice trade at Makassar, the VOC trading fort on the island of Sulawesi. The modern version, with a crew of a dozen, is similar in design but longer and larger (up to 350 tons), with navigational equipment and a diesel engine. The *pinisi* no longer carry cloves, nutmeg, and other spices. Most were unloading tropical hardwoods such as camphor, meranti, and mahogany, logged in Kalimantan or Sulawesi, and taking on cement, sand, bricks, and other building materials.

I asked my port guide to describe a typical voyage. "One week from South Sulawesi to Jakarta with a cargo of wood," he said. "Load up with cement and then three days to Jambi [a river port in central Sumatra], and back to Jakarta with a cargo of coconuts." Although a few small cranes and winches were in operation, most of the loading was done by laborers, hoisting wooden planks on their shoulders and cement sacks on their backs. For transporting bulk materials across the archipelago, *pinisi* are still the cheapest and most efficient option.

The Dutch Imperial Jewel

The East Indies were the jewel in the Dutch imperial crown—the largest and richest colony in an empire that looked, at least on the world map, as if it had been stitched together from scraps left over by the British and French. At one time or another, the Dutch established trading posts in such far-flung places as Ghana, Sri Lanka, Taiwan, Japan, Australia, Iran, Pakistan, Brazil, and, of course, New York. Few lasted long. The Cape Colony in South Africa survived for 150 years, and Suriname was a colony for three centuries until 1975. In the Caribbean, St. Maarten, Aruba, and the Netherlands Antilles are still overseas territories. No colony rivaled the East Indies for its size, location, and wealth, which is why the Dutch fought so hard to acquire and then hold onto it.

After booting the English out of Jayakarta, Coen and his successors set about building a commercial empire. In Java, they took advantage of warring factions to divide the island into two kingdoms, both subject to VOC control. The company's fortunes declined in the late eighteenth century when it lost its monopoly of the spice trade, and new commodities—coffee, tea, and sugar—began to dominate exports. A Dutch government investigation revealed rampant mismanagement and corruption. In 1799 the company was dissolved, and its territories handed over to the state.

With the decline in the spice trade, the Dutch had to figure out how to turn a profit from their colony. The solution was a system of forced labor, under which farmers had to cultivate government-owned cash crops on 20 percent of their land or work on government plantations for sixty days a year. Java became a major exporter of tea, sugar, coffee, and rubber. The commodities helped save the Netherlands from bankruptcy, but at a huge social cost. Because they had to use land for cash crops, farmers could not grow enough rice. In the 1840s, Java suffered famine and epidemics. Public opinion in the Netherlands forced the government to end the forced labor policy, but as the population increased and large plantations were established, less land was available for rice production.

In the early twentieth century, the colonial administration extended its direct authority beyond Java to the rest of the archipelago, taking control from traditional leaders and suppressing minor rebellions. It encouraged farmers to migrate from Java to less-populated islands, founded industries, and attempted to improve roads, railways, and communications. New educational opportunities benefited mostly the Javanese upper and middle classes and inadvertently sowed the seeds of revolution. As in other colonial empires, many of the intellectual and political leaders of Indonesia's nationalist movement received their education courtesy of the government they would later help to overthrow.

The Independence Struggle

Sukarno, the Javanese-born leader of the independence struggle, received his primary and secondary education at Dutch schools and an engineering degree from the Dutch technical institute at Bandung, where he was influenced by socialist and anti-imperialist ideologies. In 1927, he founded the Partai Nasional Indonesia (PNI), which became the leading secular party campaigning for independence. In 1930, he was sentenced to four years in prison. The PNI was banned, along with other Islamic and secular nationalist parties, including the communist party, the Partai Kommunis Indonesia (PKI).

In early 1942, as Japanese forces advanced through Southeast Asia, the Dutch abandoned their colony. Landing in Java, the Japanese claimed to be liberators, freeing another Asian people from colonial oppression; symbolically, they carried the red and white Indonesian flag along with the Japanese rising sun. Sukarno and other nationalist leaders were given positions in the Japanese wartime administration. Militias trained by the Japanese later transformed themselves into *pemuda* (youth groups) that joined the Republican army.

On August 17, 1945, two days before the Japanese emperor's surrender, Sukarno declared independence. The Dutch government rejected the declaration but could exert only diplomatic pressure; devastated and bankrupted by the war, it needed to focus on rebuilding its own cities and economy. By September, Republican *pemuda* had taken over most cities in Java and set up their own newspapers and radio stations. Under the terms of the surrender, Japanese troops were supposed to maintain order until they surrendered to the Allies. Some were unwilling to risk their lives for the powers that had just defeated Japan and handed over their weapons to the *pemuda*. In the chaos that followed, members of European, Chinese, and other ethnic groups suspected of opposing independence were threatened, robbed, kidnapped, and murdered by extreme nationalist groups.

When British troops landed in October to repatriate the Japanese and free prisoners-of-war, an already confusing situation turned chaotic with battles between *pemuda* and Japanese troops, and continued attacks on civilians. In November, thousands died in the bloody battle for Sura-baya, Indonesia's second-largest city. After their commander was killed by a bomb, six thousand British Indian troops with tanks and air sup-port fought *pemuda* units in the streets, eventually driving them out of the city. Although the nationalists suffered a military defeat, the heroic defense of Surabaya—now celebrated as Heroes Day—was a psycho-logical victory, increasing support for independence.

The British, already struggling to deal with partition in India and unrest in other colonies, were not ready to become embroiled in a con-flict on behalf of another colonial power. In January 1946, Dutch forces landed in Java, imprisoned Republican leaders, and drove their forces out of urban centers. The Dutch air force bombed two cities in Sumatra; in south Sulawesi, the Dutch commander was accused of terror tactics for the mass murder of *pemuda* and their supporters. The Republicans were forced to move their capital to Yogyakarta, under the patronage of its new sultan. Three years of conflict followed, with peace agreements concluded and broken, two major military offensives by the Dutch, and infighting among the Republicans, particularly between the PNI and the PKI. Although the Dutch controlled most cities and towns in Java and Sumatra, they were never able to control the rural areas. Reports of human-rights abuses led to condemnation by the UN Security Coun-cil and a threat by the US Congress to withdraw Marshall Plan aid for postwar reconstruction in the Netherlands. Facing a costly, unwinnable war and international condemnation, the Dutch government backed down. On December 27, it formally handed over power to the Republic of Indonesia.

When Sukarno proclaimed independence, as one shrewd and sea-soned Indonesia observer puts it, "he was liberating a nation that didn't really exist, imposing a notional unity on a ragbag of islands that had only a veneer of shared history, and little common culture."[6] With the Dutch gone, there was no common enemy to hold the nation together. Divisions arose along regional, ethnic, and religious lines, coupled with resentment against the Javanese political elite. Sukarno's government faced massive challenges: providing enough food for a fast-growing population, restoring an export economy battered by years of conflict, improving schools and public health facilities. New political parties competed for power, forcing Sukarno to broker deals to form a series of coalition governments.

In 1960, Sukarno dissolved the elected parliament. He proclaimed a regime of "guided democracy" where the president and an appointed parliament and cabinet exercised power. He ramped up his anti-imperialist rhetoric, attacking the Dutch, who still occupied Papua; the British, whose former colony of Malaysia controlled the northern states of Kalimantan (Borneo); and the Americans, who maintained military bases in the Philippines. Western governments withdrew aid, forcing the government to abolish subsidies and increasing poverty levels. Sukarno came to depend on the Soviet Union and China for aid and on the PKI for political support. When, at the urging of Chinese premier Zhou Enlai, he proposed establishing a people's militia, independent of the armed forces, the generals, already alarmed by the rising power of the PKI, acted. They accused the PKI of attempting a coup and launched an anticommunism purge, with thousands arrested and executed. General Suharto, who had earned his nationalist spurs by leading the defense of Yogyakarta against the Dutch in 1949, took over leadership of the armed forces and set about maneuvering Sukarno from power. The PKI was banned, pro-Sukarno troops and officials arrested, and thousands of civil servants dismissed.

On March 17, 1968, a parliament packed with his supporters elected Suharto president. He realigned Indonesia's foreign policy toward the West and was rewarded with foreign investment and the restoration of aid. Western governments celebrated another defeat for communism. It did not mark a new political era: for three decades, Suharto's so-called New Order regime, supported by the military, clamped down on opposition from political and religious groups and ruthlessly suppressed social conflict.

Unity in Diversity?

Indonesia has the fourth largest population in the world—more than 265 million in 2017—and it is growing fast. With almost 90 percent identifying themselves as Sunni Muslims, it also has the world's largest Muslim population. Christianity comes a distant second at around 10 percent, but it's all a matter of proportion. With about 25 million Christians (two-thirds Protestant, one-third Catholic), Indonesia has the second-largest Christian population in Southeast Asia after the Philippines; Christians are a majority in Papua and a significant minority in North Sumatra,

Kalimantan, and the provinces of Maluku and Sulawesi. There are smaller populations of Hindus (mostly in Bali), Buddhists, Confucians, and members of other faiths.

Since the colonial era, Indonesia's economy has been based on commodities—mineral resources (coal, tin, oil, and natural gas) and cash crops (coffee, tea, cocoa, sugar, palm oil, rubber, and indigo). Commodities make up about 60 percent of the value of exports. "For its entire modern history," notes the *Economist*, "money grew on trees, bubbled up from beneath the sea and was dug out of mines."[7] When commodities are booming—particularly when China is buying—Indonesia prospers; when demand and prices slump, Indonesia suffers. Even during the good times, the wealth is spread unevenly. Java and the capital Jakarta have prospered, as have regions of Sumatra and Kalimantan rich in minerals and natural resources, and Bali, with its tourism industry. The islands of Eastern Indonesia, lacking good roads and port facilities, have lagged behind; political and business leaders claim they are short-changed by governments dominated by the Jakarta political elite. Annual GDP per person in Papua is roughly one-third of what it is in Java; in Maluku, it's less than one-tenth. Of course, economic averages do not tell the whole story: there are many poor people in Java, living in shanties along Jakarta's polluted canals or eking out a living on hillside rice terraces. But many in the east remain impoverished and feel forgotten. Elizabeth Pisani, who worked for Reuters in Indonesia and later spent two years traveling almost fifteen thousand miles throughout the country by boat, bus, and motorbike, writes that the country's diversity "is not just geographic and cultural: different groups are essentially living at different points in human history, all at the same time."[8]

With more than seven hundred languages and ethnic groups scattered across an archipelago wider than the continental United States, economic, social, and political conflicts are to be expected. Indonesia's national motto, *Bhinneka Tunggal Ika*, meaning "unity in diversity," reflects the critical importance that the nation's founders placed on traditions of tolerance, pluralism, and inclusiveness. Under Suharto's highly centralized New Order regime, discussions of ethnic, religious, racial, and intergroup relations were restricted. When disputes occurred, they were often ruthlessly suppressed by the Indonesian military.

Suharto was forced to resign in 1998 after the Asian economic crisis plunged the country into recession and led to social unrest. The fall of the New Order regime signaled a new era of political freedom, with dozens of political parties and leaders emerging, and the rapid expansion of media, especially television. However, economic problems and the weakening of central government authority sparked conflicts over land, mineral resources, environmental issues, and political power. The struggle for autonomy in Aceh is mirrored in other regions where religion, ethnicity, and economic rivalries have coalesced. "Among the most common complaints," writes Michael Malley, "are human rights abuses by Indonesian security forces, loss of land and resources to outside investors and immigrants, and lack of political autonomy such that major policies affecting the region are made almost entirely by people from outside the region."[9]

At times of economic crisis, Indonesia's small yet wealthy ethnic Chinese population is often the scapegoat; in the late 1990s, mobs looted and burned Chinese-owned shops and warehouses in Jakarta and other cities. Violence has flared in other regions, most seriously in Kalimantan, Maluku, and Central Sulawesi. Although some conflicts have been portrayed as religious in nature, with attacks by militias and gangs on mosques and churches, many observers say religion is a pretext for economic conflicts over land, fisheries, and mineral resources, or for political power grabs.

In 1969, the Dutch handed over their last colonial territory, Papua (Irian Jaya), the western part of the island of New Guinea. A sporadic independence struggle has been going on ever since. In the late 1990s, Indonesian forces gunned down Papuans who raised their independence flag. The military maintains a large presence in Papua, the only region for which a special travel permit is still required. As in Aceh, the economic stakes are high; Papua is rich in minerals, with the world's largest gold mine, the US-owned Freeport-McMoRan mine, Indonesia's single largest taxpayer. The conflict also has a cultural dimension; Papuans are a Melanesian people, in contrast to the Malay-Polynesians who populate much of Indonesia, and most are Christian.

Most conflicts are less violent in nature. As cities have expanded and property prices risen, private developers, with the connivance of local officials, have taken advantage of unclear legal titles to seize land—the same kinds of land grab that have played out in rural Madagascar, the slums of Hyderabad, and along the river banks outside Dhaka. The government has granted huge logging concessions in Kalimantan, eroding traditional land rights and forcing groups that relied on forest resources for their livelihoods to leave. Indonesia produces more than half the world's palm oil, used in cooking and cosmetics and as a biofuel and food additive. In Kalimantan and Sumatra, plantation owners, again taking advantage of muddled land laws, have cleared vast forest areas for planting.

Every year, slash-and-burn agriculture creates massive fires that darken the skies and force authorities to close schools, hospitals, and businesses. In 2015, when a dry spell caused by the El Niño weather pattern made the fires more severe than usual, dozens died and thousands were sickened by the choking fumes; for almost one month, according to the *Economist*, "greenhouse gases released by those fires exceeded the emissions of the entire American economy." The smoke settled over Singapore and Malaysia and reached as far as Cambodia, Vietnam, and the Philippines. Indonesia's vice president, Jusuf Kalla, did not endear himself to the region's leaders when he derided the complaints: "For 11 months," he said, "our neighbors enjoyed nice air from Indonesia and they never thanked us."[10]

The Enemy Is Faceless

A decade after the fall of the New Order regime, the Indonesian journalists we met were still groping their way through a forest of shifting political and business alliances, balancing newfound freedoms against new pressures. They talked earnestly about the role of media in educating people, to make them aware of democracy and to serve as a watchdog on government and special interests. At the same time, they were conscious of the responsibilities that freedom brings in a diverse society.

"Before 1998, there was friendly persuasion," Luki Sutrisni of the national newspaper *Media Indonesia* told us. "The censors would call and tell you to be careful about what you wrote on an issue. It wasn't direct interference. We camouflaged how we felt and hid behind words." Those who resisted faced economic and legal pressures; in June 1994, Suharto ordered the closure of the leading news magazine, *Tempo*, and two other weeklies.

Most formal restrictions on news were removed after Suharto's fall, but old habits of media repression die hard. Political and religious groups, corporations, and the military still attempt to influence coverage and are not afraid to wield a range of weapons—from pressure on advertisers and expensive-to-defend libel suits to physical intimidation. Mobs have attacked newspaper offices, destroying equipment and injuring staff, and forced radio and TV stations to suspend broadcasting. "The enemy is faceless—you don't know who you'll offend when you cover a demonstration," said Arief Suditomo, editor-in-chief of the TV network RCTI.

Indonesia's muddled laws and regulations provide ample opportunities to punish or deter journalists. A new law, passed in 1999 after Suharto's fall, expanded press freedoms by prohibiting the government from banning media and allowing the formation of journalists' unions and associations. It led to the establishment of an independent press council, without government representatives, to adjudicate complaints about unbalanced coverage, unreliable sources, breaches of privacy, indecency, blackmail, racism, and perceived insults. The council tries to resolve disputes amicably but has the power to levy fines.

Instead of referring complaints to the press council, powerful figures turn to the largely unreformed criminal code, many of whose articles were inherited from the colonial era. It includes penalties for criminal defamation and articles related to ill-defined concepts such as "misuse of information." Some journalists charged with libel have lost their jobs, and others have endured lengthy, expensive trials. A string of guilty verdicts in civil and criminal libel cases have shown that the legal system is still heavily influenced by political and business elites. Journalists complain that the police and courts offer little protection from harassment. Journalists have learned to be cautious and to exercise a degree of self-censorship.

There is also a history of corruption, the practice of "envelope journalism," where reporters are paid to present stories with a certain slant. One reason is economic: journalists' salaries, particularly in the provinces, are often very low. Culture is also a factor: in Indonesian society, it is considered rude to reject a gift. Many journalists who accept "the envelope" form close relationships with business and political elites. Those who refuse or criticize the practice have been harassed by the police and others in power.

Conflict coverage is particularly sensitive. A tried-and-trusted tactic by government and military officials to restrict coverage is to accuse the media of inciting violence through its reporting. "We try to avoid stories that could cause disorder," one Metro TV journalist told us, while admitting that it was impossible to predict the impact of a story. "We try not to show footage of victims and bodies, and we identify combatants by their villages, not by their religion." Another who had covered the conflict in Maluku said that he was able to provide balanced reports by traveling with two press cards: one identified him as Muslim, one as a Christian.

In his office in central Jakarta, we met the grand old man of Indonesian journalism, the modest, soft-spoken Jakob Oetama. Born into a middle-class Catholic family in Central Java in 1931, he worked as a teacher before becoming editor of a weekly newspaper. In 1965, he and a colleague, the ethnic Chinese P. K. Ojong, with the support of the Catholic political party, started the newspaper *Kompas* (Compass) to counter propaganda from the PKI. A few years later, with Suharto in power and the PKI crushed, *Kompas* dropped its political affiliations to become an independent newspaper, or at least as independent as any could be under the New Order regime. Its daily circulation grew from under five thousand to more than half a million in 2015, making it the largest national newspaper in Indonesia. Oetama, now in his 80s, manages the *Kompas Gramedia* empire, with at least fifty print publications, a TV network, and interests in the property sector. He is still active in journalism, campaigning for professional standards and independence.

"I am a Catholic, educated by Jesuits, but the newspaper is for general readers," Oetama told us. "I believe in freedom with social responsibility. Freedom has its limits. We try to express this positively and when we cover religious issues, we are careful not to hurt any parties." Oetama worries about his country's fragile democracy and political institutions. "Democracy is in the making, in transition. I am concerned how it can survive with so many political parties and factions. Every issue needs to be discussed in parliament, so progress is slow. Our nation is a talking democracy—what we need is a working democracy." Too much talk creates divisions, said Oetama. "There are strong splintering forces. Each legislator wants to get resources for his own district. This would be OK if the country was above the socioeconomic average, but with so many poor and unemployed there is internal disorder. Every day there are direct conflicts with the police. To me there is no place in democracy for violence."

I wondered how, in such a volatile situation, *Kompas* and its sister media maintained their independence. Oetama smiled. "It's simple," he said. "We are not a publicly traded company. If we were, we would lose our independence."

Another perspective on rights and responsibilities came at *Republika*, Indonesia's largest mainstream Islamic newspaper. It was founded by Islamic scholars in 1993, with future Indonesian president B. J. Habibie as its first chairman. Although it has less than half the daily circulation of *Kompas*, its owners claim each copy is read by at least four people and is shared among students at *pesantrens*, the Islamic boarding schools. Today, *Republika* is part of a group that includes media for general and targeted audiences—TV and radio stations, a Mandarin-language newspaper, and sports magazines, including the Indonesian *Golf Digest*. As radical Islamic groups have gained strength, *Republika* has attempted to represent many views while ultimately serving as the voice of moderate Islam.

"Muslims must turn to Mecca five times a day to pray," said then editor-in-chief Syaiful Syam, "but *Republika* needs to turn both right and left because of the diversity of the Muslim community. Our message is that every Muslim must create peace within himself. Islam should spread peace and protect every group in society."

Syam said that there was little difference between *Republika* and secular newspapers in the topics covered—the usual mix of politics, business, culture, and sports—but the sources and perspectives differed. "We focus on the mainstream Islamic community while still providing a forum for liberal and fundamentalist views," he said. In conflict reporting, *Republika* journalists, like their colleagues at Metro and other media, avoid words that identify religious groups. But, as Syam noted, "it's not easy to run an Islamic newspaper and offer balance." He cited the example of polygamy, which is legal in Indonesia. "Modern Muslims reject polygamy, but if the newspaper does not support it, some leaders get mad and we have demonstrations outside the office."

Leaving on a Jet Plane

The US journalists found plenty to admire about their Indonesian colleagues. They had camped out with GAM guerrillas in the jungles of Aceh, gone undercover to report on human trafficking in Kalimantan, been threatened and beaten up by police, soldiers, and hired thugs, been accused of inciting social and religious discord, faced lawsuits from politicians and business owners, and seen their organizations pressured by special interests and advertisers.

David Smith, a photojournalist from Cincinnati TV station WXIX, said that their experiences made his own daily concerns pale by comparison. "They're facing real danger," he said, "and we're complaining about the parking situation at city hall."

On the last night of the tour, we joined the Jakarta-based members of the group for a farewell dinner at an outdoor restaurant, Pulau Dua (Two islands). The evening ended, as it often does in Indonesia, with karaoke. David joined Kamellia Soenjoto, our program assistant, on stage for a duet. They gazed into each other's eyes as they launched into John Denver's 1966 composition "Leaving on a Jet Plane," most famously recorded by Peter, Paul and Mary in a 1969 *Billboard*-topping hit.

Was it my imagination? Or did they fix their gazes even more intensely on the line, "Tell me that you'll wait for me"?

Sunset on Jimbaran Bay

Less than nine months later, I was back in Indonesia, standing in the sand at sunset on South Bali's Jimbaran Bay as David and Kamellia exchanged their vows. Fortunately, news of the impending nuptials arrived after I had submitted the final program report to the US Department of State. If it hadn't, I would have had to list "one marriage" as a program outcome under "intercultural relationship building" or some innocuous bureaucratic category.

Stephanie and I jumped at the opportunity to attend, spend Christmas in Bali, and then do some traveling. A few weeks after the invitation arrived, David asked if I would play an official role in the marriage. It had been a whirlwind romance, and preparations for the wedding were rushed. David's family (from the Chicago area) was not able to travel at short notice. He needed a stand-in family. Would I be his father?

I'm a few years older than David, although not old enough to have changed his diapers. However, appearances had to be maintained, so I agreed. David assembled the appropriate number of brothers and sisters from among the Jakarta-based journalists in our group, and his new kin drove over to Kamellia's family home in Jakarta for the *lamaran*— the formal Javanese ceremony in which David's family asked her father to approve the match. Sitting on the floor, with one of the journalists translating, I made a short formal speech, listing David's qualities. He was patient, kind, modest, hardworking—in other words, a keeper.

Fortunately, Kamellia's father did not ask me to provide evidence of these virtues; he simply smiled, graciously thanked me, and agreed to the marriage. David spoke eloquently of his love for Kamellia and annoyingly called me "Dad." Then we presented gifts to the family and had a feast, prepared by one of Kamellia's four sisters (she's the oldest of seven).

Because interreligious marriages are prohibited in Indonesia, David had to make a fast, mostly technical, conversion to Islam. This consisted, apparently, of filling out forms and reciting one verse from the Koran in Arabic. It's a formality, but a necessary one. Four days later, Kamellia's family and friends (including four of the journalists) flew in from Jakarta for the wedding on Jimbaran Bay.

South Bali has long been a popular destination for beach vacationers and surfers, but for many years Jimbaran was a backwater, a fishing village with a daily market. That started to change in the 1980s, and Jimbaran is now home to upscale beach resorts and posh villas on the high ground above the bay. It's been dubbed, probably by local tourism promoters, the "Beverly Hills of Bali." Superlatives may be justified because the location is stunning—a crescent-shaped stretch of white sand facing west toward the sunset. Kamellia wore a decorated orange dress and veil and was barefoot (as were all the guests). The wedding took place literally on the beach, with tables, chairs, and a stage set up on the sand. It was a simple Islamic ceremony, with readings from the Koran and prayers. Guests swarmed around the table where the marriage official conducted the ceremony, taking pictures. A little further off, tourists on the beach stopped to gawp, swig their bottles of Foster's, and take pictures of the bride and groom. David was making an unusual beach fashion statement, barefoot and dressed in a dark Western suit, shirt, and tie.

After the ceremony, we enjoyed a buffet dinner of barbecued fish, shrimp, and mussels, while a gamelan band and Balinese dancers performed on stage, with Kamellia dancing with them. Bali's population is predominantly Hindu, and the dances are traditionally performed in temples during ceremonies honoring Hindu gods. The dancers were followed by a singer who invited us to join her in karaoke renditions of Indonesian pop songs. It was bizarre to see her strutting around the stage in her skintight pants while the gamelan band, dressed in traditional costumes, sat quietly, waiting for the dancers to return. Musical fusion followed when the percussion players joined in on a couple of techno-beat numbers.

FIGURE 11.5 Sunset wedding on Jimbaran beach, Bali. Who ordered the birds?

There is no reliable estimate of the number of photos taken that evening, but Jimbaran's drop-dead-beautiful sunset must have featured in at least half of them. We watched the slide show by the wedding photographer at the hotel the next morning: David and Kamellia facing each other with the sunset framed between them; David and Kamellia gazing out toward the sunset; David and Kamellia kissing as two flocks of birds flew toward each other. I hadn't noticed the birds, so I asked the photographer about them. "Photoshop," he said. "Everyone wants birds in their wedding pictures." When you've got a wedding location like Jimbaran, it's difficult to avoid visual clichés.

Jammed in Jabodetabek

It's fortunate that most Indonesians have a flexible attitude to time. In many Asian and African countries, there's a sliding scale on the value of timeliness, based on location, the business at hand, and those involved. Business meetings in the capital city are expected to start within ten to fifteen minutes of the scheduled time; in a provincial city, people will show up thirty minutes late without apology; in a village, the meeting will happen when it happens. Social events also operate on a loose schedule, and so Kamellia's *lamaran* started when we had assembled

David's stand-in family, who were traveling from different parts of Jakarta. No one complained about it starting "late."

Jakarta residents, who are expected to be more punctual than people in other places, find it more difficult to be so because of the city's legendary traffic snarls. With a population of more than ten million, Jakarta is the largest city in Southeast Asia. Its metropolitan area is so large that it has its own name, Jabodetabek (the first letters of Jakarta, Bogor, Depok, Tangerang, and Bekasi combined); with a population of more than thirty million, it's the second-largest urban agglomeration in the world. Most residents of the largest—Tokyo-Yokohama—rely on public transport. In Jabodetabek, where public transport is slow and unreliable, many take to the roads; every day, Jakarta's population is swelled by millions traveling into the city to work and trade. Even outside the official rush hours, it can take three hours to travel across the city (about ten miles). The only sure way to arrive anywhere on time is by motorcycle, weaving in and out of the traffic. One of the fastest-growing e-commerce businesses is Go-Jek, a play on *ojek,* the word for the popular motorcycle taxi. The *ojek* is not as safe as a traditional taxi, or even the three-wheel auto rickshaw *bajaj,* but if you need to travel fast, this two-wheeled version of Uber is the best option. Taking advantage of the fact that Indonesia is the world's fourth-largest mobile phone market (it has more SIM cards in use than there are people, according to the *Economist*), Go-Jek lets users use an app to call a driver for a ride or a delivery.

Stephanie and I sampled most forms of public transport—minibus, train, taxi, bus, and *bajaj*—during our three-day stay in Jakarta before flying to South Bali. We didn't expect to travel by *ojek.* Then the rains came and the side street leading to the guest house was blocked by flooding. Jakarta lies in a low coastal plain, with canals (many of them heavily polluted) running throughout the city. Here, the drains had been blocked by trash, and the water was about nine inches deep. We were about to start wading through it when someone suggested we could get through on motorbikes. We set off on two machines through the muddy water, the drivers weaving around stalled vehicles and floating furniture and over invisible speed bumps. They had a remarkable sense of balance at slow speeds.

Driving Lessons

As we left Jakarta for Bali, I repeated a phrase I've often used after experiencing Asian traffic. "I would *never* drive in this country." A few days later, I was forced to eat my words. The day after the wedding, we took a road trip with David, Kamellia, and other guests to the volcanic region dominated by the dormant Gunung Agung, at more than ten thousand feet Bali's highest peak. We stopped for lunch at a restaurant, hoping the clouds would lift so we could view the volcano. At the entrance, Stephanie slipped on the tiled floor, dislocating her shoulder. A local doctor said he could do nothing, so we drove the three hours south to a hospital in Bali's capital, Denpasar, where a doctor put the shoulder back in its joint and told Stephanie to keep her arm in a sling. We abandoned our plan, which involved touring Bali on local buses and minibuses; it would be too difficult and dangerous. Instead we rented a car for seven days.

It had been thirty years since I left Britain for the United States, believing my days of driving on the left-hand side of the road were over. I quickly regained the art of driving with the wheel on the right and gear shift on the left, although for the first day I tended to signal a right-hand turn with the windshield wipers, not the flasher. The challenges were the roads, rain, motorbikes, and lack of road signs. In rural Bali, the narrow and often-potholed roads require shifting and weaving, especially when a bus or truck is barreling toward you. One day, in the mountains, driving in heavy rain, the runoff flooded sections of the road; I drove through standing water, not having any idea of whether we'd get through. When I wasn't dodging potholes and rocks, I was dodging motorbikes. There seems to be no age limit (lower or upper) on who can ride them, no limit on how many people can pile onto one machine, or how much luggage can be stacked on the carrier. There are certainly no rules of the road. Motorbikes pass on the left or right, cut across in front of you, and drive on the wrong (right) side of the road before cutting across. Road signs are scarce, especially when you're truly lost, as we were a few times. In places, they are obscured by tree branches or large political posters. Sometimes they are just plain confusing, with the same town listed as both straight ahead and to the left. Which one is the scenic route?

The Two Balis

For many people, Bali conjures up images of long, pristine beaches, palm trees, and some of the best surf west of Waikiki. That's South Bali, the destination for most tourists. After decades of real-estate and

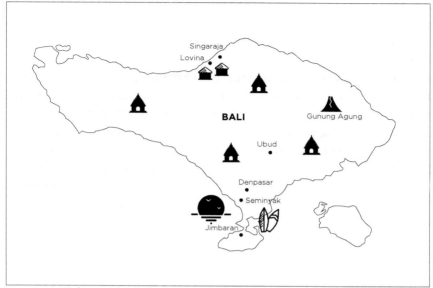

MAP 11.2 Bali (map by Belén Marco Crespo)

commercial development, it isn't exactly a tropical paradise any more, but it's still a lovely place, where ancient Hindu temples and rice paddies back onto swanky resorts and spas, and simple *warung* (local restaurants), hole-in-the-wall laundries, and barber shops, vegetable stalls, and motorbike repair sheds crowd onto the same block as night clubs, high-priced art galleries, and boutiques.

For the wedding, Stephanie and I stayed in a small hotel in Seminyak, down a shady lane away from the traffic, and a two-minute walk from the beach. I'm not much of a beach person, but I have to say that it was breathtakingly beautiful, with all the elements—warm, clean sand and clear water, coconut palms waving in the breeze, and bronzed Australian surfers who looked as if they've stepped out of magazine covers. Most people expected us to be Australian, so I temporarily dropped my carefully learned Indonesian greetings (there are five, depending on the time of day) and adopted "Gid'dy" (sometimes adding "mite" if it was a man). In some ways, Bali is for Australians the equivalent of what Cancun represents for American tourists or Majorca for the British—in a recognizably different country, but with familiar sights and sounds. We had dinner one night at the Bush Telegraph, one of the four or five Aussie pubs near the hotel. The menu featured Australian steaks, meat pies, and fish and chips. None of the faux décor of an Outback restaurant with its "Blokes" and "Sheilas" signs on the restrooms. Just Australian Rules football on TV and Foster's on draft. A place where an Australian can feel at home.

Despite the rampant tourism development in the south, much of Bali has been little touched by the beach crowd. After leaving the sprawl of Denpasar, the road north through the mountains offers vistas of rice paddies and small villages. We stayed two nights in Ubud, a string of fourteen villages famed as a center of Balinese arts, dance, and culture. Then north again along twisting mountain roads, passing dormant volcanoes with dense jungle slopes, Hindu temples and communal meeting houses, and coffee plantations. We stopped at *warungs* for simple, tasty meals. Grilled river fish, *sate* (chicken, pork, and fish), fried rice and noodles, chicken and fish curries, and roast suckling pig. Fresh fruit juices—lemon, lime, mango, papaya, watermelon, pineapple. And wonderful snacks, especially the banana fritters.

Along the roads, the most common (but temporary) landscape features were the flags and posters of political parties. Regional elections were coming up, and all the parties were showing their colors. Because of low literacy rates, all candidates were identified by number, not name. Each poster featured a picture of the candidate, looking businesslike or religious or youthful or just well-dressed, with the party's symbol and color, a patriotic backdrop, and a sample ballot with the number checked. Stephanie conducted an informal windshield survey and came up with her own political punditry: "No. 12 looks shifty, No. 4 looks too young to vote, No. 9 looks good in blue, No. 23 needs a haircut." Basically, she decided that all the men looked pompous or incompetent and that most of the women should be elected. We agreed that in a society with paternalistic traditions, it was a sign of progress that many women were running for office.

It's Christmas in Yogyakarta

By an accident of timing, I made two trips to Indonesia in mid-December, avoiding the pre-Christmas commercial frenzy in the United States. On the first, I stayed at a hotel at a suburban mall in Jakarta, where the sight of artificial Christmas trees and an inflatable Santa Claus twisting in the hot wind in the parking lot seemed slightly surreal. Although I knew that some people in Jakarta celebrated Christmas, and maybe even went to church, I put it down to the retail marketers, who did not care which religious tradition they appropriated to move merchandise. As I grabbed my morning coffee, I grimaced at the sign over the counter: Dunkin' Donuts Wishes You Merry Christmas. Surely, I thought, in this Muslim-majority country, Christmas was a sideshow.

In 2008, the artificial Christmas trees and decorations were out in South Bali, but I knew that was mostly to appeal to Australian and European tourists. I did not expect Christmas to be celebrated in the ancient city of Yogyakarta, the cultural and religious center of Java. Yet on the main shopping streets, Christmas carols blared from store loudspeakers, window displays were decorated in red and white, and street hawkers offered plastic Christmas trees and ornaments. Christmas was being celebrated, and not just at the cash register. One morning, we were awoken by the sound of electric guitars, drums, and singing. At 7:00 a.m., the congregation at the evangelical church next door was in good voice and rocking away.

The first sounds and sights of the morning are in some ways a microcosm of the diversity of the country. In Jakarta, it was the call to prayer, the rising din of car engines and horns, and the smog; in South Bali, the birds and the sounds of the ocean, the sunny, blue skies, and hotel staff making silent offerings at a Hindu shrine; in North Bali, a morning chorus of bullfrogs and roosters and the mist rising over the volcanic mountains.

Elizabeth Pisani, who knows Indonesia better than most *bule* (foreigners), describes it as an "improbable country," full of contrasts and surprises. She quotes the concise 1945 declaration of independence: "We, the people of Indonesia, hereby declare the independence of Indonesia. Matters relating to the transfer of power etc. will be executed carefully and as soon as possible." Indonesia, she writes, "has been working on that 'etc.' ever since." As Pisani traveled, she began to think of the country as "one giant Bad Boyfriend," charming, intimate, and sharing, yet at the same time deceptive and unpredictable. Yet her attraction was stronger than her doubts, and she kept returning. Indonesia's downsides include incompetence, corruption, conflict, and the kind of sudden political change that one retired general described to her as "nation-building by trial and error." Yet "Indonesia's upsides—the openness, the pragmatism, the generosity of its people, their relaxed attitude to life—are ultimately the more seductive traits, and the more important."[11]

twelve

East of Boston

On a steamy hot morning in August 1978, at an anonymous exit on Interstate 64 in southern Indiana, I climbed down from the cab of a truck and pulled on my backpack. The restaurant sign, "Eat at Steve's and Get Gas," did not inspire confidence, but I was hot, tired, and looking forward to air-conditioning almost as much as breakfast.

I had arrived in the United States from Britain two weeks earlier and was on my way to the University of Kansas to begin postgraduate studies and (although I didn't know it at the time) a new life and career in the United States. I didn't have much money. After staying with friends in New York City and Washington, DC, I took a Greyhound bus to Charleston, West Virginia, and hitchhiked west.

It was cool and shady inside the restaurant. It was late morning, and I was the only customer. The waitress was chatty.

"You're not from around here?" She phrased it as a question but didn't wait for an answer. My accent—some mixture of London suburban and Yorkshire—was enough to convince her that I was not from Indiana, or even the Midwest. She returned with my meal.

"Boston—it must be Boston," she declared triumphantly, as if she had solved a mystery of origins. I shook my head. "No, east of Boston." She looked puzzled. When she refilled my coffee, she was ready to challenge me. "But there's *nowhere* east of Boston."

We can take this story two ways. First, it tells us something about the world as seen from southern Indiana, or other US states where I've lived and worked, including Kansas, Ohio, and West Virginia. For some people, a trip to the state capital (for shopping at the mall, a day at the state fair, or the high school basketball playoffs) is about as far as they go most years. They are content to live in the communities where they grew up, close to family and friends. A trip to New York or Washington, DC—two cities I had already visited in my short time in the United States—was a major expedition. I sometimes envy their sense of place, their attachment to a community. I also fear that much of what they know or think about the rest of the world—the continents east of Boston—is incomplete and mediated through TV and the Internet.

Second, the story provides a brief glimpse into what academics sometimes term the "other," an imagined world of peoples so different in race, culture, religion, food ways, and belief systems from what we know and trust that they are at best misunderstood, at worst suspected and feared. In trying to locate me, the waitress came up with a place where English was still spoken but that seemed about as far as possible from her own world. *Boston.*

Of course, the "othering" goes both ways. Some New Yorkers and Bostonians are not nearly as cosmopolitan as we would like to believe. A 1976 *New Yorker* cover cartoon, "The View from 9th Avenue," briefly acknowledges "Jersey" and then compresses the rest of the continental United States into an amorphous blob. The Hudson River—the western boundary of the civilized world as we know it—is half as wide as the Pacific Ocean. Japan, Russia, and China are vague shapes on a far horizon.

A World of Stereotypes

What do people think of when they hear the names of the countries of *Monsoon Postcards?*

For Madagascar, it may be lemurs, baobab trees, vanilla, or penguins, the latter a reference to the improbably titled *Penguins of Madagascar,* the 2014 DreamWorks animated cartoon. The film was premiered in China, which may account for why "penguins" is also the leading autocomplete result when you type "Madagascar" into the search box on Baidu, China's leading search engine.

India? Curry, yoga, tea, cricket, and customer service call centers. A study of the most frequent queries about Asian countries on Google is not encouraging. The top questions that come up when you ask, "Why is [country name]?" focus on wealth and size. For India and Bangladesh, it's "so poor." For Indonesia, it's "Muslim."[1]

Ignorance—or perhaps ignore-ance is a better word—of the "other" is often portrayed as a peculiarly US disease (even though I find it rampant elsewhere). If epidemiologists were to investigate, they might ascribe it partly to the sheer size of the United States—you do not need a passport to experience a range of landscapes and cultures—and partly to a secondary education system that compresses geography, history, sociology, anthropology, and who-knows-what-else into a watered-down social studies curriculum that does not encourage most students to learn more. At an International Education Week forum at a community college in the Midwest, I was dismayed that students could not tell me a single significant thing about four countries with large populations and economies—Brazil, Nigeria, Turkey, and Indonesia. In a pre-Internet and multichannel world, I can understand why the waitress at Steve's did not know much about anything east of Boston. These students, who had grown up with cable or satellite TV and could find information in seconds on their smart phones, had no excuse. They were simply not curious.

Ignorance of small or medium-sized countries that lack economic and political clout is perhaps excusable, except for diplomats and policy wonks. I'm concerned at how little people know about countries with large populations and fast-growing economies. India, with an estimated 1.3 billion people, has the second-largest population in the world after China; Indonesia, with 263 million, is fourth (the United States, with more than 325 million, is third). Elizabeth Pisani recounts her frustration in trying to introduce her Bad Boyfriend at parties in London or New York. "I have become used to seeing a mildly panicked look in people's eyes when I mentioned Indonesia. . . . I can see them thinking: 'Oh God, Indonesia . . . is that the new name for Cambodia, Vietnam, those places near Thailand . . . ?'"[2]

And then there's Bangladesh, which with 165 million people has the eighth-largest population in the world, ahead of Russia, Mexico, and Japan. All of them live in a country less than one-hundredth the size of Russia. Even granted that large areas of Arctic Russia cannot support much more than nomadic herding, the contrast points to the first reason we should care about the Indian Ocean region—population pressure and migration.

For centuries, the lands around the Indian Ocean have experienced major population shifts. Internal and external migrations are most often driven by economic factors: to clear forest and expand agricultural production, to find new grazing grounds, to exploit mineral resources, to trade. The Indian Ocean slave trade and colonial-era transportation of indentured laborers to plantations resulted in the resettlement of ethnic groups; in some countries, the internal slave trade produced population shifts. Traders, entrepreneurs, and missionaries, supported by armies and navies, ventured wherever there were new business opportunities to exploit or souls to save.

Economic opportunity and poverty continue to drive migration. In Madagascar, people who cannot make a living on the land move to urban areas to work as *pousse-pousse* drivers or laborers or engage in *petite commerce*. Similar rural-urban migration patterns occur in India, Indonesia, and Bangladesh, triggered by lack of cultivable land, high rents, low prices, and, seasonally, by monsoon flooding. The discovery of minerals draws wildcat miners to rough camps, where they fight over muddy plots of ground.

Others become official migrant workers. Throughout South and Southeast Asia, companies recruit construction workers, laborers, and service staff; annually, more than half a million Bangladeshis work on short-term contracts outside the country, most in the Middle East, Malaysia, and Singapore. Their remittances support their families and boost domestic GDP, yet many are in a similar position to the indentured laborers of the colonial era, living in poor conditions and deprived of their civil rights. Other Bangladeshis cross illegally to India to seek work, leading to a clampdown by authorities who are building an electric fence along the twenty-five-hundred-mile border. To Indians, Bangladesh represents "poor immigrants." It's India's Mexico.

Some migrations are caused by natural disasters such as hurricanes, earthquakes, or climatic shocks. Yet the most disruptive population movements are occasioned by war, civil conflict, or political change—the Merina conquest of Madagascar and the failed 1947 rebellion against France, the 1947 partition of British India, Bangladesh's 1971 Liberation War, separatist movements and conflicts in regions of Indonesia.

Each country faces a difficult, perhaps impossible, balance between developing its economy, with the goal of reducing poverty and raising living standards, and the social and environmental impacts of growth. Everywhere, government agencies, foreign and domestic business interests, international agencies, environmental groups, and local communities are engaged in high-stakes conflicts over land, natural resources, and water.

The forests that once supported a population of hunters and gatherers and helped absorb carbon emissions are fast disappearing—cleared for agriculture or palm oil plantations, cut for charcoal, harvested for lumber. Do governments have the resources and political will to preserve what is left, to curb slash-and-burn agriculture and illegal logging? And if they do, will the restrictions consign more people to poverty?

Water is a source of conflict at all levels—between neighbors, communities, states and regions, urban and rural populations, national governments. Who has the right to drill a well into the aquifer, or divert a stream to water a rice paddy? With rivers crossing state and national boundaries, does one party have the right to restrict water supply to another? If India holds back too much water from the Ganges behind the Farakka dam to generate hydroelectricity or to irrigate its own farmland, the rice crop in regions of Bangladesh will fail. If it does not control the release of water, large areas will be submerged, and the rice crop will be lost.

In all four countries, fish are a major source of protein in the diet, especially for poor people. Unregulated fishing has depleted river and ocean fish stocks, forcing fishing boats to travel further and raising prices. What can governments do to reverse this trend, short of dramatic gestures such as Indonesia's blowing up of fishing boats? The most sustainable option is commercial farm fishing. Like most agricultural crops, it depends on a reliable water supply; in the 2017 Bangladesh floods, rising waters washed away fish farms.

For some countries, the fastest route to economic growth lies underground. Despite fluctuations in commodity prices, world demand for oil, gas, coal, uranium, iron, copper, and other metals will likely increase. The market for gold, silver, platinum, rare metals, and precious stones is growing. This should be good news for a country such as Madagascar, which has all these minerals and a lot more besides, plus offshore oil and gas reserves. To exploit them will require considerable investment—not only in building and operating mines, but in roads, railways, and port facilities. Companies are more likely to invest if they can be confident that the government officials with whom they have negotiated will still be in office next week, or that their successors will honor agreements without hitting them up for another "processing fee." Multinational companies routinely bribe ministers and bureaucrats to obtain licenses and permits, or to look the other way on environmental violations, but they also assume that the bribe will be "good," so to speak, at least for a year or two. Only India finishes in the top half of the 176 countries in Transparency International's Corruption Index (at 79); Indonesia is in 90th place, and Bangladesh and Madagascar are locked in an undesirable dead heat at 145th. Scores for all countries have not changed much over the last five years.[3]

The balance between economic growth and carbon emissions is the greatest challenge. The three most populous countries, India, Bangladesh, and Indonesia, are on course to bringing millions out of poverty through rural electrification, but much of the electrical capacity will be generated by fossil fuels. Restricting traffic in major cities may help reduce pollution levels, but at what cost to commerce? Until cost-effective alternatives are available, farmers will continue to burn stubble to prepare their fields for planting, and the smoke will engulf urban areas, forcing authorities to close schools and businesses and increasing the death rate from chronic respiratory diseases.

Environmentalists have called on the United Nations Development Programme to add a new measure to its Human Development Index (HDI), which currently ranks countries according to a composite statistic of life expectancy, years of education, and an average per person income level, adjusted to local prices. If a per person carbon footprint was added, the table of countries would look different, with some Western countries, including the United States, moving down the rankings, and some developing countries moving up. On average, each Indian contributes about one-tenth as much carbon dioxide as each American. Developing countries need to curb carbon emissions, but per person rather than absolute targets may be more realistic. Indeed, increasing emissions in one area may reduce them in another. If rural families use electric stoves, the increased emissions from coal-fired power plants may be more than offset by the fall in emissions from charcoal and coal stoves and fires.

Measuring the economic progress or health of a country is a tricky business, best left to economists and statisticians. I am neither, but at least I know what goes into the most common calculation of the size of an economy, Gross Domestic Product (GDP)—the sum of private consumption, investment, government spending, and net exports, that is, exports minus imports. And the concept of Purchasing Power Parity (PPP), folksily interpreted by the *Economist* in its "Big Mac Index," which uses the price of a Big Mac as the benchmark. Gross National Income (GNI) takes GDP, adds foreign remittances, and subtracts income earned by foreigners in the country to come up with an approximation of average incomes. That's as far as I'll go here, because beyond this point economics really becomes the "dismal science." What I will say is that these measures, so widely quoted by politicians, business leaders, and journalists and used to tweak interest and foreign exchange rates, do not mean much to most people.

India, Indonesia, and Bangladesh are classified by the World Bank as low middle-income countries, with a GNI per capita between $1,006 and $3,955; Madagascar is a low-income country, with less than $1,005. These averages, useful though they may be for shaping economic and fiscal policy, disguise vast wealth gaps—between regions, communities, and classes. The *Economist* comparison of the GDP PPP of Indian states to countries (see "What If Uttar Pradesh Declared Independence?" in chapter 5) offers one way to visualize this. Three large northern states and all the northeast states, if they were countries, would fall into the low-income category. India's average is pulled up by a few states where the economy has been growing and by urban areas that, if ranked individually, would likely make the World Bank's high-income category. The aggregation of India as a low middle-income country does not tell us the whole story.

Figuring out how many people live in poverty is a precarious exercise, because each country adopts a different standard for determining the poverty line. Governments tend to fiddle with the model, sometimes for political reasons or to send a message to foreign donors—either to earn praise for progress made, or to show that they still need more aid. In any case, "poverty" is as much culturally as economically defined; many "poor" people do not feel poor because everyone they know has similar living standards; by the same token, middle-class homeowners struggling to pay mortgages and credit card debts may feel "poor."

Religion and Politics

In all four countries, religion has always played a key role in politics. The Merina kings welcomed Protestant and Roman Catholic missionaries, not so much for the religion they brought as for their industrial skills. Today, any ambitious politician in Madagascar seeks the support of one or more of the large religious federations. In India, a secular democracy, the Hindu nationalist Bharatiya Janata Party (BJP) came to national power for the first time in 2014. Under Prime Minister Modi, its policies have focused mostly on economic reform and infrastructure development, but its ideology of cultural nationalism potentially poses a threat to the rights of non-Hindus. Religion is interpreted more dangerously at the state level, as in Telangana, where Chief Minister Kalvakuntia Chandrashekhar Rao's beliefs in astrology, numerology, and traditional Hindu architecture, and his expensive offerings at Hindu temples, worry secular politicians and the business community.

Within the Indian Ocean region, notes Robert Kaplan, "lies the entire arc of Islam, from the eastern fringe of the Sahara Desert to the Indonesian archipelago."[4] Indonesia has the largest Muslim population in the world (more than 225 million), followed by India (about 190 million); Bangladesh is fourth (after Pakistan) with about 150 million. Historically, all three countries have experienced religious-based violence, most notably during the 1947 partition of India, the 1971 Bangladesh Liberation War, and regional conflicts in Indonesia. Religion continues to play an important role in politics, with Islamic parties represented at all levels of government. Although governments have cracked down on religious extremists—some of whom conveniently turn out to be members of opposition parties—the balance is a delicate one. Perceived offenses to Islam often meet a violent response, as in the hacking to death of secular bloggers in Bangladesh. However, attitudes to religion are more relaxed than in some Middle Eastern countries and Pakistan, and citizens are generally more tolerant of other faiths. Sharia law may be applied in civil and family matters—marriage, divorce, and inheritance—but not in criminal matters, except in Indonesia's Aceh province, where offenses such as gambling, alcohol use, and inappropriate dress may be punished by public caning.

It's just eleven square miles and has no harbor or mineral resources. Its only permanent residents are green sea turtles and birds, although a team flies in now and again to maintain the automated weather station. Who would want to own Île Europa (Europa Island), a tiny coral atoll between Madagascar and Mozambique? France.

From the 1950s onward, France surrendered a vast colonial empire, from Indochina to north and west Africa. It held onto some islands, so today French *départements* are scattered across the globe, from French Polynesia and New Caledonia in the Pacific to the Caribbean islands of Guadalupe and Martinique to Réunion (formerly Île Bourbon) in the Indian Ocean, a French colony since the mid-seventeenth century. Some have agricultural and mineral resources and are popular vacation destinations for French tourists. But there's no good reason to visit Île Europa.

France fiercely defends its claim to the island and the other Îles Éparses de l'Océan Indien (Scattered Islands of the Indian Ocean) not because of what's on them but because of what's around them—the two-hundred-nautical mile Exclusive Economic Zone (EEZ). Although the surface is open to all shipping, what lies beneath is national property. Historically, the convention has been used mostly to protect fishing industries, but the discovery of minerals in the ocean bed has made the real estate much more valuable. Tiny Île Europa has an EEZ of almost fifty thousand square miles. France has already issued oil exploration licenses to companies for other areas around Îles Éparses in the Mozambique Channel.

France controls the largest EEZ in the world, covering almost 4.5 million square miles. The potential revenue from direct exploitation of resources and licensing is huge. No wonder Madagascar, the Comoros, and Mauritius all dispute France's territorial claims to various Îles Éparses. In the late eighteenth century, the Merina chieftain Andrianampoinimerina boasted that his kingdom would have "no frontier but the sea." Madagascar's modern leaders may wish that he had had grander territorial ambitions.

The nations of the Indian Ocean region, whose boundaries were drawn by colonial powers, will continue to have border squabbles with each other and their neighbors. Major disputes, such as that between

India and Pakistan over Jammu and Kashmir, may still result in war. China remains a security threat to India's vulnerable Siliguri Corridor and along the northeastern border in Arunachal Pradesh. However, the new battles are just as likely to be at sea. Some Indian analysts worry about China's increased naval presence in the Indian Ocean and want to see more attention paid to the "southeastern border" of the Andaman and Nicobar Islands, where Myanmar also has territorial ambitions.

Indonesia is working hard to count and claim all its islands to protect its fishing industry and mineral rights. It has a long-standing spat with Australia over the maritime boundaries of the Timor Gap, the three-hundred-mile strait between Timor (divided between the Indonesian province of West Timor and Timor-Leste) and the Northern Territory. The more serious territorial disputes are to the north, where Indonesia faces off against Malaysia, Brunei, the Philippines, Vietnam, and, most ominously, one of its largest investors, China. Since 2014, Indonesia has blown up hundreds of foreign fishing vessels seized while illegally fishing in its waters. It has beefed up its military presence in the Natuna Islands, northwest of Borneo, a region with large fish stocks and undersea oil and gas resources. Indonesia renamed the northernmost part of its EEZ the "North Natuna Sea," a defiant challenge to China's territorial ambitions in the South China Sea.[5]

Artificial Borders

In *The Coming Anarchy,* Kaplan describes "the map of the world, with its 190 or so countries, each signified by a bold and uniform color" as "an invention of modernism, specifically of European colonialism." The notion of "frontier" did not exist in the feudal mind. Drawing on Benedict Anderson's concept of imagined communities, Kaplan writes that the state "is a purely Western notion, one that until the 20th century applied to countries covering only three per cent of the earth's land area. Nor is evidence compelling that the state, as a governing ideal, can successfully be transported to areas outside the industrialized world."[6]

In this view, the four countries of *Monsoon Postcards* are all artificial constructs. In each one, a European power, pursuing its own economic and strategic interests, cobbled together tribes, ethnic groups, and princely states into a colony, imposed a system of governance, and used the colony to supply cheap labor, cash crops, and mineral resources and to serve as a market for manufactured goods. At independence, the colony was suddenly reborn as a nation state and expected to shake off its colonial legacy and function as an independent economic and political unit. It was a lot, perhaps too much, to ask.

Despite the fragility of the nation state, "this inflexible, artificial reality staggers on, not only in the United Nations but in various geographic and travel publications . . . that still report on and photograph the world according to 'country.'"[7] Kaplan admits to falling into the "country" trap. I do too, while recognizing that language, culture, and ethnicity are more powerful forces than regimes or cartography. The politically correct "We are all Malagasy" line glosses over the Merina domination of the *côtiers* and former slaves, as well as today's socioeconomic divisions. India is *inexplicable* because of its diversity in language, religion, culture, and ethnicity, and Indonesia *improbable* for some of the same reasons. Bangladesh may be the only country that genuinely came together out of a sense of shared culture and language, although it took a brutal liberation war to achieve it, and a united Bengal is still only a pipedream.

If, indeed, we view the nation state as a passing phase in history, then perhaps we need to return to the Indian Ocean world as a concept.

Indian Ocean World

In the family of oceans, the Indian is usually listed third, overshadowed in size and perceived importance by its big brothers, the Atlantic and Pacific, although still ahead of the Arctic and Southern (Antarctic). The order seems surprising, because historically the Indian Ocean has been more traveled than the others; because it forms an arc, from southern Africa to western Australia, it has been a highway for commerce and settlement for thousands of years. World maps that place the Western hemisphere in the center push the Indian Ocean to the edges, or literally the sidelines. Americans, writes Kaplan, "are barely aware of the Indian Ocean, concentrated as they are, because of their own geography, on the Atlantic and the Pacific. World War II and the Cold War confirmed this bias, with Nazi Germany, Imperial Japan, the Soviet Union and Communist China all with Atlantic or Pacific orientations." Yet this is the ocean "to which Marco Polo devoted almost an entire book of his travels near the end of the 13th century."[8] In the nineteenth-century Great Game, the Russian Empire dreamed of securing land routes across British India to the warm water ports in the Indian Ocean. For centuries, the China trade has depended on shipping through the Straits of Malacca, one of what Kaplan calls the "main navigational choke points of world commerce." Today, China is exploring new routes to the Indian Ocean as part of its trillion-dollar Belt and Road Initiative. It is planning a road and rail route from Kunming in the southwest across Myanmar to the container port of Chittagong in Bangladesh, where it is investing in infrastructure. Other routes across India have been considered but will probably need to wait until relations between the countries improve.

Throughout history sea routes have been more important than land routes because they carry bulk goods economically. The 120-mile Suez Canal, opened in 1869, transformed world trade by providing a short cut from the North Atlantic and Mediterranean Sea to the Indian Ocean and the markets of the Persian Gulf, East Africa, India, southeast Asia, and China. The canal cut the distance from the North Atlantic to the Northern Indian Ocean by about forty-three hundred miles. Today, the Indian Ocean carries about half the world's container traffic and two-thirds of its petroleum products. "This is truly a global ocean, its shores home to an agglomeration of peoples of the fast-developing former 'third world' but not to any superpower unlike the Atlantic or Pacific," writes Kaplan.[9]

It's an ocean world where culture, religion, technology, and ideas have flowed alongside trade and migration, and whose boundaries have shifted in time and space as military, economic, and cultural empires have risen and fallen. A world that stretches far beyond coastal areas—in other words, a region linked to, but not limited by, the body of water. The four countries I've described are worth knowing for themselves but need to be understood within the broader frame of an interconnected Indian Ocean world, where migration, commerce, religion, and culture have always transcended national boundaries.

East of Australia

Stephanie and I stopped for lunch at a *warung* near the resort area of Lovina on the north coast of Bali. We sat on a pleasant, covered terrace with wooden tables and chairs overlooking the beach and gazed out to the horizon. Somewhere in this archipelago, more than a thousand years earlier, a brave group of souls had set out from a place like this, passing through the Straits of Malacca into the Indian Ocean proper. By accident or design, some ended up in Madagascar, more than four thousand miles west, perhaps after a journey lasting several years. Yet theirs was one of thousands of journeys around the Indian Ocean that connected distant lands and resulted in migration, the development of agriculture, the spread of religions, exploration, and conquest. The Indian Ocean was *global* long before the word became fashionable.

We ordered *nasi goreng* and fried fish. We were the only customers, and the waiter wanted to practice his English.

"You are from Australia?" he asked politely. Most *bule* customers were from Australia. "No, east of Australia," I offered.

He beamed. "The United States of *America*. I would love to visit. I have a friend in a place that sounds like Indonesia. Indiana. Do you know it?"

Acknowledgments

This book, like *Postcards from Stanland: Journeys in Central Asia*, is the result of serendipity rather than design. When I started writing about Madagascar, India, Bangladesh, and Indonesia, my goal was simply to record my experiences and share them with family, friends, and colleagues in e-mailed essays and blogs. It was only after several journeys that I realized how my somewhat scattered observations could be blended with research into a narrative.

Although I recount two trips with my wife, Stephanie Hysmith—to northeast India and to Indonesia—most of the time I was traveling for work. My thanks to the US Department of State (Bureau of Educational and Cultural Affairs), the Asia-Pacific Institute for Broadcasting Development, Population Reference Bureau, UNESCO, and, since 2013, UNICEF for the opportunity to visit interesting places, most of them off the usual tourist beat, to conduct workshops and research projects, and then to write about my experiences. I've benefited from the insights of well-traveled colleagues: independent consultants Karen Greiner and Ami Sengupta, Andrew Carlson (Metropolitan State University, St. Paul), Amy Chadwick (Ohio University), Nicola Christofides (University of the Witwatersrand, Johannesburg), and Waithira Gikonyo and Neha Kapil of UNICEF. Special thanks to Suruchi Sood of Drexel University for sharing her stories of partition and the 1971 Bangladesh Liberation War, and for serving as my interpreter on the tour of the Liberation War Museum.

I am especially grateful to those who helped me better understand a country and its culture. Much of my learning was informal—conversations during long road trips, while waiting for a plane, or over dinner. On Madagascar—anthropologist (and sometime zebu herder) Luke Freeman, UNICEF staff member Hoby Razakasoavina, and Richard Samuel from the University of Antananarivo. It's a long list for

India: my colleagues from the University of Hyderabad—Vasuki Bela-vadi, Vinod Pavarala, and Usha Raman; from Tezpur University—Joya Chakraborty and Abhijit Bora; and Rina Gill, Khalid Syed, Bhrigu Taluk-dar, and (again) Suruchi Sood. On Bangladesh—UNICEF C4D specialist Yasmin Khan, Vijai Kapil (on the 1971 Liberation War), and my former graduate student Masudul Biswas from Loyola University, Maryland. On Indonesia—the TV journalists in the Department of State study group, my Ohio University colleague Mary Rogus, and the happy cou-ple, David Smith and Kamellia Soenjoto.

I asked my graphic designer, Belén Marco Crespo, to match my off-beat narrative style in the maps; she did so superbly, combining solid cartography with artistic flair and humor. The director of the Ohio Uni-versity Press, Gill Berchowitz, and managing editor Nancy Basmajian, were reliable guides and thoughtful critics throughout the writing and production process; I also had excellent input from two fellow West Vir-ginia writers, Fran Simone and Kathy Manley.

Finally, my deepest gratitude to my wife, Stephanie Hysmith, who loves travel as much as I do and is always prepared to go with the flow. She has always supported me in my travels and encouraged me to write about them.

Charleston, West Virginia, 2018

Notes

Chapter 1: Traveling with a Purpose

1. Thomas Swick, "A Moving Experience," *Morning News*, December 3, 2013, reprinted in *The Best American Travel Writing 2014*, ed. Paul Theroux (Boston: Houghton Mifflin Harcourt, 2014).

2. Alfonso Gumucio Dagron, "Playing with Fire: Power, Participation, and Communication for Development," *Development in Practice*, 19, nos. 4–5 (2009): 453–65.

3. Alfonso Gumucio Dagron, "The New Communicator" (seminar presentation, Rockefeller Foundation Communication for Social Change, New York, August 1998).

Chapter 2: Indian Ocean World

1. S. Arasaratnam, "Writing the History of the Indian Ocean, 1500–1800," *Asian Studies Association of Australia* 11, no. 87 (2007): 32.

2. Michael Pearson, ed., *Trade, Circulation, and Flow in the Indian Ocean World* (New York: Palgrave Macmillan, 2015), 2.

3. Robert D. Kaplan, *Monsoon: The Indian Ocean and the Future of American Power* (New York: Random House, 2010), 13.

4. Shashi Tharoor, "The Price of Empire," Project Syndicate, February 20, 2017, https://www.project-syndicate.org/commentary/uk-india-relations-colonization-by-shashi-tharoor-2017-02?barrier=accessreg.

Chapter 3: Land of the Merina

1. Maarten J. de Wit, "Madagascar: Heads It's a Continent, Tails It's an Island," *Annual Review of Earth and Planetary Sciences* 31 (May 2003): 213–48.

2. "Thirty Lost Souls: How Africa's Largest Island Was Colonized by Asians," *Economist*, March 24, 2012; Martin Lewis, "New Evidence on the Settlement of Madagascar," GeoCurrents, March 28, 2012, http://www.geocurrents.info/news-map/art-and-culture-news/new-evidence-on-the-settlement-of-madagascar.

3. Mervyn Brown, "Madagascar: Island of the Ancestors," *Anthropology Today* 3, no. 1 (February 1987): 16.

4. David Graeber, "Dancing with Corpses Reconsidered: An Interpretation of 'Famadihana' (in Arivonimamo, Madagascar)," *American Ethnologist* 22 (1995): 258–78.

5. May-Ying Lam, "The Plague, Alive and Well in Madagascar," *Washington Post*, March 9, 2016.

6. Mervyn Brown, interview by Malcolm McBain, British Diplomatic Oral History Programme, Churchill College Cambridge, October 24, 1996, https://www.chu.cam.ac.uk/media/uploads/files/Brown.pdf.

7. "Clinton Deploys Vowels to Bosnia; Cities of Sjlbvdnzv, Grzny to Be First Recipients," *The Onion*, December 1995.

8. Malcolm McBain, interview by John Hutson, British Diplomatic Oral History Programme, Churchill College Cambridge, April 27, 2000, https://www.chu.cam.ac.uk/media/uploads/files/McBain.pdf.

9. "Madagascar's Two Presidents: Bombing Bridges, Not Building Them," *Economist*, May 9, 2002.

Chapter 4: On and Off the Road in Madagascar

1. "Rio Tinto Threatens to Exit Madagascar after CEO Is Trapped by Protestors," *Telegraph*, January 11, 2013; Jessica Hatcher, "The White Stuff: Mining Giant Rio Tinto Unearths Unrest in Madagascar," *Time*, February 8, 2013.

2. Mervyn Brown, *A History of Madagascar* (Princeton, NJ: Markus Wiener, 2000), 133–57, 185–98.

3. Burkhard Bilger, "The Path of Stones," *New Yorker*, October 2, 2006, 66–79; "New Frontiers—Madagascar Is Becoming an Attractive Mining Destination," *Economist*, March 15, 2007; Aaron Ross, "A Cursed Land—Inside the Boom and Bust of a Madagascar Frontier Town," *Slate.com*, February 14, 2014.

4. Brown, *A History of Madagascar*, 38–42.

Chapter 5: Inexplicable India

1. "An Indian Summary," *Economist*, June 21, 2011.

2. Shashi Tharoor, *Inglorious Empire: What the British Did to India* (London: Hurst, 2017).

3. Shashi Tharoor, "The Price of Empire," Project Syndicate, February 20, 2017, https://www.project-syndicate.org/commentary/uk-india-relations-colonization-by-shashi-tharoor-2017-02?barrier=accessreg; "'But What about the Railways . . . ?' The Myth of Britain's Gifts to India," *Guardian*, March 8, 2017; William Dalrymple, "One Sure Way for Britain to Get Ahead—Stop Airbrushing Our Colonial History," *Guardian*, September 2, 2015.

4. Yasmin Khan, *The Great Partition: The Making of India and Pakistan* (New Haven, CT: Yale University Press, 2007), reviewed in *Economist*, July 21, 2007.

5. Tharoor, "What about the Railways?"

6. Tharoor, "The Price of Empire."

7. Quoted in Soutik Biswas, "What Is Wrong with India's Bureaucracy?" *BBC News* blog, June 10, 2010.

8. "What's Holding India Back?" and "Battling the Babu Raj," *Economist*, March 6, 2008.

9. "India's Bureaucracy Is 'the Most Stifling in the World,'" *BBC News*, June 3, 2010; "India's Bureaucracy Is 'Worst in Asia,'" *BBC News*, January 12, 2012.

10. Quoted in "Battling the Babu Raj," *Economist*.

11. "Air Clean-Up Act: PM10 out of Emergency Levels, PM2.5 to Follow Soon," *Hindustan Times*, November 11, 2017; Vidhi Dishi and Cleve R. Wootson Jr., "New Delhi's 'Gas Chamber' Smog Is So Bad That United Airlines Has Stopped Flying There," *Washington Post*, November 11, 2017; Aseem Prakash, Nives Dolšak, Thomas Bernauer, and Liam McGrath, "Delhi Is Blanketed with Toxic Smog. This Is Why," *Washington Post*, November 11, 2017.

12. "India and the Environment: Catching up with China," *Economist*, October 10, 2015; "Urban Pollution in India: Particular about Particulates," *Economist*, January 16, 2016.

13. "India: Special Report," *Economist*, March 30, 2013.

Chapter 6: A Tale of Three Cities

1. William Dalrymple, "The Lost World," *Guardian*, December 8, 2007; "Hyderabad, India: On the Trail of the White Mughals," *Telegraph*, August 31, 2015.

2. Dalrymple, "Lost World."

3. Ibid.

4. Neelkanth Mishra and Ravi Shankar, "India Market Strategy," *Credit Suisse*, July 9, 2013; "Informal Workers, Making Up 90% of Workforce, Won't Get a Good Deal till Netas Notice Them," *Economic Times*, October 25, 2013; "India's informal economy: Hidden value," *Economist*, October 3, 2013.

5. "One Country, But No Single Market," *Economist*, January 2, 2016; "Farming in India: In a Time Warp," *Economist*, June 27, 2015.

6. "GST Effect: Hundreds of Thousands Laid Off Despite Growth," *Reuters*, September 5, 2018.

7. "Nor Any Drop to Drink," *Economist*, August 24, 2002; "India's Water Nightmare: Unholy Woes," *Economist*, May 14, 2016.

8. "Floods and India's Coromandel Coast: Next Time by Water," *Economist*, December 12, 2015.

Chapter 7: The Seven Sisters

1. Ankit Panda, "Geography's Curse: India's Vulnerable 'Chicken's Neck,'" *Diplomat*, November 8, 2013.

2. Luit is another name for Brahmaputra.

3. "'Ashta Lakshmi' of NE States Will Bloom Only If BJP in Centre: Modi," *News Bharati*, February 8, 2014; Prabin Kalita, "Pranab Mukherjee: Northeast Country's Ashtalakshmi," *Times of India*, February 1, 2017.

4. "India's North-East: The Spoils of Peace," *Economist*, August 8, 2015.

5. Quoted in Naresh Mitral, "Tezpur: Memories of Chinese Aggression Still Fresh in People's Minds," *Times of India*, October 4, 2012.

Chapter 8: Joy Bangla (Victory to Bengal)

1. "Recognise Genocide of 1971," *Daily Star*, February 16, 2017.

2. "PM Slams Chief Justice for Pakistan Comparison," *Dhaka Tribune*, August 22, 2017; "Hanif Urges CJ to Go to Pakistan," *Daily Sun*, August 23, 2017.

3. Shaheed Suhrawardy, press statement, *Hindu*, April 29, 1947.

4. "Declaration of Independence," Banglapedia, http://en.banglapedia.org /index.php?title=Declaration_of_Independence.

5. Simon Dring, "Tanks Crush Revolt in Pakistan—7,000 Slaughtered: Homes Burned," *Daily Telegraph*, March 30, 1971.

6. "'Indians Are Bastards Anyway,'" *Asia Times*, June 23, 2005, http://www .atimes.com/atimes/South_Asia/GF23Df04.html.

7. This section is based on my interview with retired naval commander Vijai Kapil, Dhaka, August 25, 2017; additional data from Vice Admiral Mihir K. Roy, *War in the Indian Ocean* (New Delhi: Lancer, 1995) and Deepto TV (Dhaka) documentary on Operation Jackpot (2016).

8. The Indian foreign intelligence agency, similar to the American CIA or the British MI6.

9. The codename Operation Jackpot was also used to refer more generally to training and military operations coordinated between the Indian Army and the *mukti bahini*.

Chapter 9: Swimming to Bangladesh

1. Steve George, "A Third of Bangladesh under Water as Flood Devastation Widens," *CNN*, September 1, 2017; "Vegetable Prices Soar as Floods Damage Farmland," *Dhaka Tribune*, August 22, 2017.

2. *Daily Star*, August 20, 2017.

3. Shohel Mamun, "What Dhaka's Transport System Might Be Like in 2019," *Dhaka Tribune*, August 22, 2017.

4. Jody Rosen, "The Bangladesh Traffic Jam That Never Ends," *New York Times Style Magazine*, September 23, 2016, https://www.nytimes.com/2016/09/23/t -magazine/travel/dhaka-bangladesh-traffic.html.

5. Tuhin Shubhra, "Swarming Bikes, Riskier Roads," *Daily Star*, September 10, 2018; "60% of Bangladeshi Motorcyclists Do Not Have Valid Licence," *Dhaka Tribune*, September 12, 2018; "Is the High Number of Motorcycles a Burden on Dhaka?" *Dhaka Tribune*, September 21, 2018.

6. "Biman's Carousel of Incompetence," *Dhaka Tribune*, August 20, 2017.

7. Adnan Morshed, "Global Media and Dhaka's Urbanization," *Daily Star*, February 23, 2017.

Chapter 10: On the Road and on the Water

1. Jim Yardley, "Bangladesh Pollution, Told in Colors and Smells," *New York Times*, July 14, 2013.

2. Tawfique Ali, "Time to Declare Turag Dead," *Daily Star*, November 6, 2016.

3. Nawaz Farhin, "Transport System in Hand of Unlicensed Drivers," *Dhaka Tribune*, August 19, 2017.

4. Pankag Karmakar, Wasim Bin Habib, and Tuhin Shubhra Adhikary, "A Warning for Reckless Drivers," *Dhaka Star*, February 23, 2017.

5. "Ineffective 3-Wheeler Ban: Quader Admits to Political Pressure," *Daily Star*, September 5, 2018.

6. Upashana Salam, "Prelude to a Spreading Nightmare," *Daily Star*, April 22, 2017.

Chapter 11: Improbable Indonesia

1. Candida Beveridge, "The Boat That Landed on a Roof and Saved 59 people," *BBC World Service*, December 24, 2014; John M. Glionna, "In Aceh, Stranded Ships a Reminder of 2004 Tsunami," *Los Angeles Times*, October 30, 2009.

2. Interview with *Sky News* December 21, 2014, https://www.youtube.com/watch?v=NRroa7UniY8.

3. "In Aceh, 'Indonesian' Is a Synonym for Foreigner," *Economist*, August 10, 2002, 39.

4. New Guinea is the second-largest island, divided between Indonesia and the independent country of Papua New Guinea. The five Indonesian provinces of Kalimantan occupy about 73 percent of the land area of Borneo; the two Malaysian states of Sabah and Sarawak and the small kingdom of Brunei occupy the rest.

5. "Indonesia Counts Its Islands to Protect Territory and Resources," *BBC Asia*, June 7, 2017; Erin Blakemore, "Indonesia's Trying to Figure Out How Many Islands It Contains," Smithsonian.com, June 9, 2017.

6. Elizabeth Pisani, *Indonesia, Etc.: Exploring the Improbable Nation* (New York: W. W. Norton, 2014), 9.

7. "Special Report: Indonesia," *Economist*, February 27, 2016.

8. Pisani, *Indonesia, Etc.*, 68.

9. Michael Malley, "Class, Region, and Culture: The Sources of Social Conflict in Indonesia," in *Social Cohesion and Conflict Prevention in Asia*, ed. Nat J. Coletta, Teck Ghee Lim, and Anita Kelles-Viitanen (Washington, DC: The World Bank, 2001), 351.

10. "A World on Fire," *Economist*, February 27, 2016.

11. Pisani, *Indonesia, Etc.*, 6, 379.

Chapter 12: East of Boston

1. Alexis Kleinman, "Google Reveals What People Really Think about Europe and Asia," *Huffington Post*, January 28, 2014.

2. Elizabeth Pisani, *Indonesia, Etc.: Exploring the Improbable Nation* (New York: W. W. Norton, 2014), 6.

3. Transparency International, Corruption Perceptions Index 2016, https://www.transparency.org/news/feature/corruption_perceptions_index_2016.

4. Robert D. Kaplan, *Monsoon: The Indian Ocean and the Future of American Power* (New York: Random House, 2010), 7.

5. Joe Cochrane, "Indonesia, Long on Sidelines, Starts to Confront China's Territorial Claims," *New York Times*, September 10, 2017.

6. Robert D. Kaplan, *The Coming Anarchy: Shattering the Dreams of the Post Cold War* (New York: Vintage Books, 2000), 38–39.

7. Kaplan, *Coming Anarchy*, 39–40.

8. Kaplan, *Monsoon*, 6–7.

9. Ibid., 6.

Index

camion-brousse (bush truck), 66
Carlson, Andrew, 1, 2, 13, 114, 287
Cathedral of St. Mary Help of Christians
  (Shillong), India, 167
Char desert, India, 86
Charminar (Old City, Hyderabad), 110, 112,
  115–16, 115fig, 124; map, 111
Chennai (Madras), 95, 96
Cherrapunjee (Meghalaya, India), 165, 168,
  169; map, 143
China, 11, 36, 54, 81, 108, 109, 136, 144, 154,
  216, 249, 252, 253, 259, 260, 275, 276, 278,
  283, 285; Belt and Road Initiative (New
  Silk Road), 108–9, 285; war with India
  (1962), 144, 156
Chittagong, 179, 180, 186, 187, 208, 235, 236,
  239, 240, 285; flooding in, 193fig, 196;
  map 175
Chittagong Hill Tracts, 211
Chowmahalla palace (Hyderabad), 121, 122
Citroën 2CV (deux chevaux), 37–38
Citroën DS, 38-39
Clive, Colonel Robert, 176, 184, 206
CNG (Compressed Natural Gas); as fuel,
  105; auto rickshaws, 196, 199, 220, 237
Coen, Jan Pieterszoon (governor of Dutch
  East Indies), 253, 256
Congress Party (India), 92, 126, 153, 155
côtiers, 23, 36, 45, 48, 72, 284
Courteen's Association, 70–71
Cox, Murray (scientist), 19
Curzon, Lord (viceroy of India), 92, 176
Cyberabad, 112, 124–25

Dagron, Alfonso Gumucio, 7–8
Dalrymple, William (historian), 91, 121–22
Das, Samir (Indian navy lieutenant), 183,
  184, 185, 186
Das, Sanjit Kumar (UNICEF), 240–41, 242
Deccan plateau, 113, 137
Delhi, 5, 77, 94, 95, 96, 98, 103, 106, 107,
  112, 113, 127, 141, 176; Great Smog
  of, 104; metro, 103; pollution, 103–5;
  population, 103; traffic, 102–3, 105, 196
Democratic Movement for Malagasy
  Renovation (MDRM), 44
Denpasar (Bali), 270, 272
development, attitudes to, 5–8
De Wit, Maarten (geologist), 18
dhaba (roadside restaurant, India), 147
Dhaka, 5, 77, 93, 176, 178, 190, 192, 201, 211,
  234, 235, 242, 243; canals and rivers,
  194-95, 217, 218, 219; economy, 203, 204,

205–6, 207, 211–12; flooding, 193fig, 194,
  195; plastic bag ban, 195; population,
  212, 218, 235; public transportation,
  198–99; traffic, 196–99, 197fig; urban
  dysfunction, 197, 199, 212. See also Old
  Dhaka
Dhaka University, 174, 212; language
  martyrs, 93, 174, 178; Operation
  Searchlight, 179–80
Dhallywood, 242–43
Doordarshan (DD), 97, 98, 102
Dring, Simon (journalist), 181
Dutch East Indies, 12, 250, 252, 253, 255–56
Dyer, Brigadier General Richard, 91

East India Company (British), 70, 71, 88,
  117, 164, 165, 169, 176, 206
East India Company (French), 206
Esra (first wife of eighth Nizam of
  Hyderabad), 122
Exclusive Economic Zone (EEZ), 251, 282,
  283

fady (taboos), 30, 61, 64
famadihana (turning of the bones), 29–31
Fatephur Sikri, Agra, 107
Fianarantsoa, Madagascar, 67, 68
Fort Dauphin (Taolagnaro), Madagascar,
  54, 64, 66, 71
France, 37, 38, 41, 45, 47, 48, 231; colonial
  period in Madagascar, 22, 23, 27, 36–37;
  Exclusive Economic Zone (EEZ), 282;
  Françafrique, policy of, 50; influence in
  Madagascar, 12, 36–37, 46, 47, 49, 50;
  territorial claims in Indian Ocean, 49,
  282
Freeman, Luke (anthropologist), 16, 20–21,
  35–37, 39, 42, 48, 53, 60, 65, 287

gamosa (traditional Assamese scarf), 142, 151
Gandhi, Indira (Indian prime minister), 189
Gandhi, Mahatma, 78, 89, 93, 177, 178
Ganges (river), 12, 145, 184, 214, 226, 278. See
  also Padma
Garo (ethnic group, northeast India), 166,
  167, 211
Garo Hills, India, 145, 225
Gerakan Aceh Merdeka (GAM), Free Aceh
  Movement, 249, 250, 265
ghat (ferry terminal), 156, 161fig, 162, 241fig,
  242
Ginsberg, Allen, 232–33
Goa (Indian Union Territory), 79, 83, 153